ROCKPORT PUBLISHERS

1000

GRAPHIC ELEMENTS
SPECIAL DETAILS FOR DISTINCTIVE DESIGNS
WILSON HARVEY: LONDON

ART DIRECTOR
PAUL BURGESS

+ DESIGN
BEN WOOD

+ LAYOUT
MEGAN JONES DESIGN

+ ARTWORK
PETE USHER

+ RESEARCH AND JUDGING
PAUL BURGESS
BEN WOOD
DAN ELLIOTT
GRAHAM FARR
ALUN STEEL

+ ALL ADDITIONAL PHOTOGRAPHY
PHIL COOK

+ FONTS
DIN + BELL

First published in the United States of America by
Rockport Publishers, Inc. a member of
Quayside Publishing Group
100 Cummings Center
Suite 406-L
Beverly, Massachusetts 01915-6101

Telephone: (978) 282-9590
Fax: (978) 283-2742
www.rockpub.com
Illustrator, Photoshop, InDesign, and
Pagemaker are all registered trademarks
of Adobe.

DESIGNED AT WILSON HARVEY: LONDON

10 9 8 7 6 5 4 3 2 1

PRINTED IN CHINA

ISBN-13: 978-1-59253-662-7

ISBN-10: 1-59253-662-X

1000

GRAPHIC ELEMENTS

ROCKPORT

INTRODUCTION

0001 0002 0003 0004 0005 0006 0007 0008 0009 0010 0011 0012 0013 0014 0015 0016 0017 0018 0019 0020 0021 0022 0023 0024 00
0051 0052 0053 0054 0055 0056 0057 0058 0059 0060 0061 0062 0063 0064 0065 0066 0067 0068 0069 0070 0071 0072 0073 0074 00
0101 0102 0103 0104 0105 0106 0107 0108 0109 0110 0111 0112 0113 0114 0115 0116 0117 0118 0119 0120 0121 0122 0123 0124 01
0151 0152 0153 0154 0155 0156 0157 0158 0159 0160 0161 0162 0163 0164 0165 0166 0167 0168 0169 0170 0171 0172 0173 0174 01
0201 0202 0203 0204 0205 0206 0207 0208 0209 0210 0211 0212 0213 0214 0215 0216 0217 0218 0219 0220 0221 0222 0223 0224 02
0251 0252 0253 0254 0255 0256 0257 0258 0259 0260 0261 0262 0263 0264 0265 0266 0267 0268 0269 0270 0271 0272 0273 0274 02
0301 0302 0303 0304 0305 0306 0307 0308 0309 0310 0311 0312 0313 0314 0315 0316 0317 0318 0319 0320 0321 0322 0323 0324 03
0351 0352 0353 0354 0355 0356 0357 0358 0359 0360 0361 0362 0363 0364 0365 0366 0367 0368 0369 0370 0371 0372 0373 0374 03
0401 0402 0403 0404 0405 0406 0407 0408 0409 0410 0411 0412 0413 0414 0415 0416 0417 0418 0419 0420 0421 0422 0423 0424 04
0451 0452 0453 0454 0455 0456 0457 0458 0459 0460 0461 0462 0463 0464 0465 0466 0467 0468 0469 0470 0471 0472 0473 0474 04
0501 0502 0503 0504 0505 0506 0507 0508 0509 0510 0511 0512 0513 0514 0515 0516 0517 0518 0519 0520 0521 0522 0523 0524 05
0551 0552 0553 0554 0555 0556 0557 0558 0559 0560 0561 0562 0563 0564 0565 0566 0567 0568 0569 0570 0571 0572 0573 0574 05
0601 0602 0603 0604 0605 0606 0607 0608 0609 0610 0611 0612 0613 0614 0615 0616 0617 0618 0619 0620 0621 0622 0623 0624 06
0651 0652 0653 0654 0655 0656 0657 0658 0659 0660 0661 0662 0663 0664 0665 0666 0667 0668 0669 0670 0671 0672 0673 0674 06
0701 0702 0703 0704 0705 0706 0707 0708 0709 0710 0711 0712 0713 0714 0715 0716 0717 0718 0719 0720 0721 0722 0723 0724 07
0751 0752 0753 0754 0755 0756 0757 0758 0759 0760 0761 0762 0763 0764 0765 0766 0767 0768 0769 0770 0771 0772 0773 0774 07
0801 0802 0803 0804 0805 0806 0807 0808 0809 0810 0811 0812 0813 0814 0815 0816 0817 0818 0819 0820 0821 0822 0823 0824 08
0851 0852 0853 0854 0855 0856 0857 0858 0859 0860 0861 0862 0863 0864 0865 0866 0867 0868 0869 0870 0871 0872 0873 0874 08
0901 0902 0903 0904 0905 0906 0907 0908 0909 0910 0911 0912 0913 0914 0915 0916 0917 0918 0919 0920 0921 0922 0923 0924 09
0951 0952 0953 0954 0955 0956 0957 0958 0959 0960 0961 0962 0963 0964 0965 0966 0967 0968 0969 0970 0971 0972 0973 0974 09

+
This book is as much about the possibilities as it is about the detail. Most projects begin with the former and arrive at the latter. The possibilities are often the justification we as designers give ourselves for all those late nights and obsessive thoughts. Possibility is what keeps us inspired, and realization is what keeps us content. Detail is the challenge that connects the two. **+** Getting the finer details to fall into place is an art form. Get it right and the project comes alive, get it wrong and the project can be a disaster. The line is fine between experimentation, exploitation, and excess, but should the design allow it, then it is a line worth exploring. **+** The work featured in this book exemplifies this exploration; 1,000 examples of work that goes the extra inch or, in some cases, the extra mile. At first glance, many seem to have started life with the perfect brief, almost to the point where the budget seems as flexible as the concepts produced—a design utopia you dream of but never experience firsthand. However, many of these solutions have emerged from hard-fought battles and persuasive designers doing whatever they can to progress their possibilities. In many cases, it's true to say "if you have nothing, the possibilities are endless"—a bad brief, a low budget, or a vague client might actually be the perfect platform to realizing those possibilities. **+** With today's ever-expanding repertoire of finishing techniques, materials, and processes, there are plenty of excuses to innovate. Some might argue that "everything's been designed before," but here are 1,000 pieces of work that beg to differ. There are common themes and processes, but each piece is as unique as the client it represents and the information it contains, a testament to the designer's possibilities. This collection is also hard proof that it doesn't always work. While there are 1,000 pieces on display here, there are plenty more on the cutting room floor. What's left is an inspiring collection. It shows the work of those seeking to push the boundaries and others who concentrate on using more standard approaches with equally stunning success. **+** If there's one common thread throughout this book, it's the desire to realize new possibilities, and for us it's inspiring to see so many designers with the courage to push those possibilities to the limit. **Paul Burgess, Ben Wood, and all at Wilson Harvey**

01

PRINTING TECHNIQUES

SCREEN PRINTING
HAND RENDERING
LETTERPRESS
VARNISHES
OVERPRINTING

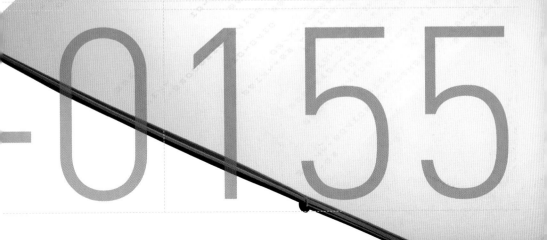

0001 **TEMPLIN BRINK DESIGN**
USA

0002 **ONE O'CLOCK GUN DESIGN CONSULTANTS**
SCOTLAND

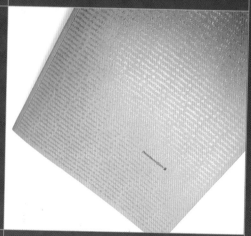

0003 **CRUSH DESIGN**
UK

0004 **SCANDINAVIAN DESIGN GROUP**
DENMARK

The Mill
New York.

The Mill
435 Hudson Street
New York NY 10014
Telephone (212) 520 3150
www.mill.co.uk

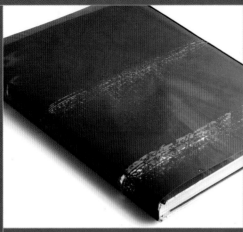

0007 **SCANDINAVIAN DESIGN GROUP**
DENMARK

0008 **PRECURSOR**
UK

0009 **MODE**
UK

0010 **PRECURSOR**
UK

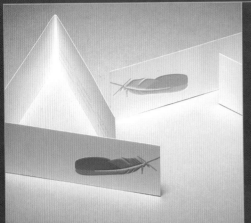

0012 **LLOYDS GRAPHIC DESIGN AND COMMUNICATION**
NEW ZEALAND

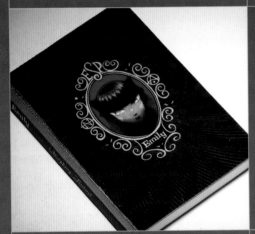

0013 **CHRONICLE BOOKS**
USA

0014 **HAND MADE GROUP**
ITALY

Sale at Viaduct
6–20 July 2002
Up to 50% off selected items
10 –15% off all orders

Onn

506
4300

Fac
650
596
2178

Web
www
oraclemobile
com

Facsimile
650
596
2178

ephone
0
06
300

ORACLE MOBILE

Onn

ORACLE MOBILE

Brad Hogan
Brand Marketing Manager, Mobile/Wireless
Oracle Worldwide Marketing

500 Oracle Parkway	Tel	Fax
MS8BP2		
Redwood Shores	650	413
CA 94065	506	581
	5543	6105

Email
brad.hogan@oracle.com

aclemobile.com

0017 **WALLACE CHURCH**
USA

0018 **TEMPLIN BRINK DESIGN**
USA

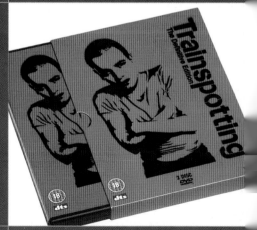

0019 **HGV FELTON**
UK

0020 **POINT BLANK DESIGN**
UK

0021 **UNTITLED**
UK ◊🖉✳**T**↑

0022 **SAMPSONMAY**
UK ◊**T**↑

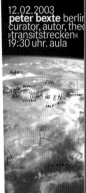

11.12.2002
horst hörtner linz
ars electronica center
»futurelab«
19:30 uhr. aula

12.02.2003
peter bexte berlin
curator, autor, theo
»transitstrecken«
19:30 uhr. aula

0023 **HESSE DESIGN GMBH**
GERMANY 🖉◊**T**↑

0024 **SCANDINAVIAN DESIGN GROUP**
DENMARK ◊🖉🖾↑

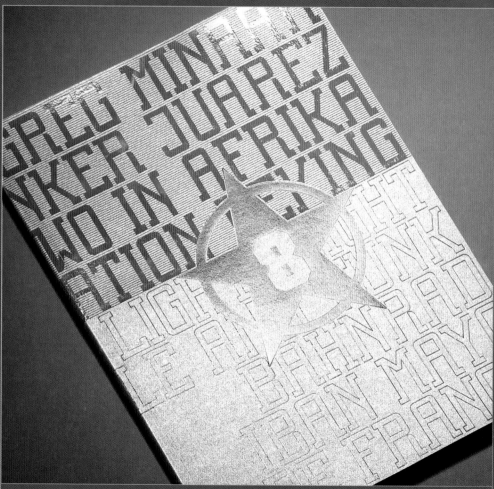

0027 **EGBG**
THE NETHERLANDS

0028 **SK VISUAL**
USA

0029 **MADE THOUGHT**
UK

0030 **FELDER GRAFIKDESIGN**
AUSTRIA

0031 **SHIH DESIGN**
TAIWAN

0032 **WEBB & WEBB**
UK

0033 **FIELD DESIGN CONSULTANTS**
UK

0034 **THE PHOENIX STUDIO**
USA

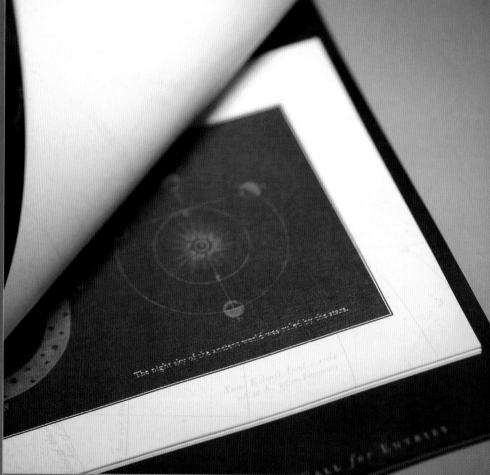

The night sky of the ancient world was ruled by the stars.

0037 **V06**
BRAZIL
 *T ↑

0038 **CRUSH DESIGN**
UK
 ◊ T ↑

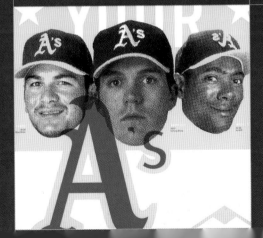

From Vernal Pool to Metropolis

0041 **LCTS**
UK

0042 **FELDER GRAFIKDESIGN**
AUSTRIA

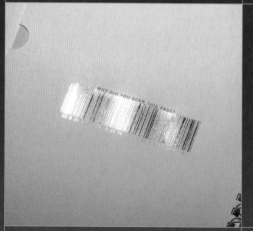

0043 **PH.D**
USA

0044 **GOUTHIER DESIGN, INC.**
USA

elve:ten

Dimensions 277 mm x 210mm
Front Colors Mix CN 40 Y100 K79
Publication Font FF Din Medium
Office Hours = 06 • After Hours = 70

Cover 4 col • Matt laminate • Spot varnish
Origination text Apple Mac
Origination text Kramer Lithrone
Avg. no. of operatives = 27
Avg. daily hot beverage intake = 4.3 cups

(03)

Graphica

IMMENSE
HIDDEN
BETWEEN
SLEEVES

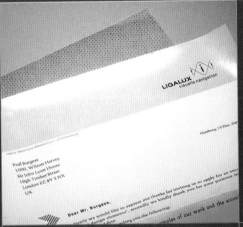

0047 **LIGALUX**
GERMANY

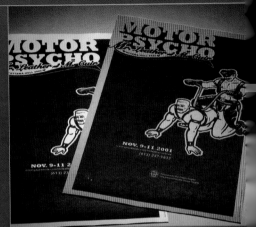

0048 **IRIDIUM, A DESIGN AGENCY**
CANADA

0049 **FORTYFOUR DESIGN**
AUSTRALIA

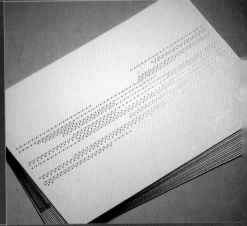

0050 **LIGALUX**
GERMANY

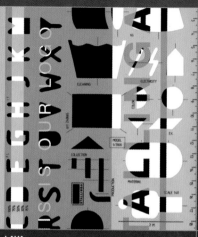

0051 **LAVA**
THE NETHERLANDS

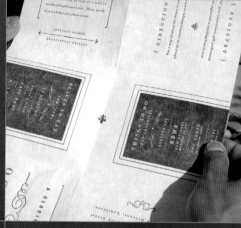

0052 **IAMALWAYSHUNGRY**
USA

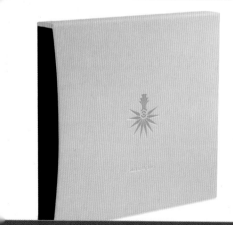

0053 **RIORDON DESIGN**
CANADA

0054 **R2 DESIGN**
PORTUGAL

0057 **NIKLAUS TROXLER DESIGN**
SWITZERLAND ◊ ◊ ◊ **T** ↑

0058 **GRAPHISCHE FORMGEBUNG,**
HERBERT ROHSIEPE
GERMANY ◊ ◊ ↑

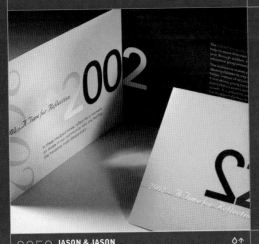

0059 **JASON & JASON**
ISRAEL ◊ ↑

0060 **SCANDINAVIAN DESIGN GROUP**
DENMARK ◊ **T** ◊ ↑

0061 **THOMPSON**
UK

0062 **PROJECT 88**
UK

0063 **WILSON HARVEY**
UK

STEVEN AND JULIE SWIRES
ARE DELIGHTED TO ANNOUNCE THE BIRTH
OF DANIEL STEVEN

0064 **LAYFIELD**
AUSTRALIA

nd Administration

CENTRE STAFFING:

The permanent staff of the Centre has been m

level commensurate with efficient operati

the financial resources of the Centre

on.

hart Chief Exe

Co

0067 **MARIUS FAHRNER DESIGN**
GERMANY

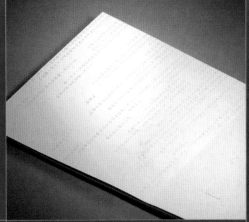

0068 **HAND MADE GROUP**
ITALY

0069 **...,STAAT**
THE NETHERLANDS

0070 **LIPPA PEARCE DESIGN**
UK

0071 **R2 DESIGN**
PORTUGAL ◊✐❋↑

ONY OURSLER THE INFLUENCE MACHI

0072 **EGGERS + DIAPER**
GERMANY ◊✐↑

0073 **MOTIVE DESIGN RESEARCH**
USA ◊✐↑

0074 **YAEL MILLER DESIGN**
USA ◊✐✄**T**❋↑

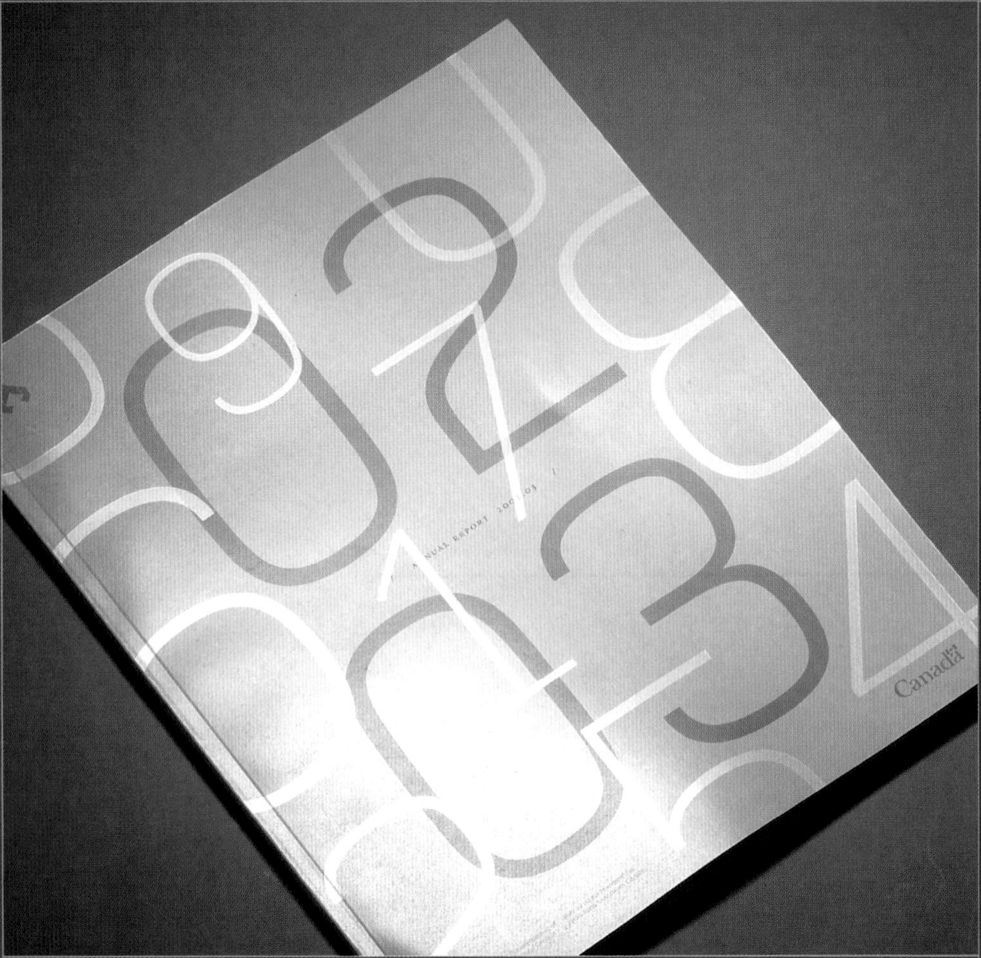

0076 **KOLEGRAM DESIGN**
CANADA

0077 **STARSHOT**
GERMANY

0078 **EMERY VINCENT DESIGN**
AUSTRALIA

0079 **DESIGN DEPOT CREATIVE BUREAU**
RUSSIA

0080 **UNDERWARE**
THE NETHERLANDS

0081 **MADE THOUGHT**
UK

◊⌀ T↑

0082 **NO.PARKING**
ITALY

◊⌀ T✻↑

0083 **CHEN DESIGN ASSOCIATES**
USA

◊⌀ ☰T✻↑

0084 **BRUKETA & ZINIC**
CROATIA

◊⌀ ✛⌀T↑

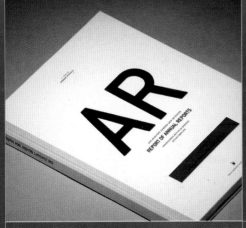

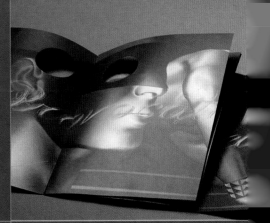

0087 **STRICHPUNKT**
GERMANY

0088 **MIRKO ILIC**
USA

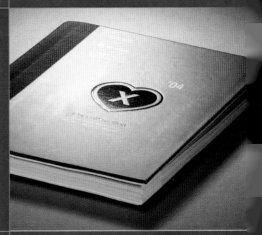

0089 **SCANDINAVIAN DESIGN GROUP**
DENMARK

0090 **STRICHPUNKT**
GERMANY

0091 **FELDER GRAFIKDESIGN**
AUSTRIA
◊ ✍ ↑

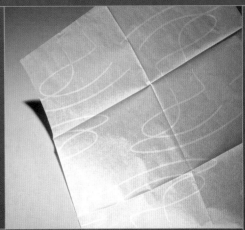

0092 **ALOOF DESIGN**
UK
◊ ✍ ↑

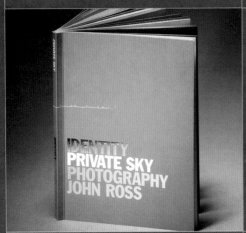

0093 **SEA DESIGN**
UK
◊ ✍ ⊘ T ↑

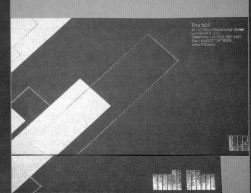

0094 **MADE THOUGHT**
UK
◊ ✍ T ☀ ↑

0097 **MODE**
UK ◊ ⬢ **T** ↑

0098 **KBDA**
USA ◊ ⬢ ⊘ + ↑

0099 **VOICE**
AUSTRALIA ◊ ⬢ ⬢ **T** ↑

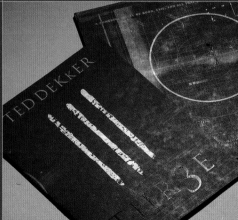

0100 **ANDERSON THOMAS DESIGN**
USA ◊ ↑

0101 **ROSE DESIGN**
UK

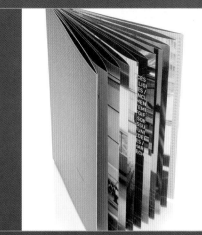

0102 **SCANDINAVIAN DESIGN GROUP**
DENMARK

0103 **IAMALWAYSHUNGRY**
USA

0104 **CDT DESIGN**
UK

0105 **GRAPHISCHE FORMGEBUNG, HERBERT ROHSIEPE**
GERMANY

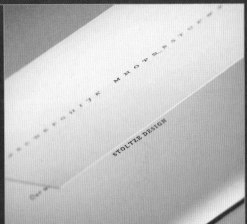

0107 **PROGRESS**
UK
◊🖌T☀↑

0108 **STOLTZE DESIGN**
USA
◊🖌✎↑

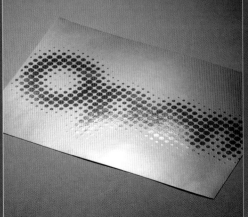

0109 **STEERSMCGILLAN**
UK
◊T↑

0110 **@RADICAL.MEDIA**
USA
◊☀🖌↑

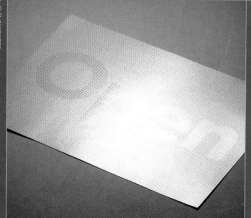

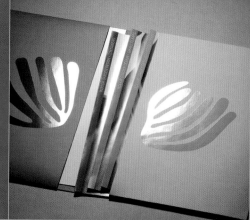

0111 **STEERSMCGILLAN**
UK

◊ T ↑

0112 **FORM**
UK

◊ ⬙ ↑

0113 **V06**
BRAZIL

◊ ⬙ ⬙ ↑

0114 **AVE DESIGN STUDIO**
USA

◊ ⬙ ⬙ ↑

0115 **JONES DESIGN GROUP**
USA

RSVP: VIA ENCLOSED
REPLY CARD

INVITATION: ADMITS ONE
ONLY PLEASE BRING IT
WITH YOU ON THE NIGHT

VISIT: THE EXHIBITION
WILL ALSO BE OPEN
FROM 10AM UNTIL 6PM
17/18/19/20/21 OCTOBER
ADMISSION FREE

INFORMATION: D&AD
+44 (0) 20 7840 1111
www.dandad.org

SPONSOR: PREMIER PAPER
DRINKS: COURTESY OF
KIRIN BEER

0116 **NB:STUDIO**
UK

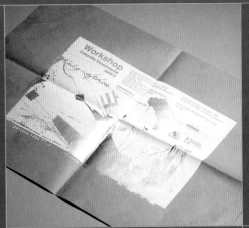

0117 **V06**
BRAZIL

0118 **PROGRESS**
UK

0119 **MIASO DESIGN**
USA

0120 **RIPE IN ASSOCIATION WITH ALCAN PRINT FINISHING**
UK

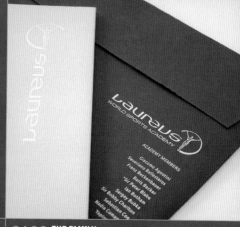

0121 **ROYCROFT DESIGN**
USA ◊T↑

0122 **THE FAMILY**
UK ◊✍↑

0123 **IRIDIUM, A DESIGN AGENCY**
CANADA ◊≡T✻↑

0124 **PRECURSOR**
UK ◊T✍✄↑

0125 **ERIC HESEN GRAPHIC DESIGN**
THE NETHERLANDS

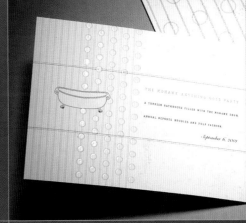

0127 **TAXI STUDIO**
UK

0128 **ROYCROFT DESIGN**
USA

0129 **CRANHAM ADVERTISING**
UK

0130 **ROSE DESIGN**
UK

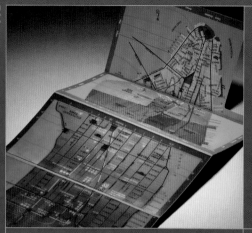

0131 **URBAN MAPPING**
USA

0132 **FELDER GRAFIKDESIGN**
AUSTRIA

INCA

INCA

Charlotte
Director

INCA Productions
The Top Floor
7–11 St Johns Hill
London SW11 1TN
United Kingdom

T +44 (0) 20 7223 5512
F +44 (0) 20 7223 4681
M +44 (0) 7976 684 273
E charlotte@incaproductions.co.uk
W www.incaproductions.com

0133 **SUM DESIGN**
UK

0134 **LIPPA PEARCE DESIGN**
UK

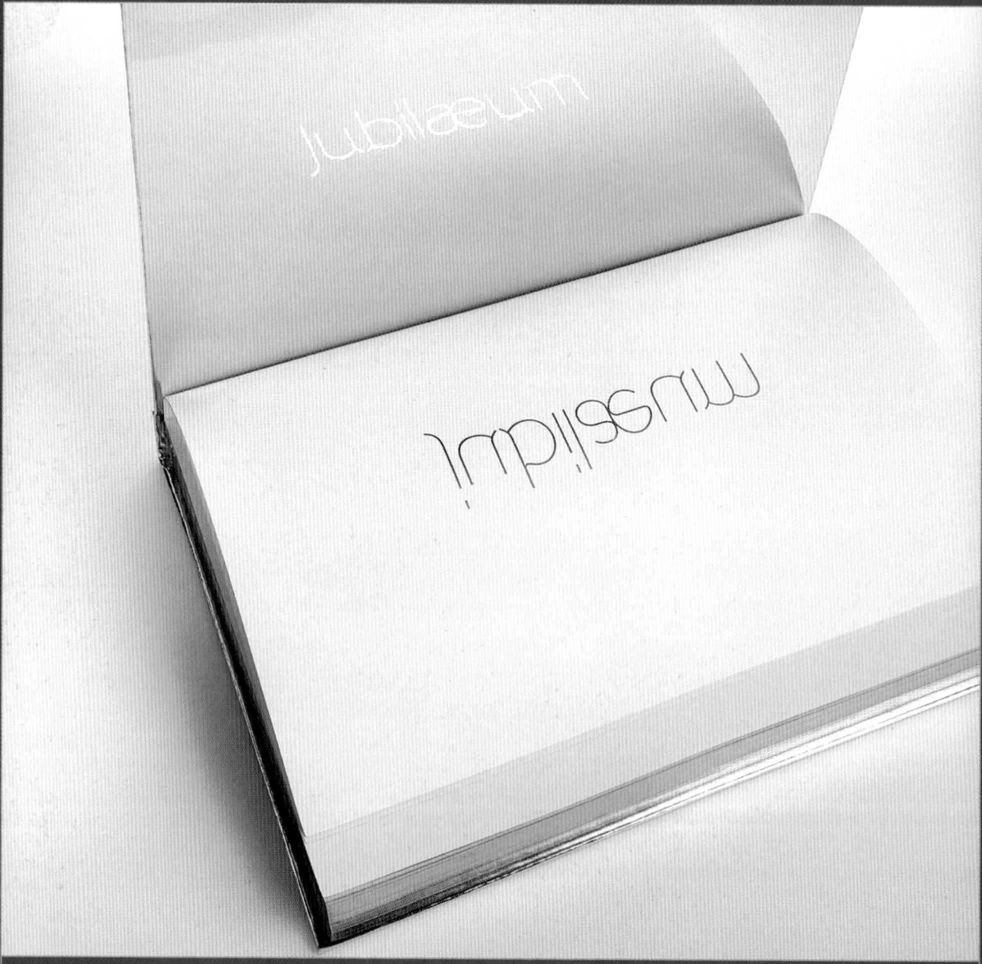

0136 **SCANDINAVIAN DESIGN GROUP**
DENMARK

0137 **ORANGESEED DESIGN**
USA

0138 **MODE**
UK

0139 **HESSE DESIGN**
GERMANY

0140 **PRECURSOR**
UK

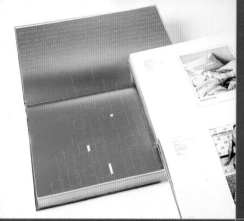

0141 **SCANDINAVIAN DESIGN GROUP**
DENMARK

0142 **MARIUS FAHRNER DESIGN**
GERMANY

0143 **CAPSULE**
USA

0144 **LIPPA PEARCE DESIGN**
UK

Ultra surface gloss

Ultra surface smoothness

Ultra white

Excellent ink lift and varnishing

Excellent dimensional stability for registration

Single sheet cutting for consistent quality

World-wide availability

...ck ink setting

115
135
150
170
200
250
300
350

B1

SRA1   SRA1

63x72   65x88   64x90   65x92   72x100 72x102

UK   UK   UK   UK   UK   UK
Mill   Mill   Mill   Mill   Mill   Mill

● ream wrapped
○ bulk/ream wrapped
○ bulk packed only

◊ + ✄ **T** ↑

0147 **QUESTION DESIGN**
USA

0148 **MAIOW CREATIVE BRANDING**
UK

0149 **ELMWOOD**
UK

0150 **11D – ELEVEN DESIGN**
DENMARK

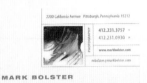

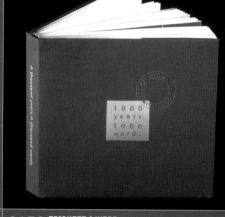

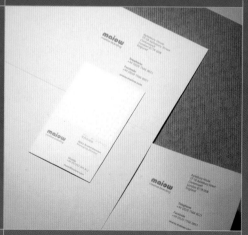

0151 **MONA MACDONALD DESIGN**
USA ◊+T✎↑

0152 **TRICKETT & WEBB**
UK ◊⊘✄↑

0153 **WILSON HARVEY**
UK ◊✎✄+↑

0154 **MAIOW CREATIVE BRANDING**
UK ◊✎✳T↑

shine

artworks
AWARDS ART DAY RESEARCH

0028 0029 0030 0031 0032 0033 0034 0035 0036 0037 0038 0039 0040
0068 0069 0070 0071 0072 0073 0074 0075 0076 0077 0078 0079 0080
0108 0109 0110 0111 0112 0113 0114 0115 0116 0117 0118 0119 0120
0148 0149 0150 0151 0152 0153 0154 0155
0348 0349 0350 0351 0352 0353 0354 0355 0356 0357 0358 0359 0360
0388 0389 0390 0391 0392 0393 0394 0395 0396 0397 0398 0399 0400
0428 0429 0430 0431 0432 0433 0434 0435 0436 0437 0438 0439 0440
0468 0469 0470 0471 0472 0473 0474 0475 0476 0477 0478 0479 0480
0508 0509 0510 0511 0512 0513 0514 0515 0516 0517 0518 0519 0520
0548 0549 0550 0551 0552 0553 0554 0555 0556 0557 0558 0559 0560
0588 0589 0590 0591 0592 0593 0594 0595 0596 0597 0598 0599 0600
0628 0629 0630 0631 0632 0633 0634 0635 0636 0637 0638 0639 0640
0668 0669 0670 0671 0672 0673 0674 0675 0676 0677 0678 0679 0680
0708 0709 0710 0711 0712 0713 0714 0715 0716 0717 0718 0719 0720
0748 0749 0750 0751 0752 0753 0754 0755 0756 0757 0758 0759 0760
0788 0789 0790 0791 0792 0793 0794 0795 0796 0797 0798 0799 0800
0828 0829 0830 0831 0832 0833 0834 0835 0836 0837 0838 0839 0840
0868 0869 0870 0871 0872 0873 0874 0875 0876 0877 0878 0879 0880
0908 0909 0910 0911 0912 0913 0914 0915 0916 0917 0918 0919 0920
0948 0949 0950 0951 0952 0953 0954 0955 0956 0957 0958 0959 0960
0988 0989 0990 0991 0992 0993 0994 0995 0996 0997 0998 0999 1000

02

MANIPULATED SURFACES

EMBOSSING
PERFORATION
FOIL BLOCKING
SPECIAL INKS
METALLICS

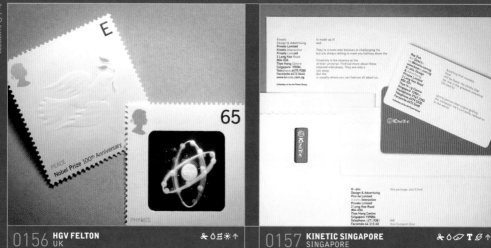

0156 **HGV FELTON**
UK

0157 **KINETIC SINGAPORE**
SINGAPORE

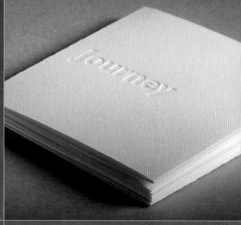

0158 **CRUSH DESIGN**
UK

0159 **WEBB & WEBB**
UK

Simon Jordan
simon@jump-studios.com

Jump London
35 Brita
London
United
Teleph
+44 0
Webs
www

Shaun Fernandes
shaun@jump-studios.com

Jump London
35 Brite
London
United
Teleph
+44 0
Web
www

Sarah Williams
sarah@jump-studios.com

Jump London
35 Britannia Row
London N1 8QH
United Kingdom
Telephone
+44 (0)20 7688 0080
Website
www.jump-studios.com

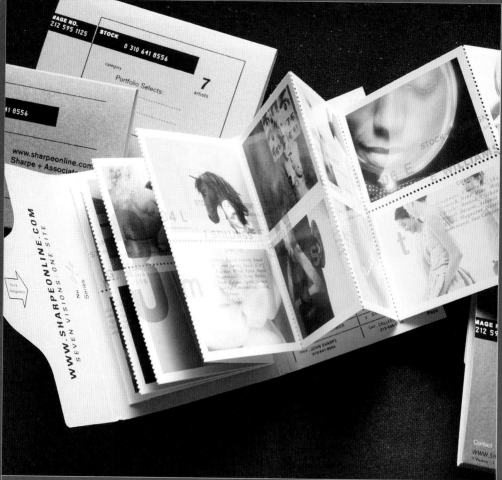

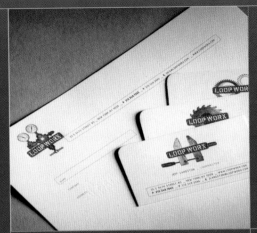

0162 **GIORGIO DAVANZO DESIGN**
USA

0163 **BBM & D**
USA

0164 **TEMPLIN BRINK DESIGN**
USA

0165 **PHILLIPS**
UK

0166 **JASON & JASON**
ISRAEL

0167 **STARSHOT**
GERMANY

the cats' home

SHAW HEAD FARM
BECKWITHSHAW HARROGATE
NORTH YORKSHIRE HG3 1QU
TEL 01423 561 897

0168 **LAYFIELD**
AUSTRALIA

0169 **MARIUS FAHRNER DESIGN**
GERMANY

0170 **ERBE DESIGN**
USA

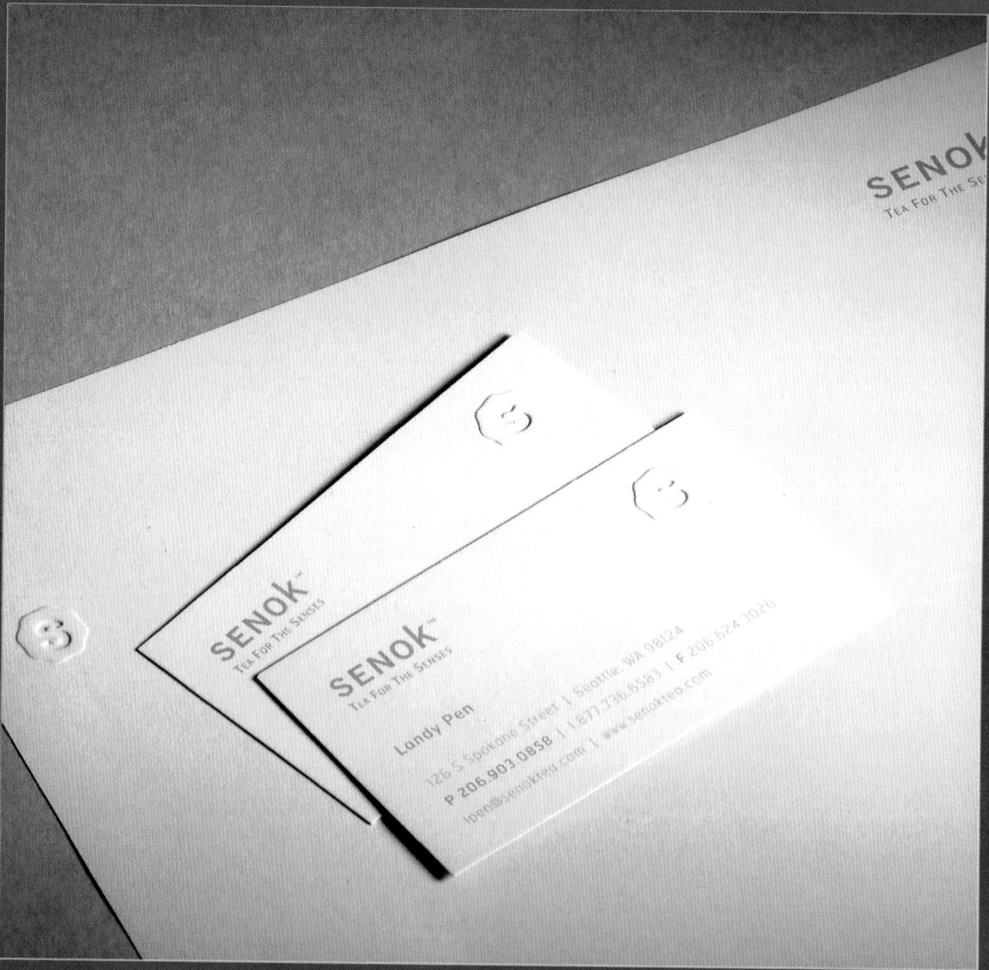

0171 **GIORGIO DAVANZO DESIGN**
USA

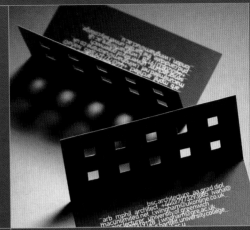

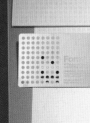

0172 **WALLACE CHURCH**
USA

0173 **KONTRAPUNKT**
SLOVENIA

0174 **AFTERHOURS CREATIVE**
USA

0175 **FORM**
UK

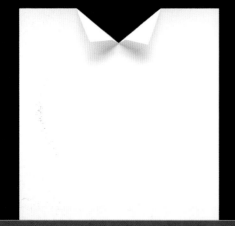

0176 **LAYFIELD**
AUSTRALIA

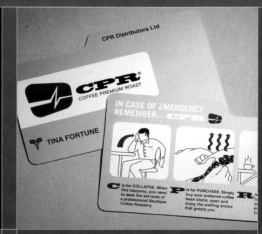

0177 **LLOYDS GRAPHIC DESIGN AND
COMMUNICATION**
NEW ZEALAND

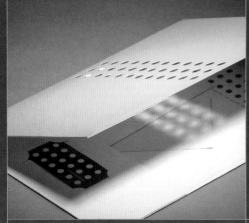

0178 **PH.D**
USA

0179 **WEBB & WEBB**
UK

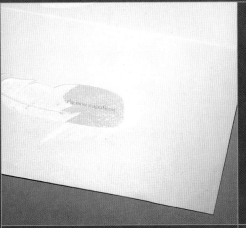

0182 **FLIGHT CREATIVE**
AUSTRALIA

0183 **FIBRE**
UK

0184 **NAVY BLUE**
UK

0185 **ULTRA DESIGN**
BRAZIL

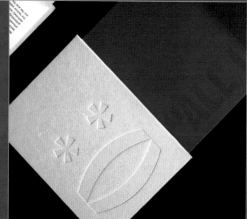

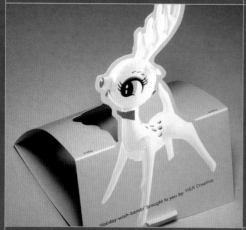

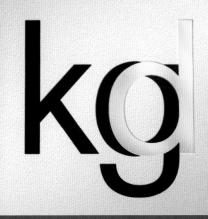

0192 **LIPPA PEARCE DESIGN**
UK

0193 **LIPPA PEARCE DESIGN**
UK

0194 **DOSSIERCREATIVE**
CANADA

0195 **NASSAR DESIGN**
USA

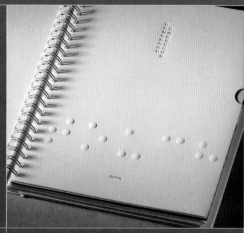

0196 **PH.D** USA

0197 **PH.D** USA

0198 **EMPIRE DESIGN STUDIO** USA

0199 **LLOYDS GRAPHIC DESIGN AND COMMUNICATION** NEW ZEALAND

Functional
Communication
Surfaces

under the Australian Government's
...nes Program

0201 **FAITH**
CANADA

0202 **NYC COLLEGE OF TECHNOLOGY**
USA

0203 **CHRONICLE BOOKS**
USA

0204 **ZIP DESIGN**
UK

0205 **GRAPEFRUIT DESIGN**
ROMANIA

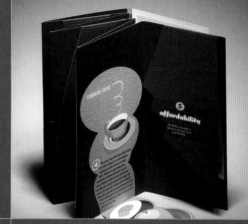

one.. hungry or peckish soup meal.. free

feeling hungry
or peckish ?

0206 **LIPPA PEARCE DESIGN**
UK

0207 **BARCELLONA**
USA

0208 **JULIA TAM DESIGN**
USA

0209 **EMERY VINCENT DESIGN**
AUSTRALIA

youth **befriending**

where do **you** fit in?

bullied

talk

together

REAL RED

SPECIAL

frien

0211   **EMERY VINCENT DESIGN**
AUSTRALIA

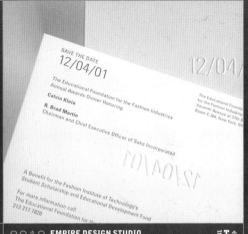

0212 **BWA DESIGN**
UK

0213 **EMPIRE DESIGN STUDIO**
USA

0214 **CASERTA DESIGN COMPANY**
USA

0215 **CHRONICLE BOOKS**
USA

0216 **CHRONICLE BOOKS** USA

0217 **HGV FELTON** UK

0218 **BETH CURTIS** UK

0219 **R2 DESIGN** PORTUGAL

BBK STUDIO
USA

Dialogue

Works by Peter Meacock
Central Workshop

0222 **BLACKCOFFEE** USA

0223 **IRIDIUM, A DESIGN AGENCY** CANADA

0224 **HORNALL ANDERSON DESIGN WORKS** USA

0225 **IRIDIUM, A DESIGN AGENCY** CANADA

0226 **IRIDIUM, A DESIGN AGENCY**
CANADA

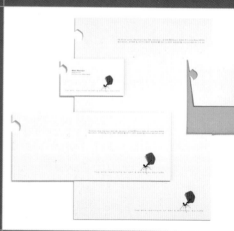

0227 **LAVA**
THE NETHERLANDS

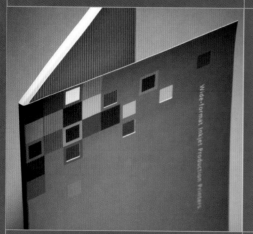

0228 **JASON & JASON**
ISRAEL

0229 **NET#WORK BBDO**
SOUTH AFRICA

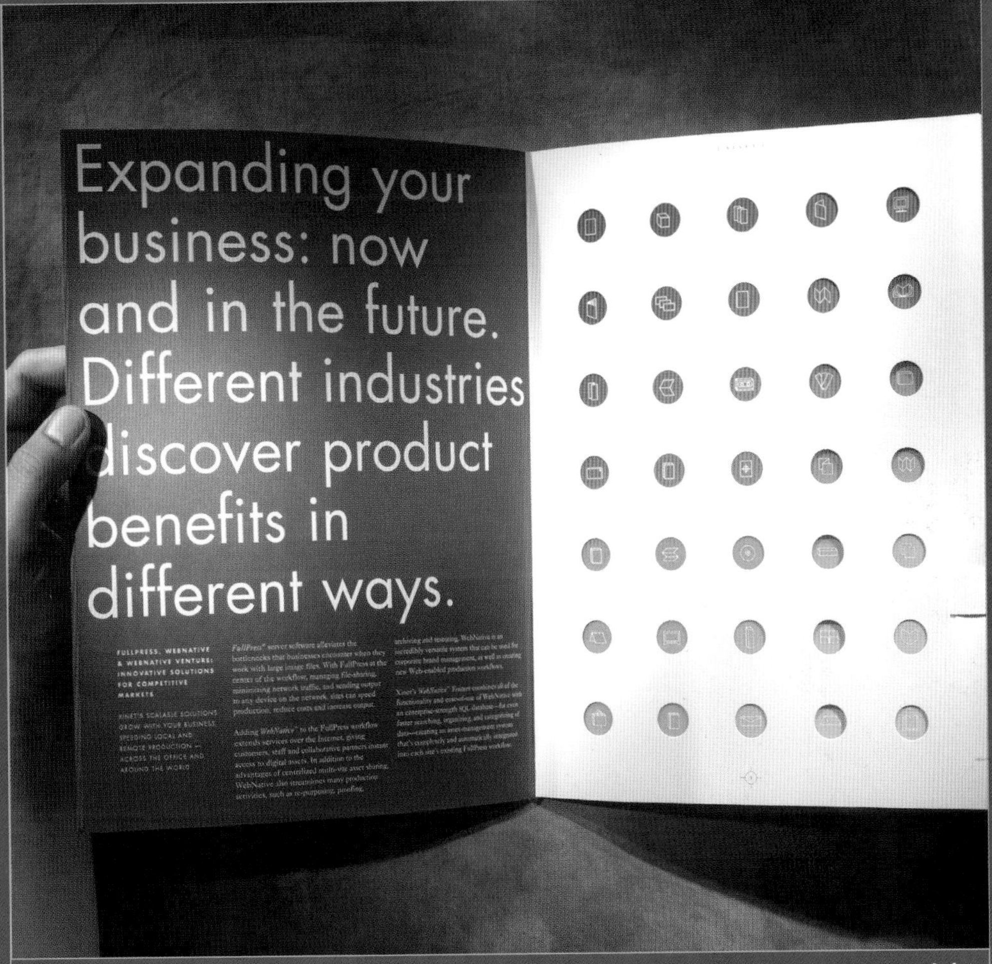

0230 **GEE + CHUNG DESIGN**
USA

0231 **MODE**
UK

people. innovation. design.

esther
franklin

0232 **BNIM ARCHITECTS**
USA

0233 **MADE THOUGHT**
UK

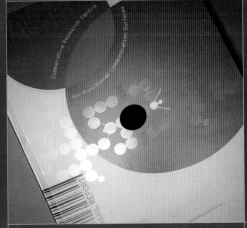

0234 **FORTYFOUR DESIGN**
AUSTRALIA

0235 **XAX CREATIVE**
USA

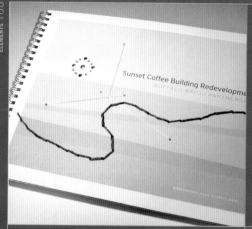

0236 **BNIM ARCHITECTS**
USA

0237 **RIORDON DESIGN**
CANADA

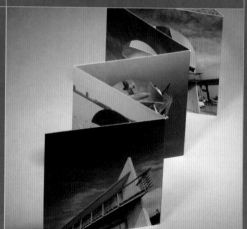

0238 **RINZEN**
AUSTRALIA

0239 **FOUR-LETTER WORD**
UK

0240 **LAVA**
THE NETHERLANDS

0242 **KINETIC SINGAPORE**
SINGAPORE

0243 **PROGRESS**
UK

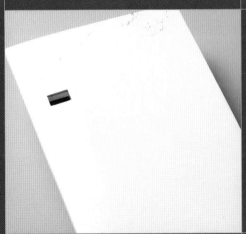

0244 **SCANDINAVIAN DESIGN GROUP**
DENMARK

0245 **KINETIC SINGAPORE**
SINGAPORE

0246 **KINETIC SINGAPORE**
SINGAPORE

0247 **PLUS DESIGN**
USA

0248 **PROGRESS**
UK

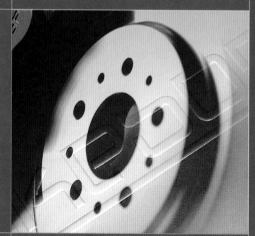

0249 **THE FAMILY**
UK

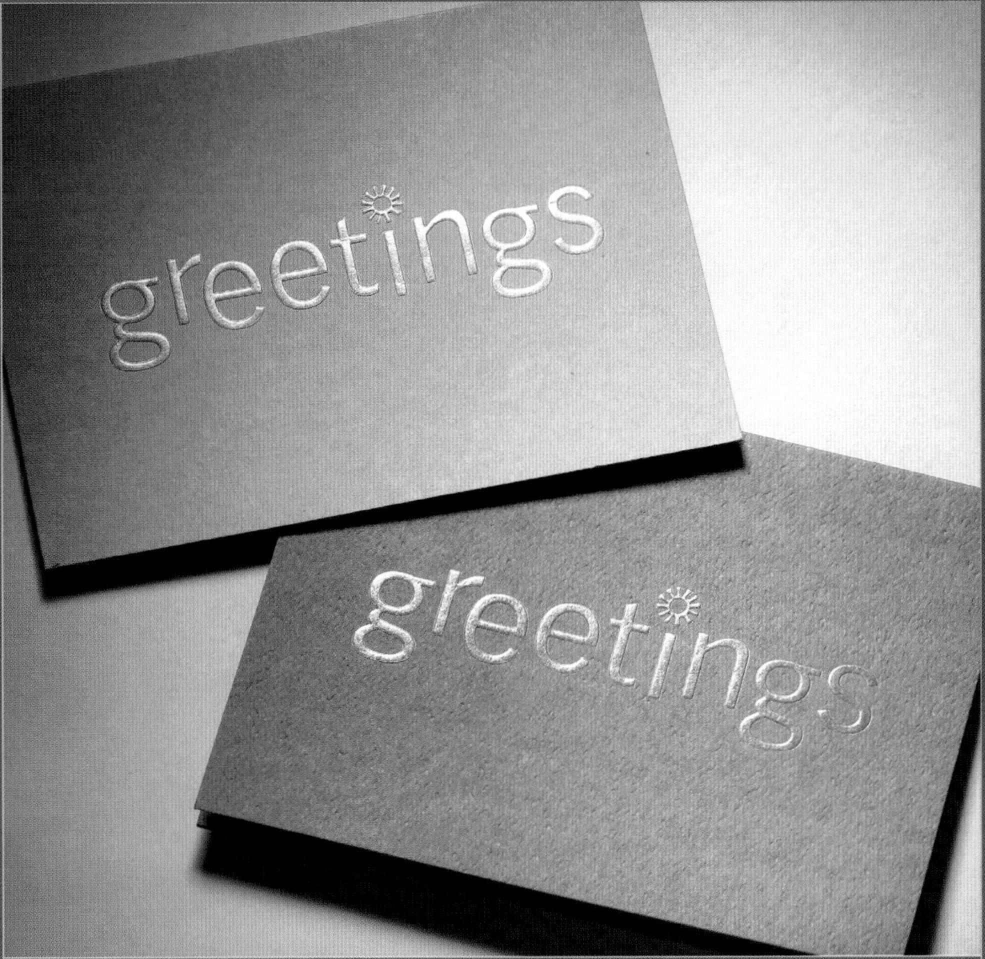

0250 **BELYEA**
USA

Händlerstempel

0252 **KESSELS KRAMER**
THE NETHERLANDS

0253 **BBK STUDIO**
USA

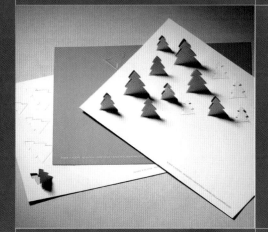

0254 **BISQIT DESIGN**
UK

0255 **JASON & JASON**
ISRAEL

0256 **HGV FELTON**
UK

0257 **HAND MADE GROUP**
ITALY

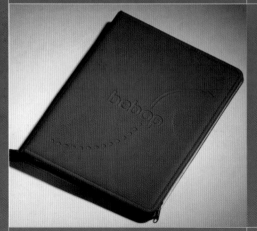

0258 **PHILLIPS**
UK

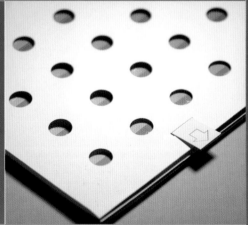

0259 **GEE + CHUNG DESIGN**
USA

0260 **MOTIVE DESIGN RESEARCH**
USA

portfolio-cph

(adress) Langangstræde 37B / DK-1468 Copenhagen K
(tel) +45 3393 6670 / (fax) +45 3393 6680 / (www) **portfolio-cph**.dk
(mail) hello@portfolio-cph.dk

Hasse Nielse

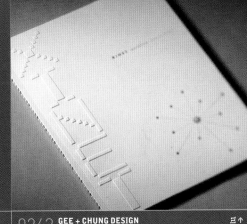

0262 **PHILLIPS**
UK

0263 **GEE + CHUNG DESIGN**
USA

0264 **MOTIVE DESIGN RESEARCH**
USA

0265 **STRICHPUNKT**
GERMANY

0266 **FAUXPAS**
SWITZERLAND

0267 **PHILLIPS**
UK

0268 **ALOOF DESIGN**
UK

0269 **ANDERSON THOMAS DESIGN**
USA

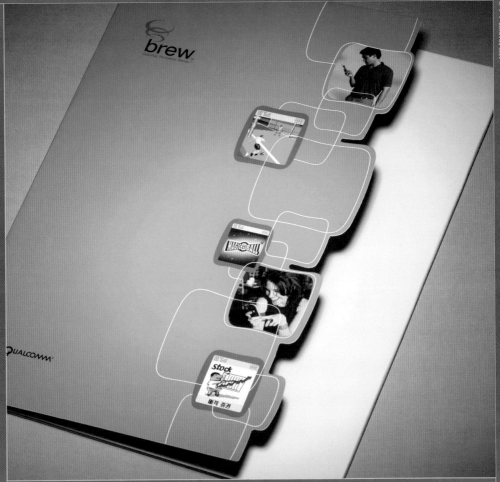

0270 **MIRES**
USA

GEORGINAGOODMAN

12/14 Shepherd Street, M

GEORGINAGOODMAN

12/14 Shepherd Street, Mayfair, London W

t +44 20 7499 8599

f +44 20 7

GEORGINAGOODMAN

0272 **STRUKTUR DESIGN**
UK

0273 **MIRES**
USA

0274 **JASON & JASON**
ISRAEL

0275 **THE FAMILY**
UK

0276 **CAPSULE**
USA

0277 **FELDER GRAFIKDESIGN**
AUSTRIA

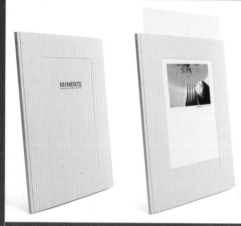

0278 **KINETIC SINGAPORE**
SINGAPORE

0279 **SCANDINAVIAN DESIGN GROUP**
DENMARK

0280 **KOLEGRAM DESIGN** CANADA

LIQUID AGENCY
USA

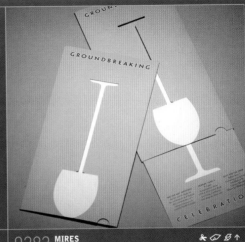

0282 **IRIDIUM, A DESIGN AGENCY**
CANADA

0283 **MIRES**
USA

0284 **KOLEGRAM DESIGN**
CANADA

0285 **KOLEGRAM DESIGN**
CANADA

0286 **BEAULIEU CONCEPTS GRAPHIQUES**
CANADA

0287 **UNA (AMSTERDAM) DESIGNERS**
THE NETHERLANDS

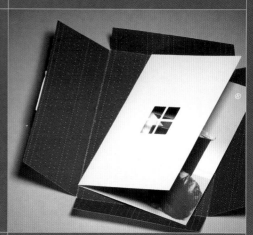

0288 **TRICKETT & WEBB**
UK

0289 **KOLEGRAM DESIGN**
CANADA

Adduci**studios**

2520 Ryan Road #36
Concord Ca 94518

925.686.4511 | office
925.787.1243 | mobile

stephen@adducistudios.com
www.adducistudios.com

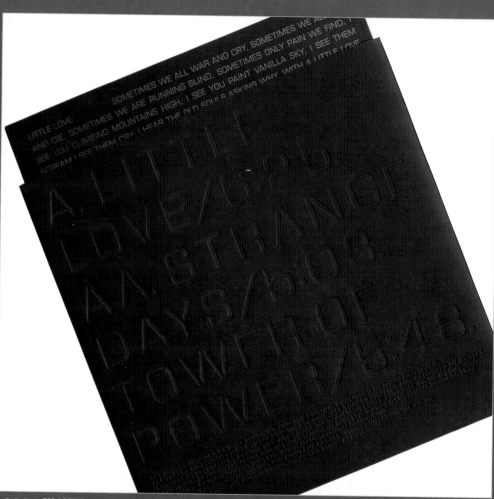

LITTLE LOVE. SOMETIMES WE ALL WAR AND CRY, SOMETIMES WE AL AND DIE, SOMETIMES WE ARE RUNNING BLIND, SOMETIMES ONLY PAIN WE FIND, SEE YOU CLIMBING MOUNTAINS HIGH, I SEE YOU PAINT VANILLA SKY, I SEE THEM SCREAM I SEE THEM CRY, I HEAR THE OLD SOULS ASKING WHY WITH A LITTLE LOVE

A LITTLE LOVE/6.26. A STRANGE AM. DAYS/6.03. TOWER OF POWER/5.48.

0292 **MORTENSON DESIGN**
USA
Ξ↑

0293 **TRACY DESIGN**
USA
Ξ⌀◊+⌀↑

0294 **PRECURSOR**
UK
&⌀ΞT✳↑

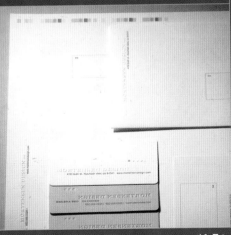

0295 **MORTENSON DESIGN**
USA
Ξ&T↑

0296 **MARIUS FAHRNER DESIGN**
GERMANY

0297 **METAL**
USA

0298 **DESIGN 5**
USA

0299 **JASON & JASON**
ISRAEL

0300 **CHEN DESIGN ASSOCIATES**
USA

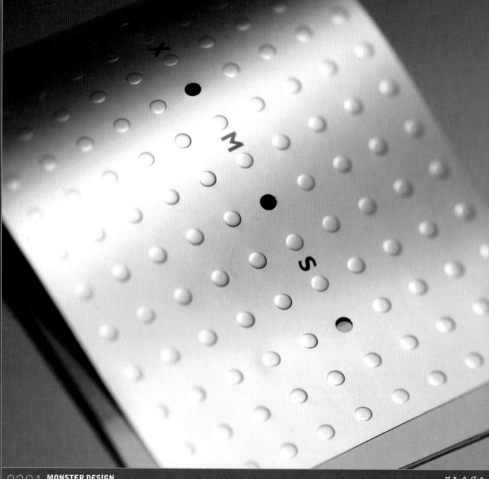

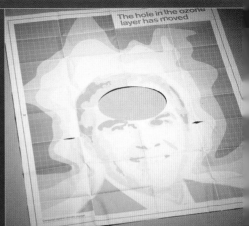

0302 **DESIGN 5** USA	0303 **JOHNSON BANKS** UK
0304 **LIPPA PEARCE DESIGN** UK	0305 **JASON & JASON** ISRAEL

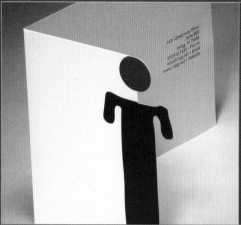

0306 **NETSUCCESS**
USA

0307 **DESIGN 5**
USA

0308 **TEMPLIN BRINK DESIGN**
USA

0309 **LIGALUX**
GERMANY

our universe is expanding...

but our name is contracting.

kbda

WHAT DOES
PROGRESS
SOUND LIKE?

0312 **AND PARTNERS**
USA

0313 **MIRIELLO GRAFICO**
USA

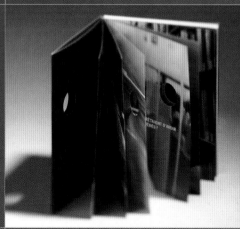

0314 **SALTERBAXTER**
UK

0315 **IRIDIUM, A DESIGN AGENCY**
CANADA

0316 **MIRKO ILIC**
USA

0317 **BUREAU GRAS**
THE NETHERLANDS

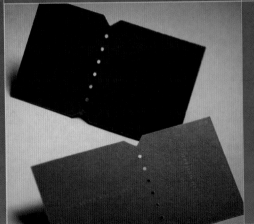

0318 **IE DESIGN**
USA

0319 **PLUS DESIGN**
USA

BLOK DESIGN
MEXICO

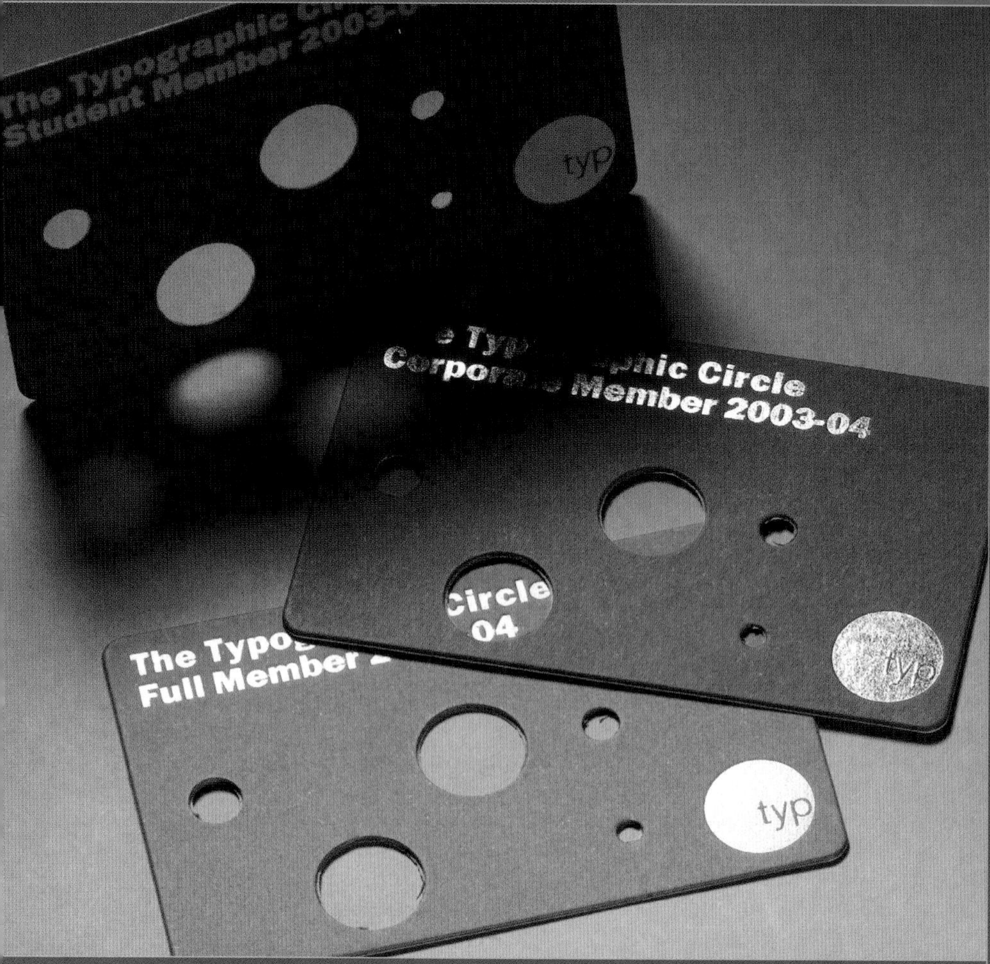

0321 **JADE DESIGN**
UK

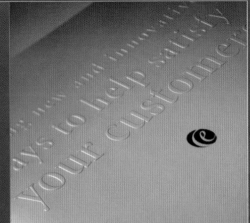

0322 **IE DESIGN**
USA

0323 **IRIDIUM, A DESIGN AGENCY**
CANADA

0324 **FELDER GRAFIKDESIGN**
AUSTRIA

0325 **IE DESIGN**
USA

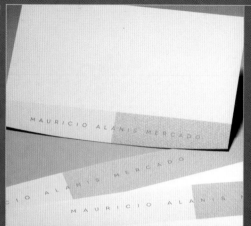

0326 **CINCODEMAYO DESIGN**
MEXICO

0327 **MARIUS FAHRNER DESIGN**
GERMANY

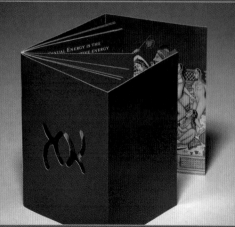

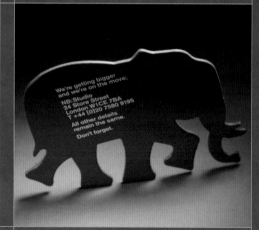

0328 **MIRKO ILIC**
USA

0329 **NB:STUDIO**
UK

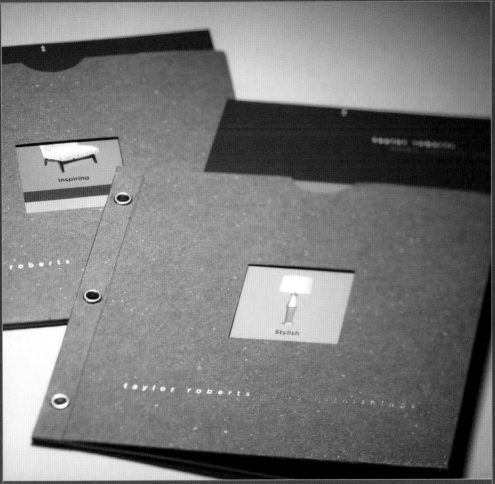

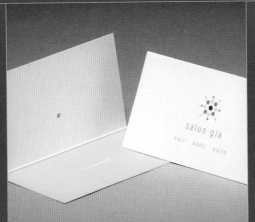

0332 **HANS DESIGN**
USA

0333 **THE WORKS DESIGN COMMUNICATIONS**
CANADA

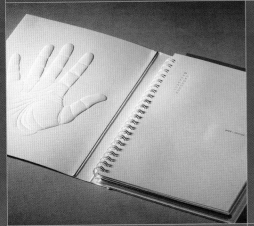

0334 **PH.D**
USA

0335 **...,STAAT**
THE NETHERLANDS

0336 **ZULVER & CO**
UK

0337 **KOLEGRAM DESIGN**
CANADA

0338 **LIPPA PEARCE DESIGN**
UK

0339 **CAPSULE**
USA

0001 0002 0003 0004 0005 0006 0007 0008 0009 0010 0011 0012 0013 0014 0015 0016 0017 0018 0019 0020 0021 0022 0023 0024 0025
0041 0042 0043 0044 0045 0046 0047 0048 0049 0050 0051 0052 0053 0054 0055 0056 0057 0058 0059 0060 0061 0062 0063 0064 0065
0081 0082 0083 0084 0085 0086 0087 0088 0089 0090 0091 0092 0093 0094 0095 0096 0097 0098 0099 0100 0101 0102 0103 0104 0105
0121 0122 0123 0124 0125 0126 0127 0128 0129 0130 0131 0132 0133 0134 0135 0136 0137 0138 0139 0140 0141 0142 0143 0144 0145
0161 0162 0163 0164 0165 0166 0167 0168 0169 0170 0171 0172 0173 0174 0175 0176 0177 0178 0179 0180 0181 0182 0183 0184 0185
0201 0202 0203 0204 0205 0206 0207 0208 0209 0210 0211 0212 0213 0214 0215 0216 0217 0218 0219 0220 0221 0222 0223 0224 0225
0241 0242 0243 0244 0245 0246 0247 0248 0249 0250 0251 0252 0253 0254 0255 0256 0257 0258 0259 0260 0261 0262 0263 0264 0265
0281 0282 0283 0284 0285 0286 0287 0288 0289 0290 0291 0292 0293 0294 0295 0296 0297 0298 0299 0300 0301 0302 0303 0304 0305
0321 0322 0323 0324 0325 0326 0327 0328 0329 0330 0331 0332 0333 0334 0335 0336 0337 0338 0339 0340 0341 0342 0343 0344 0345
0361 0362 0363 0364 0365 0366 0367 0368 0369 0370 0371 0372 0373 0374 0375 0376 0377 0378 0379 0380 0381 0382 0383 0384 0385
0401 0402 0403 0404 0405 0406 0407 0408 0409 0410 0411 0412 0413 0414 0415 0416 0417 0418 0419 0420 0421 0422 0423 0424 0425
0441 0442 0443 0444 0445 0446 0447 0448 0449 0450 0451 0452 0453 0454 0455 0456 0457 0458 0459 0460 0461 0462 0463 0464 0465
0481 0482 0483 0484 0485 0486 0487 0488 0489 0490 0491 0492 0493 0494 0495 0496 0497 0498 0499 0500 0501 0502 0503 0504 0505
0521 0522 0523 0524 0525 0526 0527 0528 0529 0530 0531 0532 0533 0534 0535 0536 0537 0538 0539 0540 0541 0542 0543 0544 0545
0561 0562 0563 0564 0565 0566 0567 0568 0569 0570 0571 0572 0573 0574 0575 0576 0577 0578 0579 0580 0581 0582 0583 0584 0585
0601 0602 0603 0604 0605 0606 0607 0608 0609 0610 0611 0612 0613 0614 0615 0616 0617 0618 0619 0620 0621 0622 0623 0624 0625
0641 0642 0643 0644 0645 0646 0647 0648 0649 0650 0651 0652 0653 0654 0655 0656 0657 0658 0659 0660 0661 0662 0663 0664 0665
0681 0682 0683 0684 0685 0686 0687 0688 0689 0690 0691 0692 0693 0694 0695 0696 0697 0698 0699 0700 0701 0702 0703 0704 0705
0721 0722 0723 0724 0725 0726 0727 0728 0729 0730 0731 0732 0733 0734 0735 0736 0737 0738 0739 0740 0741 0742 0743 0744 0745
0761 0762 0763 0764 0765 0766 0767 0768 0769 0770 0771 0772 0773 0774 0775 0776 0777 0778 0779 0780 0781 0782 0783 0784 0785
0801 0802 0803 0804 0805 0806 0807 0808 0809 0810 0811 0812 0813 0814 0815 0816 0817 0818 0819 0820 0821 0822 0823 0824 0825
0841 0842 0843 0844 0845 0846 0847 0848 0849 0850 0851 0852 0853 0854 0855 0856 0857 0858 0859 0860 0861 0862 0863 0864 0865
0881 0882 0883 0884 0885 0886 0887 0888 0889 0890 0891 0892 0893 0894 0895 0896 0897 0898 0899 0900 0901 0902 0903 0904 0905
0921 0922 0923 0924 0925 0926 0927 0928 0929 0930 0931 0932 0933 0934 0935 0936 0937 0938 0939 0940 0941 0942 0943 0944 0945
0961 0962 0963 0964 0965 0966 0967 0968 0969 0970 0971 0972 0973 0974 0975 0976 0977 0978 0979 0980 0981 0982 0983 0984 0985

0028 0029 0030 0031 0032 0033 0034 0035 0036 0037 0038 0039 0040
0068 0069 0070 0071 0072 0073 0074 0075 0076 0077 0078 0079 0080
0108 0109 0110 0111 0112 0113 0114 0115 0116 0117 0118 0119 0120
0148 0149 0150 0151 0152 0153 0154 0155 0156 0157 0158 0159 0160
0188 0189 0190 0191 0192 0193 0194 0195 0196 0197 0198 0199 0200
0228 0229 0230 0231 0232 0233 0234 0235 0236 0237 0238 0239 0240
0268 0269 0270 0271 0272 0273 0274 0275 0276 0277 0278 0279 0280
0308 0309 0310 0311 0312 0313 0314 0315 0316 0317 0318 0319 0320
0348 0349 0350 0351 0352 0353 0354 0355 0356 0357 0358 0359 0360
0388 0389 0390 0391 0392 0393 0394 0395 0396 0397 0398 0399 0400
0428 0429 0430 0431 0432 0433 0434 0435 0436 0437 0438 0439 0440
0468 0469 0470 0471 0472 0473 0474 0475 0476 0477 0478 0479 0480
0508 0509 0510 0511 0512 0513 0514 0515 0516 0517 0518 0519 0520
0548 0549 0550 0551 0552 0553 0554 0555 0556 0557 0558 0559 0560
0588 0589 0590 0591 0592 0593 0594 0595 0596 0597 0598 0599 0600
0628 0629 0630 0631 0632 0633 0634 0635 0636 0637 0638 0639 0640
0668 0669 0670 0671 0672 0673 0674 0675 0676 0677 0678 0679 0680
0708 0709 0710 0711 0712 0713 0714 0715 0716 0717 0718 0719 0720
0748 0749 0750 0751 0752 0753 0754 0755 0756 0757 0758 0759 0760
0788 0789 0790 0791 0792 0793 0794 0795 0796 0797 0798 0799 0800
0828 0829 0830 0831 0832 0833 0834 0835 0836 0837 0838 0839 0840
0868 0869 0870 0871 0872 0873 0874 0875 0876 0877 0878 0879 0880
0908 0909 0910 0911 0912 0913 0914 0915 0916 0917 0918 0919 0920
0948 0949 0950 0951 0952 0953 0954 0955 0956 0957 0958 0959 0960
0988 0989 0990 0991 0992 0993 0994 0995 0996 0997 0998 0999 1000

03

FORMATS
AND
BINDINGS

STITCHING
FOLDING
SCREWING

-0560

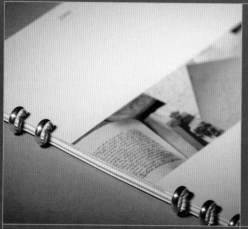

0341 **ZULVER & CO**
UK
⊘↑

0342 **SCANDINAVIAN DESIGN GROUP**
DENMARK
⊘T✳↑

0343 **SCANDINAVIAN DESIGN GROUP**
DENMARK
⊘T✳↑

0344 **JONES DESIGN GROUP**
USA
⊘ℬ↑

⊘ ⦵ **T** ◇ ☀ ↑

0346 **STRUKTUR DESIGN**
UK

0347 **BWA DESIGN**
UK

0348 **WALLACE CHURCH**
USA

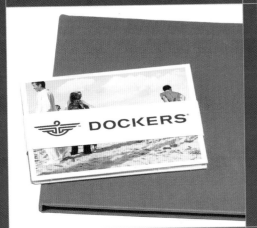

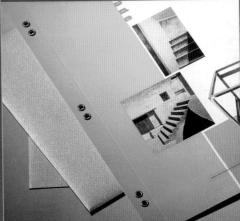

0349 **POINT BLANK DESIGN**
UK

0350 **BELYEA**
USA

0351 **BBK STUDIO**
USA

0352 **TAXI STUDIO**
UK

0353 **SAS**
UK

0354 **TEMPLIN BRINK DESIGN**
USA

0355 **IRIDIUM, A DESIGN AGENCY**
CANADA

0357 **TAXI STUDIO**
UK

0358 **LEWIS COMMUNICATIONS**
USA

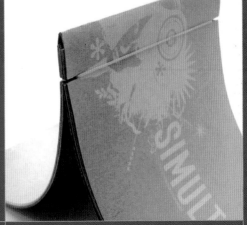

0359 **STOLTZE DESIGN**
USA

0360 **CRUSH DESIGN**
UK

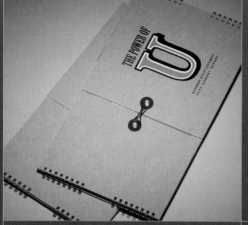

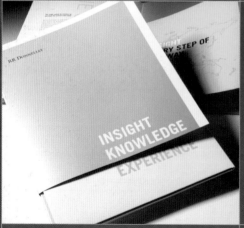

0361 **POPCORN INITIATIVE**
USA

0362 **KOLEGRAM DESIGN**
CANADA

0363 **JASON & JASON**
ISRAEL

0364 **LIQUID AGENCY**
USA

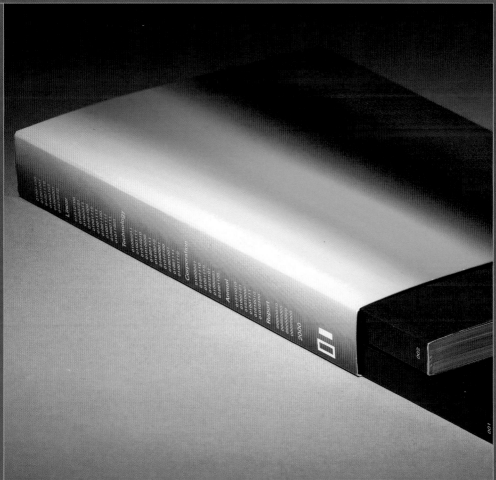

0365 **CAHAN & ASSOCIATES** USA

⌀ **T** ✳ ↑

MIRKO ILIC
USA

heather Ruhrman
505 North park Dr
Apartment 4
Arlington, Virginia

DOCKERS

because
some things just
fit better*

0367 **HEATHER BIANCHI DESIGN**
USA

0368 **POINT BLANK DESIGN**
UK

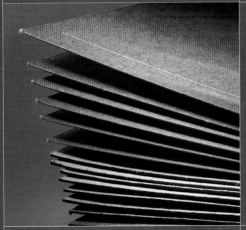

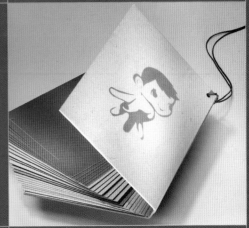

0369 **R2 DESIGN**
PORTUGAL

0370 **R2 DESIGN**
PORTUGAL

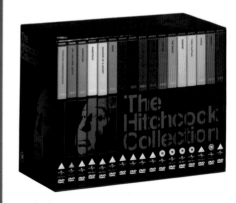

0371 **TEMPLIN BRINK DESIGN**
USA

0372 **KEARNEY ROCHOLL**
GERMANY

0373 **NB:STUDIO**
UK

0374 **POINT BLANK DESIGN**
UK

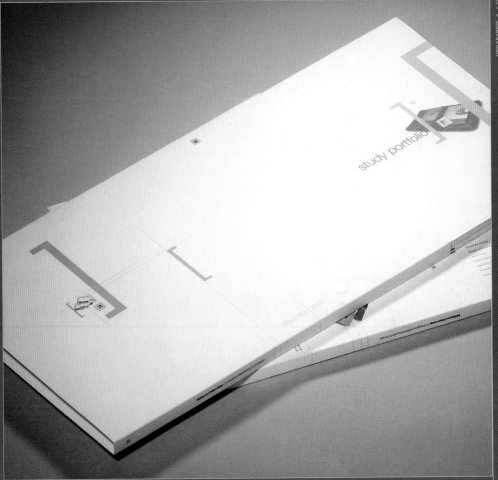

0376 **ROSE DESIGN**
UK

⌀ ✂ ↑

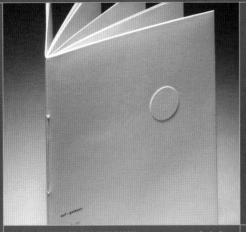

0377 **FELDER GRAFIKDESIGN**
AUSTRIA

0378 **DESIGN HOCH DREI**
GERMANY

0379 **LIPPA PEARCE DESIGN**
UK

0380 **SAS**
UK

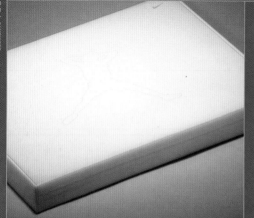

0381 **FIBRE**
UK

0382 **CHIMERA DESIGN**
AUSTRALIA

0383 **IRIDIUM, A DESIGN AGENCY**
CANADA

0384 **IAMALWAYSHUNGRY**
USA

PRINTING/FINISHING TECHNIQUE

CMYK

PERFORATION

MICRO

PRINTING/FINISHING TECHNIQUE

CMYK + PMS

FOIL BLOCKING

PRINTING/FINISHING TECHNIQUE

CMYK

SCORING

FOILBLOCKING

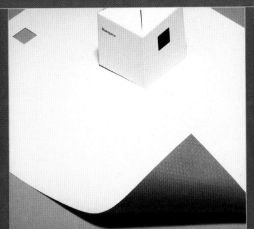

0387 **AFTERHOURS CREATIVE**
USA

0388 **BARCELLONA**
USA

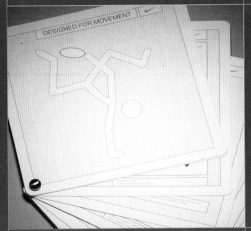

0389 **FIBRE**
UK

0390 **RICKABAUGH GRAPHICS**
USA

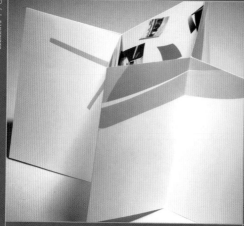

0391 **FLIGHT CREATIVE**
AUSTRALIA

0392 **GILLESPIE DESIGN**
USA

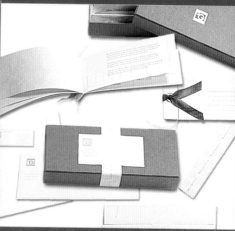

0393 **THE FORMATION**
UK

0394 **IE DESIGN**
USA

MADE TO MOVE
03

0397 **OCTAVO DESIGN**
AUSTRALIA

0398 **DAWN HOSKINSON**
UK

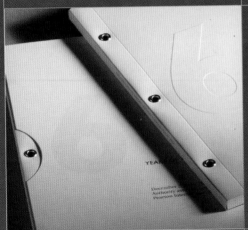

0399 **THE WORKS DESIGN COMMUNICATIONS**
CANADA

0400 **IMAGINATION (GIC)**
UK

0401 **PH.D**
USA

0402 **PH.D**
USA

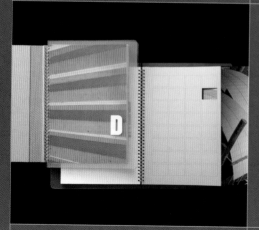

0403 **LIPPA PEARCE DESIGN**
UK

0404 **SUSSNER DESIGN**
USA

ACHIEVEMENT

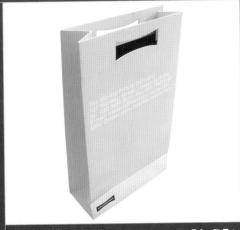

0407 **FORM**
UK

0408 **LAVA**
THE NETHERLANDS

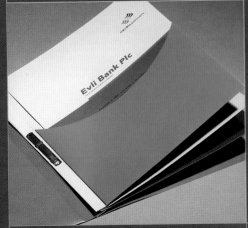

0409 **SHARP COMMUNICATIONS**
USA

0410 **R2 DESIGN**
PORTUGAL

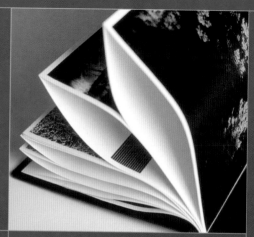

0411 **EMPIRE DESIGN STUDIO**
USA

0412 **EMERY VINCENT DESIGN**
AUSTRALIA

0413 **FORM**
UK

0414 **CHIMERA DESIGN**
AUSTRALIA

better wrap up

we want to brighten up your christmas in more
ways than one. so when you've finished with this
card, don't out it out and transform it into festive
wrapping paper. please reuse it and give it a
new lease of life!

UNDERWARE
THE NETHERLANDS

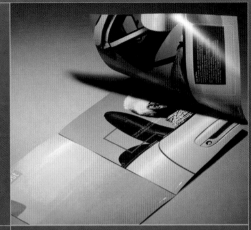

0417 **LLOYDS GRAPHIC DESIGN AND COMMUNICATION**
NEW ZEALAND ⊘ ✄ **T** ↑

0418 **WILSON HARVEY**
UK ✄ **T** ↑

0419 **BWA DESIGN**
UK ✄ ✎ ↑

0420 **BNIM ARCHITECTS**
USA ⊘ ✄ ✎ ☀ ↑

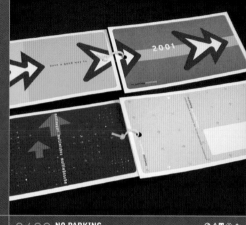

DOOM
2000

2010
BOOM ☆ DESIGN YORKSHIRE EXISTS TO IMPRESS THE LIVES OF THE PEOPLE
OF THE REGION AND RAISE YORKSHIRE'S INTERNATIONAL PROFILE BY
DEVELOPING A CULTURE OF DESIGN AND INNOVATION

Ø ✄ T ✳ ↑

0427 **CHRONICLE BOOKS**
USA

0428 **HGV FELTON**
UK

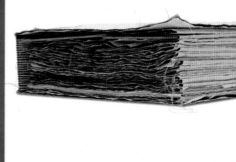

0429 **BBK STUDIO**
USA

0430 **BIRMINGHAM INSTITUTE**
OF ART & DESIGN
UK

0431 **BLACKCOFFEE**
USA

0432 **RADLEY YELDAR**
UK

PART PF-001 DESIGN SKILLS

0433 **RINZEN**
AUSTRALIA

0434 **FOXINABOX**
UK

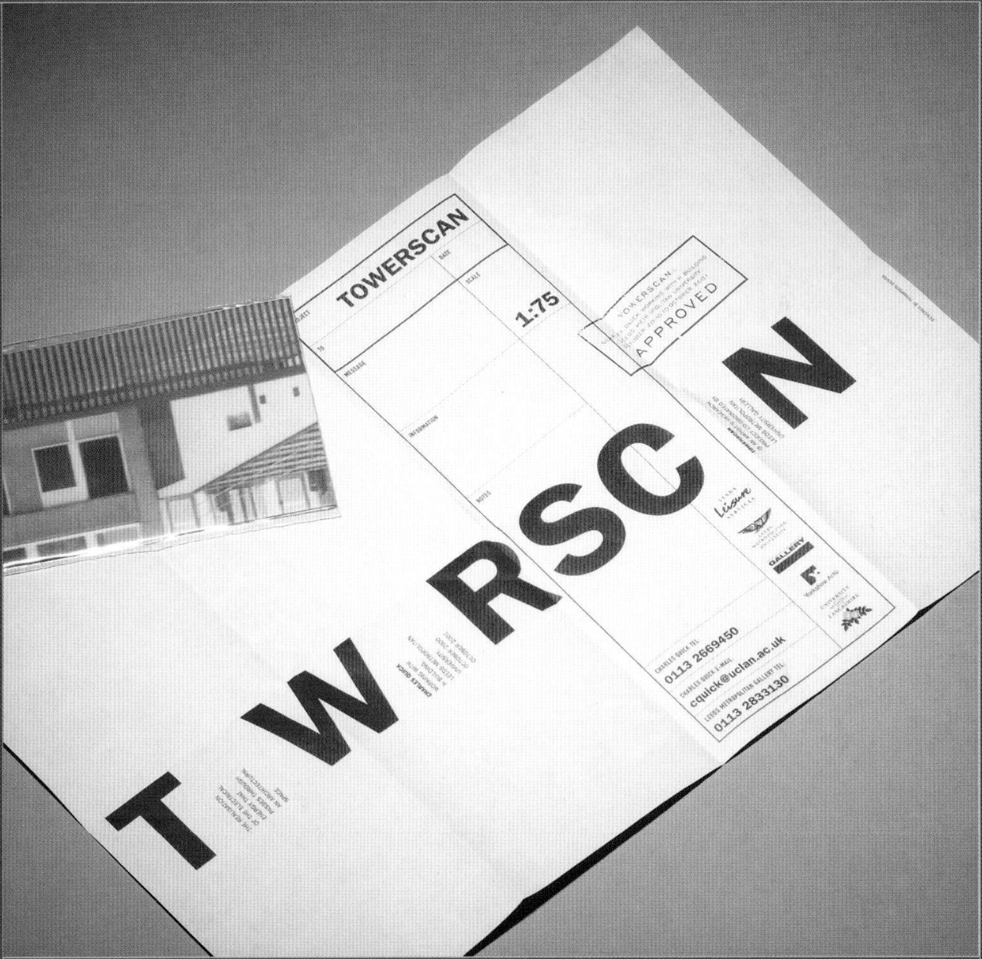

0435 **THOMPSON**
UK

Yours.

do

Haven't we seen y...
Yours,
do.

3...2...1...

This is the 3rd edition of do future. The sequel to the sequel.
Scream 12. Die Hard IX. Rocky 67. Titanic the Revenge. do
Future 3.

Welcome back or hello.

do future was (is) written by over 30 authors from all over the
planet, who felt a great urge to discuss with you that thing someone
misleadingly called youth culture.
(Are you out there? We'd like to meet you.)

By the very nature of a book like do future, some pages have
become as out of date as WAP phones and e-commerce (we're
talking about the future remember).

Until that day, each new edition is brought up to date by scribbling
over the old editions.

This way, you can see the bare bones of do future; take a peek at
how things have evolved.

Only this first page is written again, since it's only polite to
re-introduce ourselves properly to you.

Inside this naked paperback you will find a mixed bag of
thoughts, stories, comments, criticisms and dreams all jostling for
position beside that by now infamous piece of global youth
research called 'do insight,' the place where over 600 of the
world's youth told us what could be happening in a neighbourhood
near you, tomorrow.

Read, enjoy, marvel, hate, disagree, ignore, wonder, rewrite, rip
up.

do future will continue printing editions of itself until interest
dries up, or we run out of space in which to scribble.
In the meantime, also try and check out 'do-tv', the book of the
internet experiment that contains ideas, arguments and alphabetic
fisticuffs in a worldwide discussion about that dream demon, alive
television. And once again, to keep the do philosophy alive
(being: do is there to be shaped by everyone who cares to get
involved), do-tv is written with views from more people than
seems possible to fit into one book. More info: dosurl.com
OK, advertisement over.

Now looks like a good time to turn the page...

2000
1999
1998

0437 **NASSAR DESIGN**
USA

0438 **SAMPSONMAY**
UK

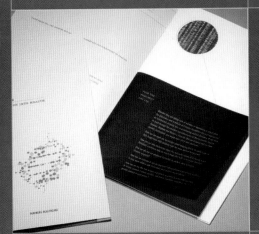

0439 **SELTZER DESIGN**
USA

0440 **ZIP DESIGN**
UK

0441 **JASON & JASON**
ISRAEL

0442 **MARIUS FAHRNER DESIGN**
GERMANY

0443 **KESSELS KRAMER**
THE NETHERLANDS

0444 **BELYEA**
USA

0445 **JASON & JASON**
ISRAEL

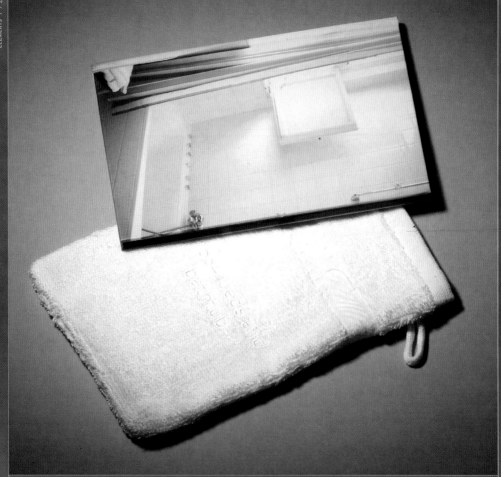

0447 **THIRTEEN**
UK

0448 **HORNALL ANDERSON DESIGN WORKS**
USA

0449 **KESSELS KRAMER**
THE NETHERLANDS

0450 **HORNALL ANDERSON DESIGN WORKS**
USA

0451 **THIRTEEN**
UK

0452 **THIRTEEN**
UK

0453 **KESSELS KRAMER**
THE NETHERLANDS

0454 **THIRTEEN**
UK

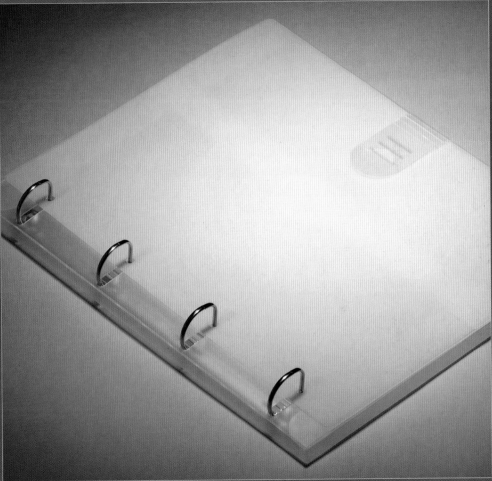

0456 **STRUKTUR DESIGN**
UK

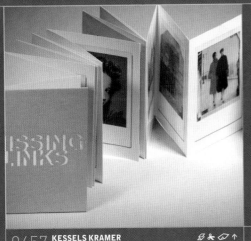

0457 **KESSELS KRAMER**
THE NETHERLANDS

0458 **KESSELS KRAMER**
THE NETHERLANDS

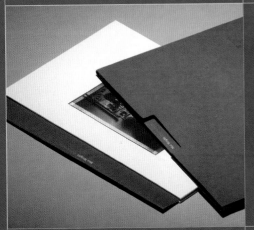

0459 **ORIGIN**
UK

0460 **KESSELS KRAMER**
THE NETHERLANDS

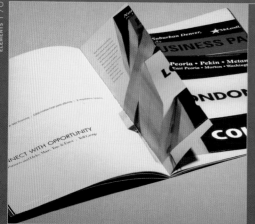

0461 **GREENFIELD/BELSER**
USA

0462 **A2-GRAPHICS/SW/HK**
UK

0463 **FELTON COMMUNICATION**
UK

0464 **COLLEGE DESIGN**
UK

0467 **SCANDINAVIAN DESIGN GROUP**
DENMARK

0468 **SCANDINAVIAN DESIGN GROUP**
DENMARK

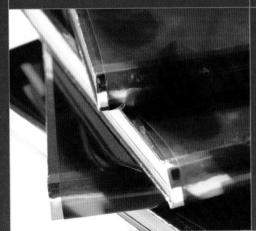

0469 **SCANDINAVIAN DESIGN GROUP**
DENMARK

0470 **KOLEGRAM DESIGN**
CANADA

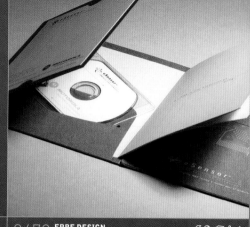

0471 **HORNALL ANDERSON DESIGN WORKS**
USA

0472 **ERBE DESIGN**
USA

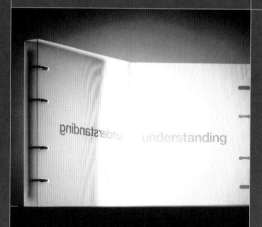

0473 **PROGRESS**
UK

0474 **THIRTEEN**
UK

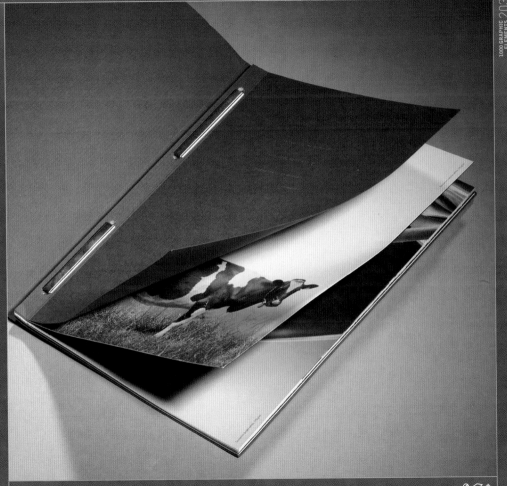

0475 **Q** GERMANY

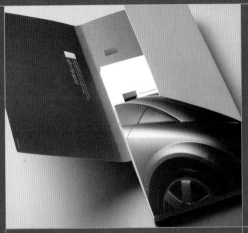

0477 **SCANDINAVIAN DESIGN GROUP**
DENMARK

0478 **SCANDINAVIAN DESIGN GROUP**
DENMARK

0479 **METAL**
USA

0480 **Q**
GERMANY

0481 **KOLEGRAM DESIGN**
CANADA

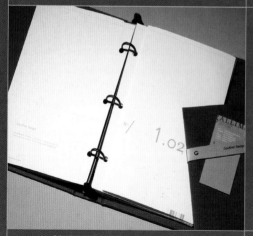

0482 **PROGRESS**
UK

0483 **GOUTHIER DESIGN**
USA

0484 **SCANDINAVIAN DESIGN GROUP**
DENMARK

& the winner

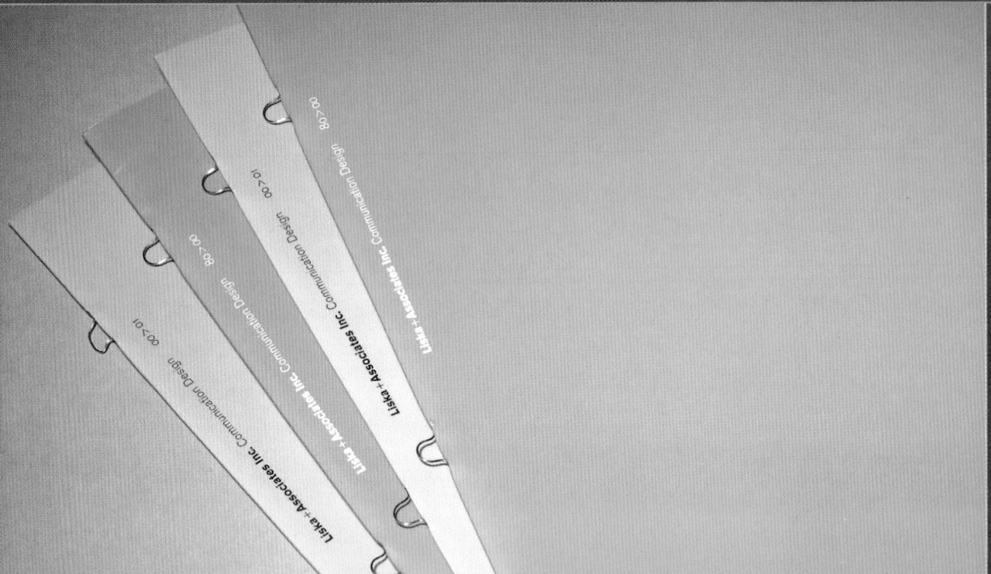

0486 **LISKA + ASSOCIATES**
USA

0487 **ANDERSON THOMAS DESIGN**
USA

0488 **BBK STUDIO**
USA

0489 **CAPSULE**
USA

0490 **FORM**
UK

0491 **GILLESPIE DESIGN**
USA

0492 **CAPSULE**
USA

0493 **STOLTZE DESIGN**
USA

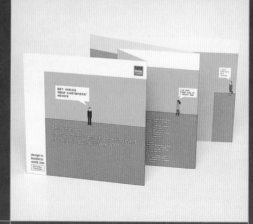

0494 **FORM**
UK

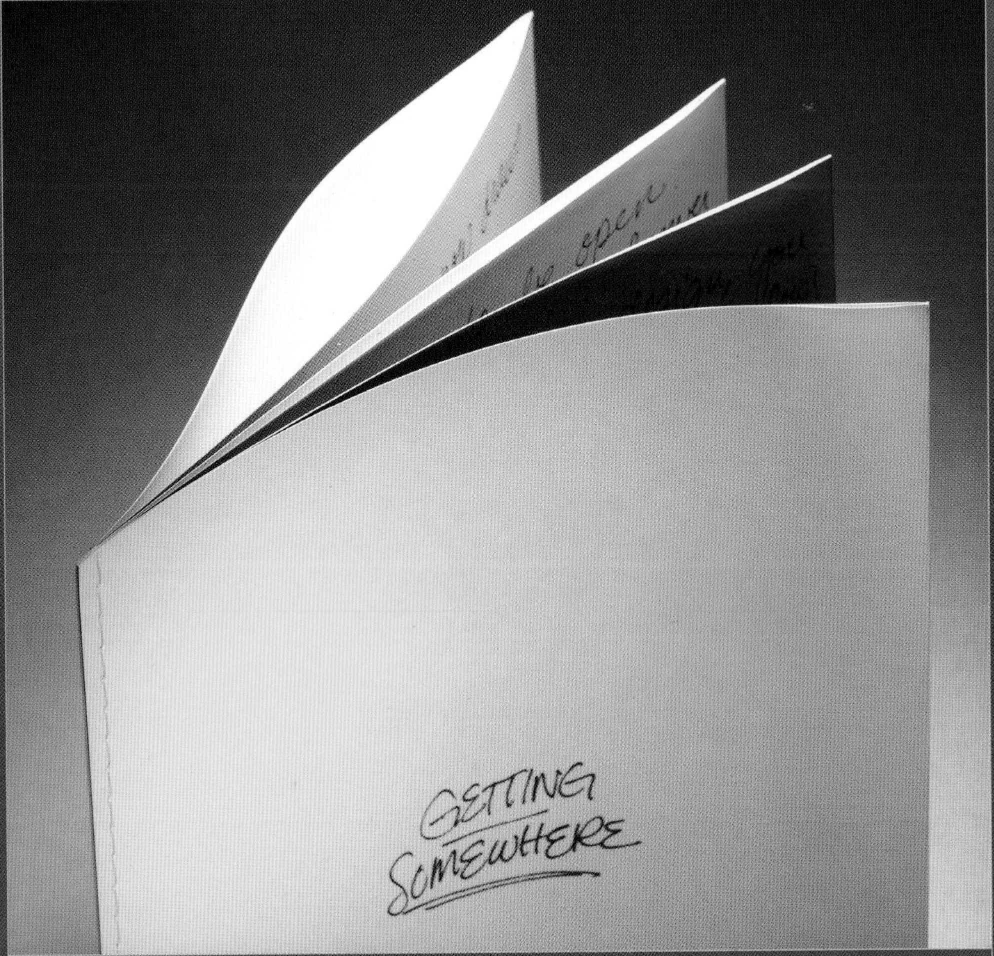

0495 **MIRES**
USA

0497 **GILLESPIE DESIGN**
USA

0498 **PRECURSOR**
UK

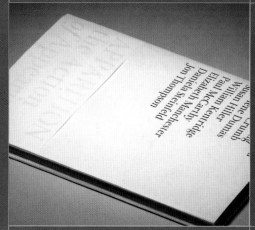

0499 **A2-GRAPHICS/SW/HK**
UK

0500 **VIVA DOLAN COMMUNICATIONS
& DESIGN**
CANADA

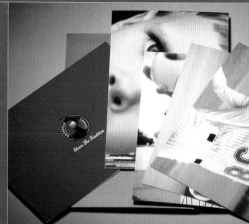

0501 **CAHAN & ASSOCIATES**
USA

0502 **LEWIS COMMUNICATIONS**
USA

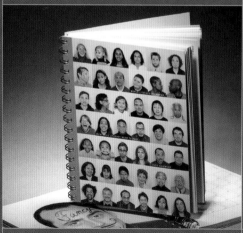

0503 **VIVA DOLAN COMMUNICATIONS & DESIGN**
CANADA

0504 **VIVA DOLAN COMMUNICATIONS & DESIGN**
CANADA

While companies look for ways to c
expenditures in response to econo
the majority of our client relations
In most cases, they strengthen.

NN Growth will also come
xecutive Programs, known
a concierge-quality service
nd profitable—with revenue
ng our full product set at the
current members, GartnerEXP
ze.

economy, it's prudent for Gartner
flow and profits. A key strategy
t of the Fortune 1000 are Gartr
annual sales potential of
pe are expanded wh
represent ar

Gartner

2001

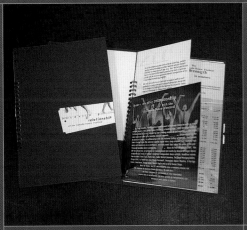

0507 **IRIDIUM, A DESIGN AGENCY**
CANADA

0508 **MONDERER DESIGN**
USA

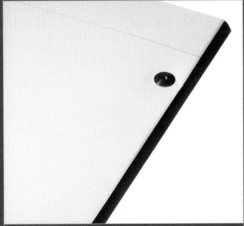

0509 **11D – ELEVEN DESIGN**
DENMARK

0510 **IRIDIUM, A DESIGN AGENCY**
CANADA

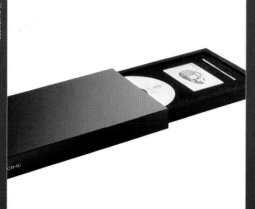

00/01

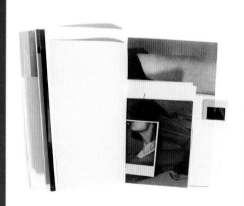

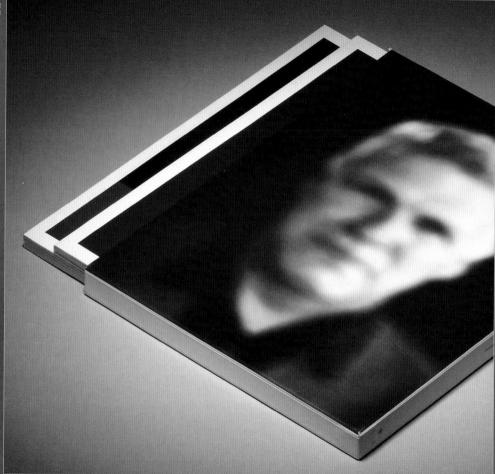

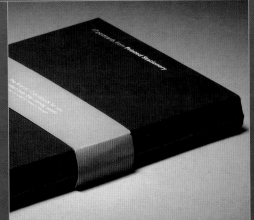

0517 **CAHAN & ASSOCIATES** USA

0518 **RADLEY YELDAR** UK

0519 **RADLEY YELDAR** UK

0520 **ZIGZAG DESIGN** USA

0521 **11D – ELEVEN DESIGN**
DENMARK

0522 **11D – ELEVEN DESIGN**
DENMARK

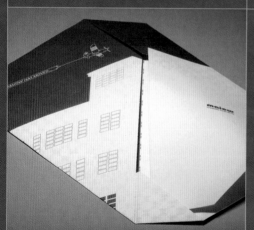

0523 **MAIOW CREATIVE BRANDING**
UK

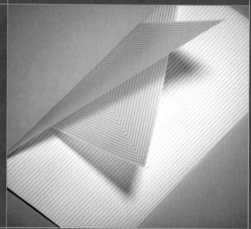

0524 **MIRKO ILIC**
USA

0527 **LEWIS COMMUNICATIONS**
USA

0528 **SAGE COMMUNICATION**
USA

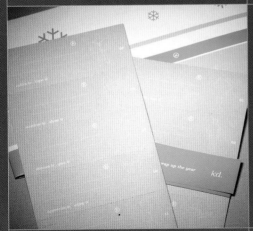

0529 **KOLEGRAM DESIGN**
CANADA

0530 **LEWIS COMMUNICATIONS**
USA

0531 **KBDA**
USA

0532 **IMAGINATION (GIC)**
UK

0533 **BWA DESIGN**
UK

0534 **DAVID CARTER DESIGN**
USA

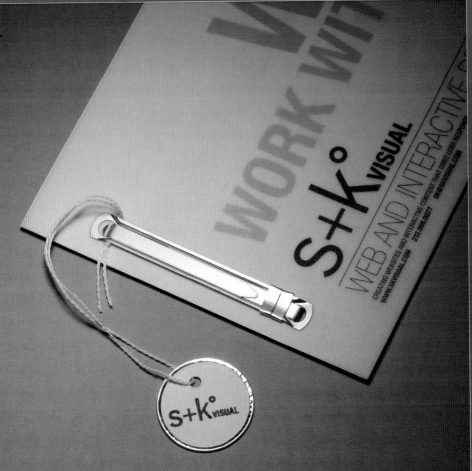

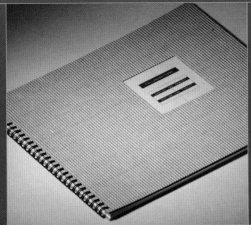

0537 **KBDA**
USA

0538 **MIRIELLO GRAFICO**
USA

0539 **NIELINGER & ROHSIEPE**
GERMANY

0540 **JOHNSON BANKS**
UK

0541 **DEW GIBBONS**
UK

0542 **NB:STUDIO**
UK

0543 **NB:STUDIO**
UK

0544 **BUREAU GRAS**
THE NETHERLANDS

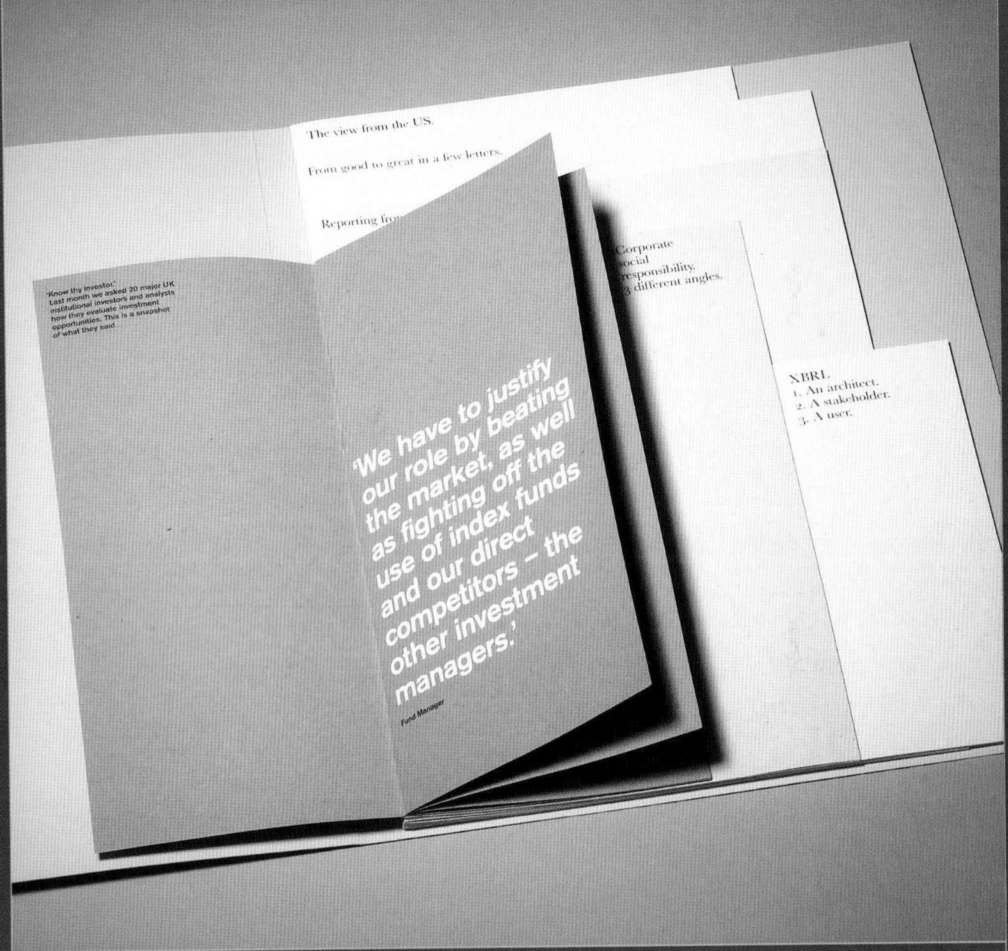

0545 **NB:STUDIO**
UK

0547 **HAND MADE GROUP**
ITALY

0548 **GRAPHISCHE FORMGEBUNG,
HERBERT ROHSIEPE**
GERMANY

0549 **RADLEY YELDAR**
UK

0550 **NBBJ GRAPHIC DESIGN**
USA

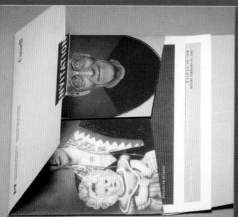

0551 **KOLEGRAM DESIGN**
CANADA

0552 **JOHNSON BANKS**
UK

0553 **SALTERBAXTER**
UK

0554 **AND PARTNERS**
USA

PRINT FINISHING STUDIO HANDBOOK
DESIGNERS WILL
BE PROSNERS
PROSECUTED NOT
Decorative Print Finishes applied to Urban Wallscapes

ALCAN

0557 **IRIDIUM, A DESIGN AGENCY**
CANADA

0558 **SUM DESIGN**
UK

0559 **HARRIMANSTEEL**
UK

0560 **SALTERBAXTER**
UK

0001 0002 0003 0004 0005 0006 0007 0008 0009 0010 0011 0012 0013 0014 0015 0016 0017 0018 0019 0020 0021 0022 0023 0024 0025
0041 0042 0043 0044 0045 0046 0047 0048 0049 0050 0051 0052 0053 0054 0055 0056 0057 0058 0059 0060 0061 0062 0063 0064 0065
0081 0082 0083 0084 0085 0086 0087 0088 0089 0090 0091 0092 0093 0094 0095 0096 0097 0098 0099 0100 0101 0102 0103 0104 0105
0121 0122 0123 0124 0125 0126 0127 0128 0129 0130 0131 0132 0133 0134 0135 0136 0137 0138 0139 0140 0141 0142 0143 0144 0145
0161 0162 0163 0164 0165 0166 0167 0168 0169 0170 0171 0172 0173 0174 0175 0176 0177 0178 0179 0180 0181 0182 0183 0184 0185
0201 0202 0203 0204 0205 0206 0207 0208 0209 0210 0211 0212 0213 0214 0215 0216 0217 0218 0219 0220 0221 0222 0223 0224 0225
0241 0242 0243 0244 0245 0246 0247 0248 0249 0250 0251 0252 0253 0254 0255 0256 0257 0258 0259 0260 0261 0262 0263 0264 0265
0281 0282 0283 0284 0285 0286 0287 0288 0289 0290 0291 0292 0293 0294 0295 0296 0297 0298 0299 0300 0301 0302 0303 0304 0305
0321 0322 0323 0324 0325 0326 0327 0328 0329 0330 0331 0332 0333 0334 0335 0336 0337 0338 0339 0340 0341 0342 0343 0344 0345
0361 0362 0363 0364 0365 0366 0367 0368 0369 0370 0371 0372 0373 0374 0375 0376 0377 0378 0379 0380 0381 0382 0383 0384 0385
0401 0402 0403 0404 0405 0406 0407 0408 0409 0410 0411 0412 0413 0414 0415 0416 0417 0418 0419 0420 0421 0422 0423 0424 0425
0441 0442 0443 0444 0445 0446 0447 0448 0449 0450 0451 0452 0453 0454 0455 0456 0457 0458 0459 0460 0461 0462 0463 0464 0465
0481 0482 0483 0484 0485 0486 0487 0488 0489 0490 0491 0492 0493 0494 0495 0496 0497 0498 0499 0500 0501 0502 0503 0504 0505
0521 0522 0523 0524 0525 0526 0527 0528 0529 0530 0531 0532 0533 0534 0535 0536 0537 0538 0539 0540 0541 0542 0543 0544 0545
0561 0562 0563 0564 0565 0566 0567 0568 0569 0570 0571 0572 0573 0574 0575 0576 0577 0578 0579 0580 0581 0582 0583 0584 0585
0601 0602 0603 0604 0605 0606 0607 0608 0609 0610 0611 0612 0613 0614 0615 0616 0617 0618 0619 0620 0621 0622 0623 0624 0625
0641 0642 0643 0644 0645 0646 0647 0648 0649 0650 0651 0652 0653 0654 0655 0656 0657 0658 0659 0660 0661 0662 0663 0664 0665
0681 0682 0683 0684 0685 0686 0687 0688 0689 0690 0691 0692 0693 0694 0695 0696 0697 0698 0699 0700 0701 0702 0703 0704 0705
0721 0722 0723 0724 0725 0726 0727 0728 0729 0730 0731 0732 0733 0734 0735 0736 0737 0738 0739 0740 0741 0742 0743 0744 0745
0761 0762 0763 0764 0765 0766 0767 0768 0769 0770 0771 0772 0773 0774 0775 0776 0777 0778 0779 0780 0781 0782 0783 0784 0785
0801 0802 0803 0804 0805 0806 0807 0808 0809 0810 0811 0812 0813 0814 0815 0816 0817 0818 0819 0820 0821 0822 0823 0824 0825
0841 0842 0843 0844 0845 0846 0847 0848 0849 0850 0851 0852 0853 0854 0855 0856 0857 0858 0859 0860 0861 0862 0863 0864 0865
0881 0882 0883 0884 0885 0886 0887 0888 0889 0890 0891 0892 0893 0894 0895 0896 0897 0898 0899 0900 0901 0902 0903 0904 0905
0921 0922 0923 0924 0925 0926 0927 0928 0929 0930 0931 0932 0933 0934 0935 0936 0937 0938 0939 0940 0941 0942 0943 0944 0945
0961 0962 0963 0964 0965 0966 0967 0968 0969 0970 0971 0972 0973 0974 0975 0976 0977 0978 0979 0980 0981 0982 0983 0984 0985

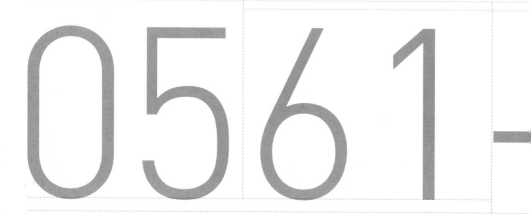

028 0029 0030 0031 0032 0033 0034 0035 0036 0037 0038 0039 0040
068 0069 0070 0071 0072 0073 0074 0075 0076 0077 0078 0079 0080
108 0109 0110 0111 0112 0113 0114 0115 0116 0117 0118 0119 0120
148 0149 0150 0151 0152 0153 0154 0155 0156 0157 0158 0159 0160
188 0189 0190 0191 0192 0193 0194 0195 0196 0197 0198 0199 0200
228 0229 0230 0231 0232 0233 0234 0235 0236 0237 0238 0239 0240
268 0269 0270 0271 0272 0273 0274 0275 0276 0277 0278 0279 0280
308 0309 0310 0311 0312 0313 0314 0315 0316 0317 0318 0319 0320
348 0349 0350 0351 0352 0353 0354 0355 0356 0357 0358 0359 0360
388 0389 0390 0391 0392 0393 0394 0395 0396 0397 0398 0399 0400
428 0429 0430 0431 0432 0433 0434 0435 0436 0437 0438 0439 0440
468 0469 0470 0471 0472 0473 0474 0475 0476 0477 0478 0479 0480
508 0509 0510 0511 0512 0513 0514 0515 0516 0517 0518 0519 0520
548 0549 0550 0551 0552 0553 0554 0555 0556 0557 0558 0559 0560
588 0589 0590 0591 0592 0593 0594 0595 0596 0597 0598 0599 0600
628 0629 0630 0631 0632 0633 0634 0635 0636 0637 0638 0639 0640
668 0669 0670 0671 0672 0673 0674 0675 0676 0677 0678 0679 0680
708 0709 0710 0711 0712 0713 0714 0715 0716 0717 0718 0719 0720
748 0749 0750 0751 0752 0753 0754 0755 0756 0757 0758 0759 0760
788 0789 0790 0791 0792 0793 0794 0795 0796 0797 0798 0799 0800
828 0829 0830 0831 0832 0833 0834 0835 0836 0837 0838 0839 0840
868 0869 0870 0871 0872 0873 0874 0875 0876 0877 0878 0879 0880
908 0909 0910 0911 0912 0913 0914 0915 0916 0917 0918 0919 0920
948 0949 0950 0951 0952 0953 0954 0955 0956 0957 0958 0959 0960
988 0989 0990 0991 0992 0993 0994 0995 0996 0997 0998 0999 1000

04

ADD-ONS   STICKERS
RUBBER BANDS
TAGS
FOILS

2003

THE GIFT OF GOOD ART

There are many ways to solve a single problem. A thousand
paths to completing the assignment. As many possibilities
for sharing your idea as there are artists and viewers sharing
this old world. We celebrate the limitlessness of artistic
possibility with this year's calendar, a selection of the works
of area high school students who have solved problems,
completed assignments, shared their ideas and exhibited their
work at the Holland Area Arts Council, in Holland, Michigan.

Enjoy.

2003

THE GIFT OF GOOD ART

There are many ways to solve a single problem. A thousand
paths to completing the assignment. As many possibilities
for sharing your idea as there are artists and viewers sharing
this old world. We celebrate the limitlessness of artistic
possibility with this year's calendar, a selection of the works
of area high school students who have solved problems,
completed assignments, shared their ideas and exhibited their
work at the Holland Area Arts Council, in Holland, Michigan.

Enjoy.

0685

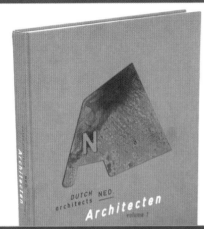

0562 **KOEWEIDEN POSTMA**
THE NETHERLANDS + ⌒ ⊘ T ↑

0563 **ROUNDEL**
UK + ⊘ T ↑

0564 **IE DESIGN**
USA + ⌒ T ↑

0565 **BIG ACTIVE**
UK + ⌒ T ↑

0566 **PROGRESS**
UK

+ ✎ ◊ **T** ↑

0567 **LAVA**
THE NETHERLANDS

+ ✄ ✎ ↑

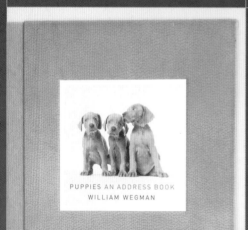

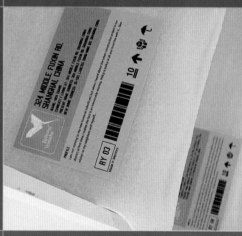

0568 **EMPIRE DESIGN STUDIO**
USA

+ ☰ ⊘ ↑

0569 **MINGZHAM HUANG**
UK

+ ✎ **T** ✳ ✍ ↑

w_ie schreibt man einen brief, liebe gruppe w_?   bremen, den 01.03.2003

wenn ihr einen brief für die gruppe w_ schreiben wollt, benutzt ihr natürlich
den extra dafür vorgesehenen briefbogen. ihr legt diesen also in euren drucker
ein. beachtet: es gibt auch eine zweite seite, falls der brief etwas länger werden
sollte. benutzt in diesem fall bitte ebenfalls das dafür extra vorgesehene blatt.

damit nun, wenn ihr euren brief ausgedruckt ha
und ihr euch nicht jedes mal überlegen müsst, '
hinkommt und wieviel leerzeilen dann folgen b
folgt. gibt es diese maske die mit dem blindtext
also nur noch diesen text markieren und eure
falls ihr wert darauf legt, das eurer name auf
wort »wer« steht könnt ihr am ende des brief
return drücken, bis euer name die gewünsch
zu gehen könnt ihr auch die hilfslinien ein

mit freundlichem gruß,
david lindemann

team challenge are you in?

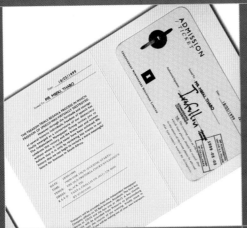

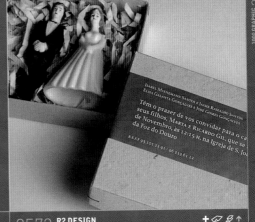

Têm o prazer de vos convidar para o ca
seus filhos, MARTA E RICARDO GIL, que se
de Novembro, às 12:15 h, na Igreja de S. Joã
da Foz do Douro

ISABEL MINNEMANN SANTOS
ELISA GALANTE GONÇALVES E JAIME RAMALHO SANTOS
JOSÉ GOMES GONÇALVES

INVITATION

ADMISSION TICKET

0572 NET#WORK BBDO SOUTH AFRICA

0573 R2 DESIGN PORTUGAL

0574 NASSAR DESIGN USA

0575 NET#WORK BBDO SOUTH AFRICA

1000 GRAPHIC ELEMENTS 244:5

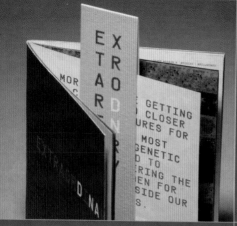

0576 **IRIDIUM, A DESIGN AGENCY**
CANADA
+ ✐ **T** ✄ ↑

0577 **TRICKETT & WEBB**
UK
+ ↑

0578 **ROBIN RAYNO**
THE NETHERLANDS
+ ✐ ↑

0579 **THE FAMILY**
UK
+ ✐ ✄ ◊◊ ↑

PΦNL
photography annual
of the netherlands

7 | m

7th issue > 1996/97 >
1147 photographs
submitted > 176 photos
selected > incl. pand
award > 208 pages

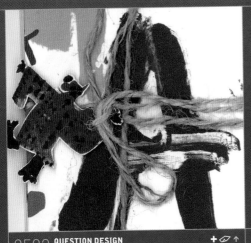

0582 **QUESTION DESIGN**
USA

0583 **LIGALUX**
GERMANY

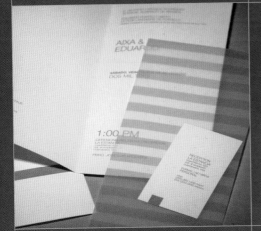

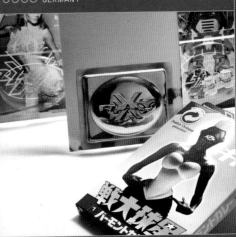

0584 **CIRCULO SOCIAL**
MEXICO

0585 **SCANDINAVIAN DESIGN GROUP**
DENMARK

0586 **UNA (AMSTERDAM) DESIGNERS**
THE NETHERLANDS + ✐ ↑

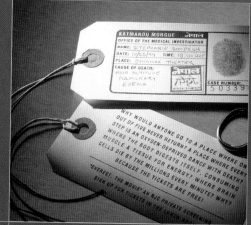

0587 **RICK JOHNSON & COMPANY**
USA + ✐ ↑

0588 **NET#WORK BBDO**
SOUTH AFRICA + ✐ ↑

0589 **TEMPLIN BRINK DESIGN**
USA + ✐ T ☀ ↑

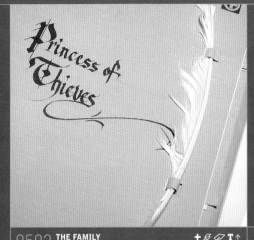

0592 **THE FAMILY**
UK

0593 **HAND MADE GROUP**
ITALY

0594 **MARIUS FAHRNER DESIGN**
GERMANY

0595 **AND PARTNERS**
USA

0596 **LIPPA PEARCE DESIGN**
UK

0597 **TEMPLIN BRINK DESIGN**
USA

0598 **BLACKCOFFEE**
USA

0599 **BNIM ARCHITECTS**
USA

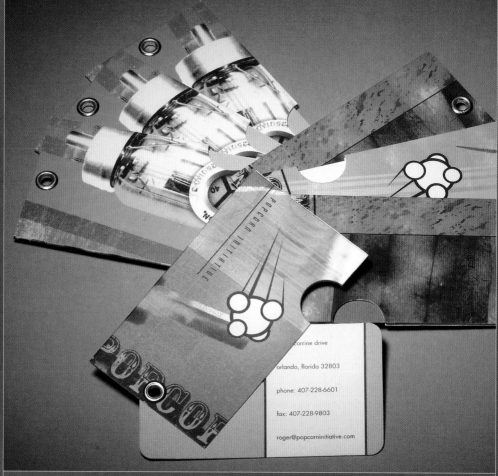

corrine drive

orlando, florida 32803

phone: 407-228-6601

fax: 407-228-9803

roger@popcorninitiative.com

0601 **POPCORN INITIATIVE**
USA

+ ⊘ ⅋ ↑

0602 **AND PARTNERS**
USA
+ 🖋 ✎ ↑

0603 **RIORDON DESIGN**
CANADA
+ ✎ ↑

0604 **RIORDON DESIGN**
CANADA
+ ✎ ↑

take me

0605 **LIPPA PEARCE DESIGN**
UK
+ ✎ 🖋 ↑

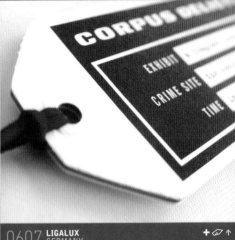

0606 **UNA (AMSTERDAM) DESIGNERS** THE NETHERLANDS + ✐ **T** ↑

0607 **LIGALUX** GERMANY + ✐ ↑

0608 **FORM** UK + ✳ ↑

0609 **GOUTHIER DESIGN** USA + ✐ ◊**T** ↑

2003
THE GIFT OF GOOD ART
There are many ways to solve a single problem. A thousand
paths to completing the assignment. As many possibilities
for sharing your idea as there are artists and viewers sharing
this old world. We celebrate the limitlessness of artistic
possibility with this year's calendar, a selection of the works
of area high school students who have solved problems,
completed assignments, shared their ideas and exhibited their
work at the Holland Area Arts Council, in Holland, Michigan.
Enjoy.

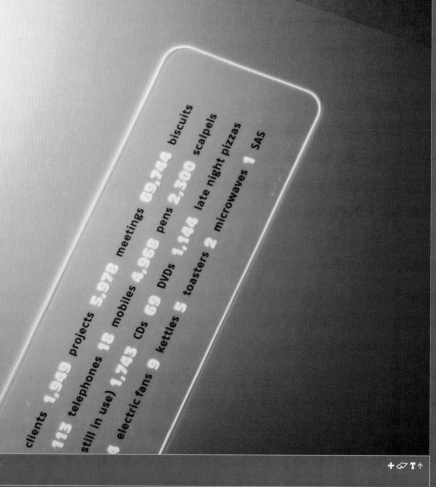

clients **1,949** projects **5,978** meetings **69,744** biscuits

113 telephones **18** mobiles **4,968** pens **2,300** scalpels

still in use) **1,743** CDs **69** DVDs **1,144** late night pizzas

4 electric fans **9** kettles **5** toasters **2** microwaves **1** SAS

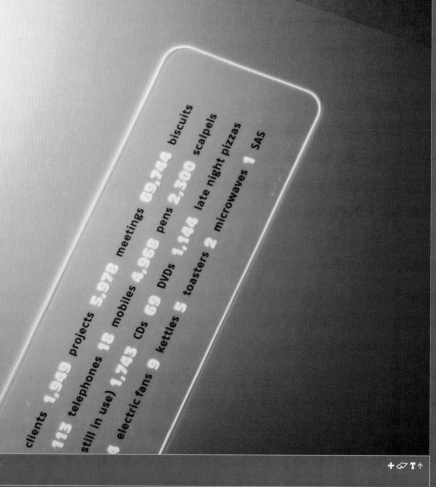

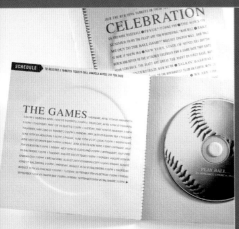

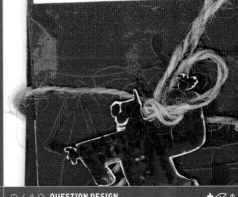

0612 **WALLACE CHURCH**
USA

0613 **QUESTION DESIGN**
USA

0614 **LIPPA PEARCE DESIGN**
UK

0615 **BIG ACTIVE**
UK

0616 **ZIGZAG DESIGN**
USA
+ ✍ ↑

0617 **MARIUS FAHRNER DESIGN**
GERMANY
+ ✍ ℬ T ❋ ↑

0618 **CHRONICLE BOOKS**
USA
+ ✍ T ↑

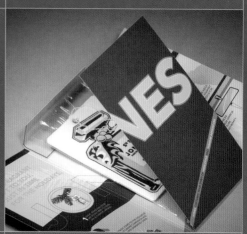

0619 **JONES DESIGN GROUP**
USA
+ ℬ ↑

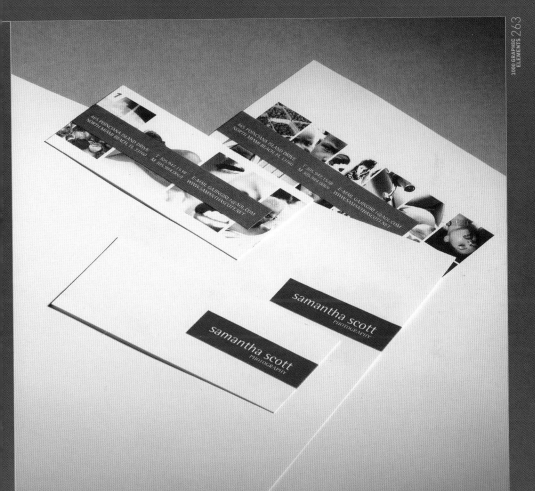

+ ⬭ **T** ⬭ ↑

0623 **THE DESIGN DELL** UK + ⬭ **T** ↑

0624 **NAVY BLUE** UK + ⬭⬭ **T** ⬭◊ ↑

0625 **IE DESIGN** USA + **T** ⬭ ↑

0626 **BECKER DESIGN**
USA

0627 **KBDA**
USA

0628 **IRIDIUM, A DESIGN AGENCY**
CANADA

0629 **SAS**
UK

think big...

DESIGN GROUP

THE POSSIBILITIES ARE ENDLESS

0632 **THIRTEEN**
UK

+ ✦ ✐ T ◊ ↑

0633 **STEERSMCGILLAN**
UK

+ ✐ ↑

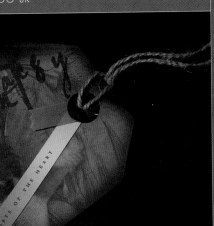

0634 **CHENG DESIGN**
USA

+ T ✐ ↑

0635 **GOUTHIER DESIGN**
USA

+ ✐ ◊ ↑

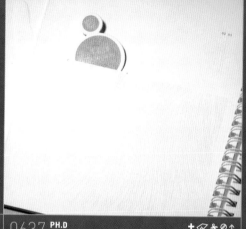

0636 **CUCKOOLAND** UK + T ◊ ✎ ↑

0637 **PH.D** USA + ✎ ✂ ∅ ↑

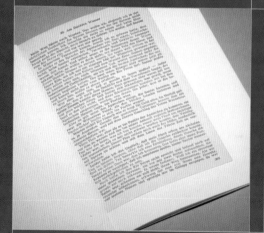

0638 **FELDER** GRAFIKDESIGN AUSTRIA + ✎ ↑

0639 **FIBRE** UK + T ✎ ◊ ✳ ↑

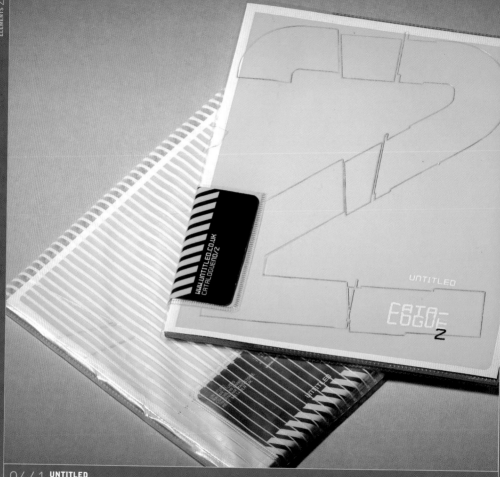

✚ ☰ ✍ **T** ◊ ✳ ✐ ⊘ ↑

0642 **TRACY DESIGN**
USA

0643 **EMSPACE DESIGN GROUP**
USA

0644 **GIORGIO DAVANZO DESIGN**
USA

0645 **AFTERHOURS CREATIVE**
USA

Bad Behaviour
from the Arts Council Collection

*Please note that this book contains artworks
that may cause offence.

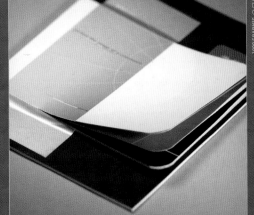

0652 **FELDER GRAFIKDESIGN**
AUSTRIA

0653 **MOTIVE DESIGN RESEARCH**
USA

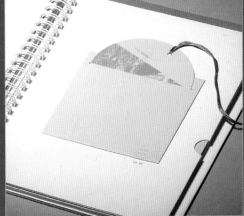

0654 **FIELD DESIGN CONSULTANTS**
UK

0655 **PH.D**
USA

0656 **KESSELS KRAMER**
THE NETHERLANDS
 + ✎ T ↑ ↑

0657 **CHRONICLE BOOKS**
USA
+ ✎ ✳ ↑

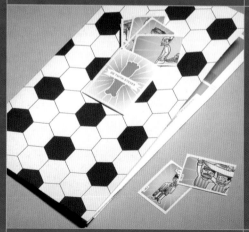

0658 **LIGALUX**
GERMANY
 + ✎ ✳ ↑

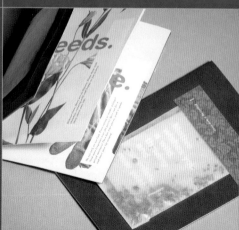

0659 **MOTIVE DESIGN RESEARCH**
USA
 + ✎ T ✳ ↑

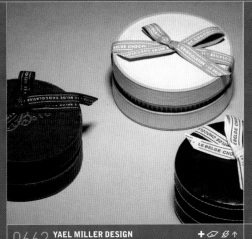

0662 **YAEL MILLER DESIGN**
USA
 + ✐ ✂ ↑

0663 **MIRIELLO GRAFICO**
USA
+ ✄ ↑

0664 **RADLEY YELDAR**
UK
+ **T** ↑

0665 **HAND MADE GROUP**
ITALY
 + ✂ ✐ ↑

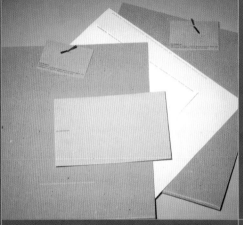

0666 **PLUS DESIGN**
USA

0667 **BISQIT DESIGN**
UK

0668 **KOLEGRAM DESIGN**
CANADA

0669 **BBK STUDIO**
USA

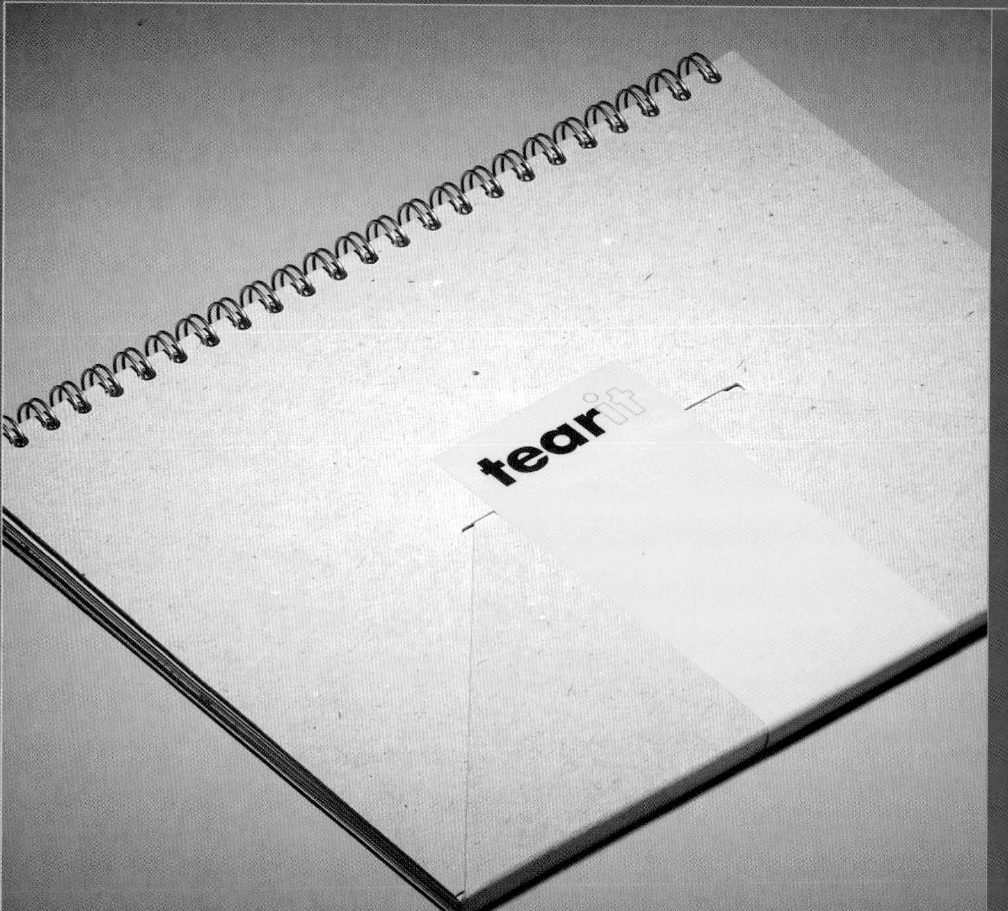

0671 **RADLEY YELDAR**
UK

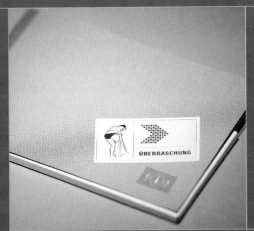

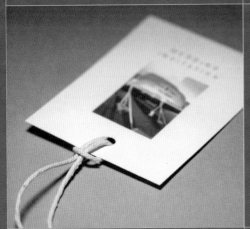

0672 **LIGALUX**
GERMANY

0673 **TWELVE:TEN**
UK

0674 **DAWN HOSKINSON**
UK

0675 **RADLEY YELDAR**
UK

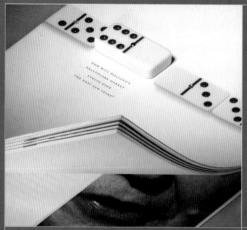

0676 **UNA (AMSTERDAM) DESIGNERS**
THE NETHERLANDS
+ ⟂ ↑

0677 **CIRCLE K DESIGN**
USA
+ ⟂ ↑

0678 **IRIDIUM, A DESIGN AGENCY**
CANADA
+ ↑

0679 **MAGMA**
GERMANY
+ ↑

PICTURE this...

0681 **SAMPSON MAY**
UK

0682 **DAVID CARTER DESIGN**
USA
+ ⊘ ✐ ↑

0683 **HAND MADE GROUP**
ITALY
+ ✐ ✐ ↑

0684 **WALLACE CHURCH**
USA
+ ↑

0685 **FELDER GRAFIKDESIGN**
AUSTRIA
+ ✐ ↑

0001 0002 0003 0004 0005 0006 0007 0008 0009 0010 0011 0012 0013 0014 0015 0016 0017 0018 0019 0020 0021 0022 0023 0024 0025
0041 0042 0043 0044 0045 0046 0047 0048 0049 0050 0051 0052 0053 0054 0055 0056 0057 0058 0059 0060 0061 0062 0063 0064 0065
0081 0082 0083 0084 0085 0086 0087 0088 0089 0090 0091 0092 0093 0094 0095 0096 0097 0098 0099 0100 0101 0102 0103 0104 0105
0121 0122 0123 0124 0125 0126 0127 0128 0129 0130 0131 0132 0133 0134 0135 0136 0137 0138 0139 0140 0141 0142 0143 0144 0145
0161 0162 0163 0164 0165 0166 0167 0168 0169 0170 0171 0172 0173 0174 0175 0176 0177 0178 0179 0180 0181 0182 0183 0184 0185
0201 0202 0203 0204 0205 0206 0207 0208 0209 0210 0211 0212 0213 0214 0215 0216 0217 0218 0219 0220 0221 0222 0223 0224 0225
0241 0242 0243 0244 0245 0246 0247 0248 0249 0250 0251 0252 0253 0254 0255 0256 0257 0258 0259 0260 0261 0262 0263 0264 0265
0281 0282 0283 0284 0285 0286 0287 0288 0289 0290 0291 0292 0293 0294 0295 0296 0297 0298 0299 0300 0301 0302 0303 0304 0305
0321 0322 0323 0324 0325 0326 0327 0328 0329 0330 0331 0332 0333 0334 0335 0336 0337 0338 0339 0340 0341 0342 0343 0344 0345
0361 0362 0363 0364 0365 0366 0367 0368 0369 0370 0371 0372 0373 0374 0375 0376 0377 0378 0379 0380 0381 0382 0383 0384 0385
0401 0402 0403 0404 0405 0406 0407 0408 0409 0410 0411 0412 0413 0414 0415 0416 0417 0418 0419 0420 0421 0422 0423 0424 0425
0441 0442 0443 0444 0445 0446 0447 0448 0449 0450 0451 0452 0453 0454 0455 0456 0457 0458 0459 0460 0461 0462 0463 0464 0465
0481 0482 0483 0484 0485 0486 0487 0488 0489 0490 0491 0492 0493 0494 0495 0496 0497 0498 0499 0500 0501 0502 0503 0504 0505
0521 0522 0523 0524 0525 0526 0527 0528 0529 0530 0531 0532 0533 0534 0535 0536 0537 0538 0539 0540 0541 0542 0543 0544 0545
0561 0562 0563 0564 0565 0566 0567 0568 0569 0570 0571 0572 0573 0574 0575 0576 0577 0578 0579 0580 0581 0582 0583 0584 0585
0601 0602 0603 0604 0605 0606 0607 0608 0609 0610 0611 0612 0613 0614 0615 0616 0617 0618 0619 0620 0621 0622 0623 0624 0625
0641 0642 0643 0644 0645 0646 0647 0648 0649 0650 0651 0652 0653 0654 0655 0656 0657 0658 0659 0660 0661 0662 0663 0664 0665
0681 0682 0683 0684 0685 0686 0687 0688 0689 0690 0691 0692 0693 0694 0695 0696 0697 0698 0699 0700 0701 0702 0703 0704 0705
0721 0722 0723 0724 0725 0726 0727 0728 0729 0730 0731 0732 0733 0734 0735 0736 0737 0738 0739 0740 0741 0742 0743 0744 0745
0761 0762 0763 0764 0765 0766 0767 0768 0769 0770 0771 0772 0773 0774 0775 0776 0777 0778 0779 0780 0781 0782 0783 0784 0785
0801 0802 0803 0804 0805 0806 0807 0808 0809 0810 0811 0812 0813 0814 0815 0816 0817 0818 0819 0820 0821 0822 0823 0824 0825
0841 0842 0843 0844 0845 0846 0847 0848 0849 0850 0851 0852 0853 0854 0855 0856 0857 0858 0859 0860 0861 0862 0863 0864 0865
0881 0882 0883 0884 0885 0886 0887 0888 0889 0890 0891 0892 0893 0894 0895 0896 0897 0898 0899 0900 0901 0902 0903 0904 0905
0921 0922 0923 0924 0925 0926 0927 0928 0929 0930 0931 0932 0933 0934 0935 0936 0937 0938 0939 0940 0941 0942 0943 0944 0945
0961 0962 0963 0964 0965 0966 0967 0968 0969 0970 0971 0972 0973 0974 0975 0976 0977 0978 0979 0980 0981 0982 0983 0984 0985

0686

028 0029 0030 0031 0032 0033 0034 0035 0036 0037 0038 0039 0040
068 0069 0070 0071 0072 0073 0074 0075 0076 0077 0078 0079 0080
108 0109 0110 0111 0112 0113 0114 0115 0116 0117 0118 0119 0120
148 0149 0150 0151 0152 0153 0154 0155 0156 0157 0158 0159 0160
188 0189 0190 0191 0192 0193 0194 0195 0196 0197 0198 0199 0200
228 0229 0230 0231 0232 0233 0234 0235 0236 0237 0238 0239 0240
268 0269 0270 0271 0272 0273 0274 0275 0276 0277 0278 0279 0280
308 0309 0310 0311 0312 0313 0314 0315 0316 0317 0318 0319 0320
348 0349 0350 0351 0352 0353 0354 0355 0356 0357 0358 0359 0360
388 0389 0390 0391 0392 0393 0394 0395 0396 0397 0398 0399 0400
428 0429 0430 0431 0432 0433 0434 0435 0436 0437 0438 0439 0440
468 0469 0470 0471 0472 0473 0474 0475 0476 0477 0478 0479 0480
508 0509 0510 0511 0512 0513 0514 0515 0516 0517 0518 0519 0520
548 0549 0550 0551 0552 0553 0554 0555 0556 0557 0558 0559 0560
588 0589 0590 0591 0592 0593 0594 0595 0596 0597 0598 0599 0600
628 0629 0630 0631 0632 0633 0634 0635 0636 0637 0638 0639 0640
668 0669 0670 0671 0672 0673 0674 0675 0676 0677 0678 0679 0680
708 0709 0710 0711 0712 0713 0714 0715 0716 0717 0718 0719 0720
748 0749 0750 0751 0752 0753 0754 0755 0756 0757 0758 0759 0760
788 0789 0790 0791 0792 0793 0794 0795 0796 0797 0798 0799 0800
828 0829 0830 0831 0832 0833 0834 0835 0836 0837 0838 0839 0840
868 0869 0870 0871 0872 0873 0874 0875 0876 0877 0878 0879 0880
908 0909 0910 0911 0912 0913 0914 0915 0916 0917 0918 0919 0920
948 0949 0950 0951 0952 0953 0954 0955 0956 0957 0958 0959 0960
988 0989 0990 0991 0992 0993 0994 0995 0996 0997 0998 0999 1000

05

UNIQUE MATERIALS

STICKERS
RUBBER BANDS
TAGS
FOILS

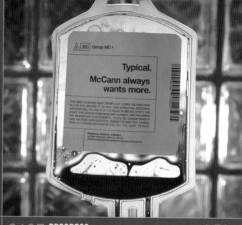

0686 **PRECURSOR**
UK

0687 **PROGRESS**
UK

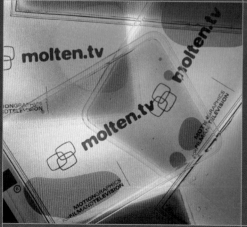

0688 **PROGRESS**
UK

0689 **NB:STUDIO**
UK

test your senses

Can you recognize a real orange?
from each of the oranges shown above
and decide which the real one is.
The right answer is at the end of the book.

0690 **BRUKETA & ZINIC**
CROATIA

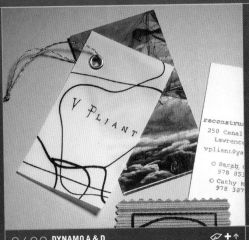

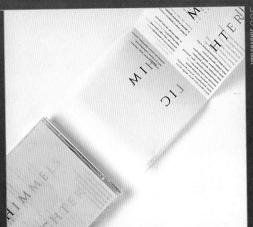

0692 **DYNAMO A & D**
USA

0693 **FELDER GRAFIKDESIGN**
AUSTRIA

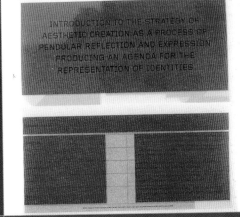

0694 **GRETEMAN GROUP**
USA

0695 **11D – ELEVEN DESIGN**
DENMARK

0696 **FORM**
UK

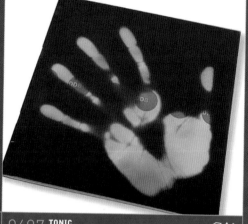

0697 **TONIC**
UK

0698 **NYC COLLEGE OF TECHNOLOGY**
USA

0699 **LIPPA PEARCE DESIGN**
UK

reveal

Solar 100g/m²

0702 **SCANDINAVIAN DESIGN GROUP**
DENMARK

0703 **FORM**
UK

0704 **PROGRESS**
UK

0705 **JADE DESIGN**
UK

0706 **MAIOW CREATIVE BRANDING**
UK

0707 **SAS**
UK

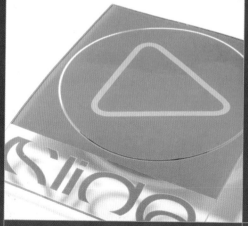

0708 **SCANDINAVIAN DESIGN GROUP**
DENMARK

0709 **BLOK DESIGN**
MEXICO

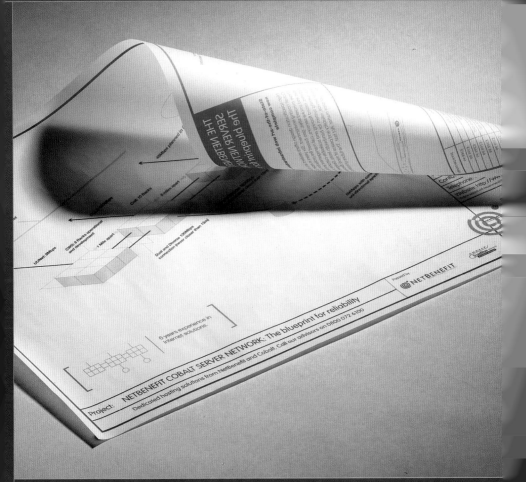

NETBENEFIT COBALT SERVER NETWORK: The blueprint for reliability

Dedicated hosting solutions from NetBenefit and Cobalt. Call our advisors on 0800 072 6100

6 years experience in internet solutions.

Project:

Prepared by
NETBENEFIT

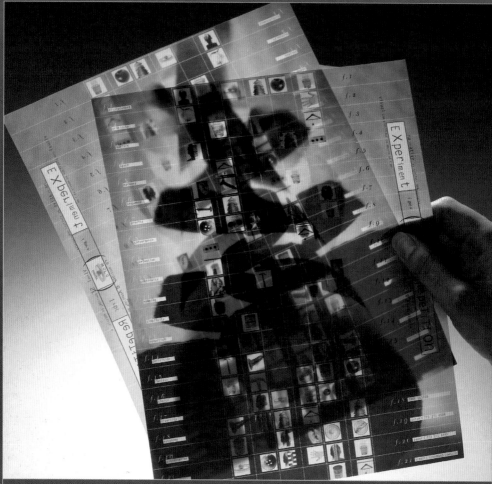

0712 **BLACKCOFFEE**
USA

0713 **PROGRESS**
UK

0714 **STEERSMCGILLAN**
UK

0715 **WALLACE CHURCH**
USA

0716 **HORNALL ANDERSON DESIGN WORKS**
USA

0717 **STEERSMCGILLAN**
UK

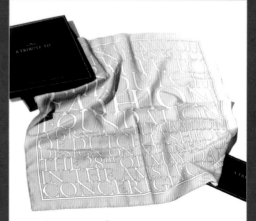

0718 **NB:STUDIO**
UK

0719 **...,STAAT**
THE NETHERLANDS

0722 **V06**
BRAZIL ⟨T⟩

0723 **AND PARTNERS**
USA

0724 **BLACKCOFFEE**
USA

0725 **BLACKCOFFEE**
USA

0726 **FOXINABOX**
UK

0727 **HAND MADE GROUP**
ITALY

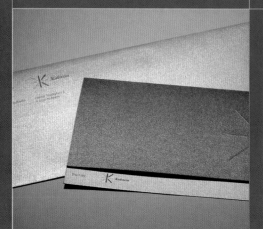

0728 **BÜRO SCHELS FÜR GESTALTUNG**
GERMANY

0729 **NO.PARKING**
ITALY

THIS IS NOT A LIFE SAVING DEVICE

USE ONLY UNDER ADULT SUPERVISION AND FOLLOW THE INSTRUCTIONS CAREFULLY

0732 **COLLEGE DESIGN** UK

0733 **DAVID CARTER DESIGN** USA

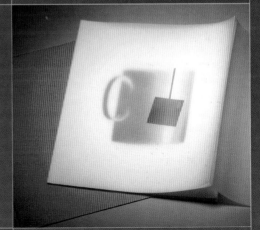

0734 **KOLEGRAM DESIGN** CANADA

0735 **RADLEY YELDAR** UK

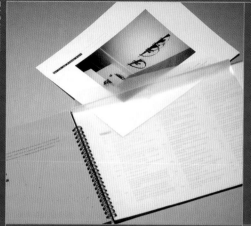

0736 **KBDA**
USA

0737 **SAS**
UK

0738 **@RADICAL.MEDIA**
USA

0739 **WAGNER DESIGN**
USA

0740 **BRUKETA & ZINIC**
CROATIA

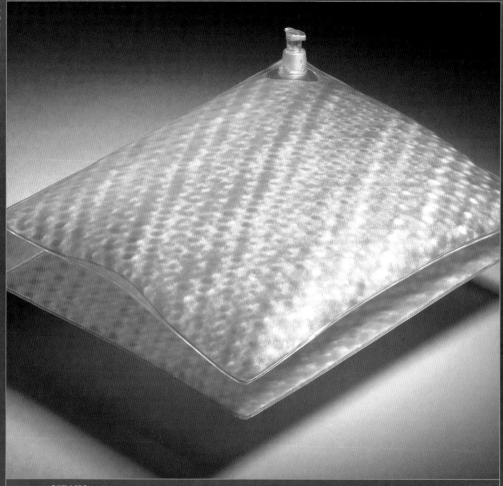

0742 **POINT BLANK DESIGN** UK

0743 **FORM** UK

0744 **AVE DESIGN STUDIO** USA

0745 **BRUKETA & ZINIC** CROATIA

0746 **PRECURSOR**
UK

0747 **BRUKETA & ZINIC**
CROATIA

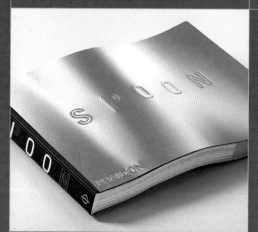

0748 **EGGERS + DIAPER**
GERMANY

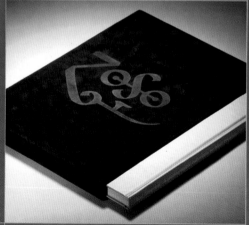

0749 **FORM**
UK

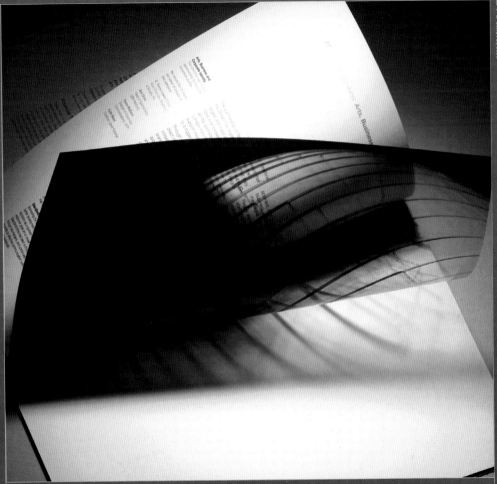

0752 **REEBOK DESIGN SERVICES**
USA

0753 **PROGRESS**
UK

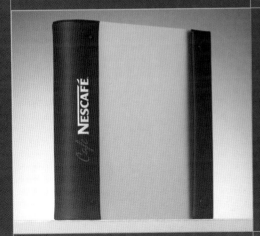

0754 **PROGRESS**
UK

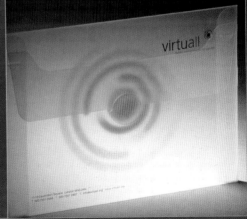

0755 **PHILLIPS**
UK

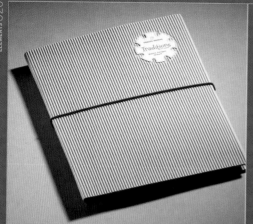

0756 **BELYEA**
USA

0757 **PROGRESS**
UK

0758 **EGBG**
THE NETHERLANDS

0759 **BELYEA**
USA

0762 **JONES DESIGN GROUP**
USA

0763 **CARTER WONG TOMLIN**
UK

0764 **HARRIMANSTEEL**
UK

0765 **POINT BLANK DESIGN**
UK

0766 **PHILLIPS**
UK

0767 **YAEL MILLER DESIGN**
USA

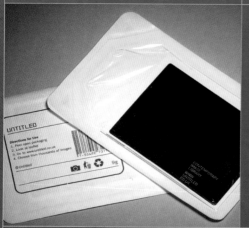

0768 **UNTITLED**
UK

0769 **PH.D**
USA

DOES YOUR DESIGN
AGENCY'S WORK WORK?

Can they claim over 60 top creative awards?
What's more, can they back them up with
4 internationally recognised Business Design
Effectiveness Awards? And a host of other
effectiveness accolades?

If not, is it time for a change.

IT'S TIME YOU CHANGED
YOUR DESIGN AGENCY.

From January 2004 there will be a brand new
design agency with over 30 years of combined
experience. HGV and Felton Communication
are about to merge our like-minded agencies
to deliver even more lateral thinking that
is logically effective. In other words, work
that works.

For more details on the new agency please
call Roger Felton on 020 7405 0900.

To see some of the work that has won over 100
creative and business effectiveness awards so
far, visit www.hgv.co.uk and www.feltoncom.com.
Our new website, www.hgvfelton.com, will be
operational from the 1st January.

0772 **...,STAAT**
THE NETHERLANDS

0773 **MAGMA**
GERMANY

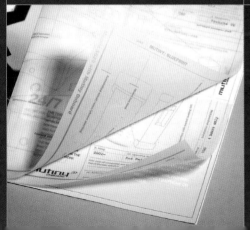

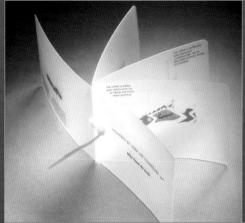

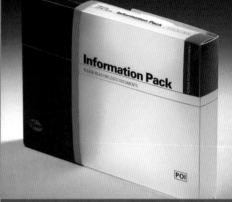

0776 **HARRIMANSTEEL**
UK

0777 **WILSON HARVEY**
UK

0778 **FAITH**
CANADA

0779 **FORTYFOUR DESIGN**
AUSTRALIA

0781 **LAVA**
THE NETHERLANDS

0782 **KEARNEY ROCHOLL**
GERMANY

0783 **CRUSH DESIGN**
UK

0784 **ELMWOOD**
UK

0785 **RIORDON DESIGN**
CANADA

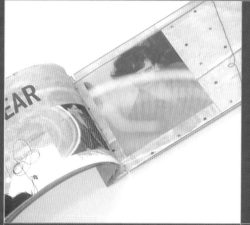

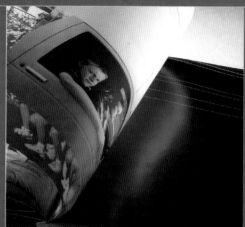

0786 **CRUSH DESIGN**
UK

0787 **DINNICK & HOWELLS**
CANADA

0788 **AFTERHOURS CREATIVE**
USA

0789 **ELMWOOD**
UK

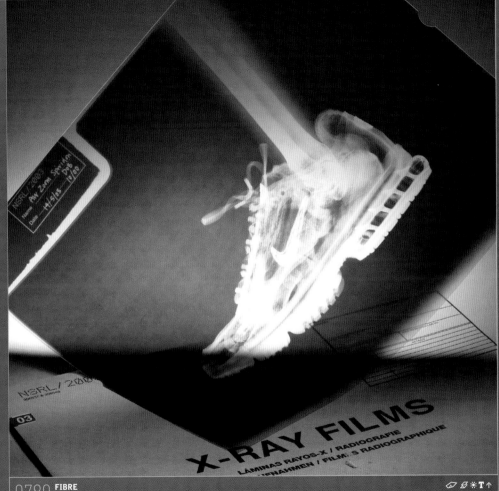

X-RAY FILMS

LÁMINAS RAYOS-X / RADIOGRAFIE
...ENAHMEN / FILM: S RADIOGRAPHIQUE

0792 **METAL**
USA

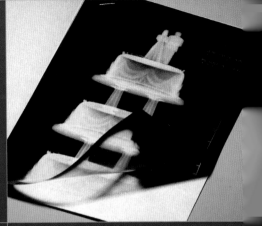

0793 **ELMWOOD**
UK

0794 **AFTERHOURS CREATIVE**
USA

0795 **FIBRE**
UK

0796 **SAS**
UK

0797 **ELMWOOD**
UK

0798 **CRUSH DESIGN**
UK

0799 **SAS**
UK

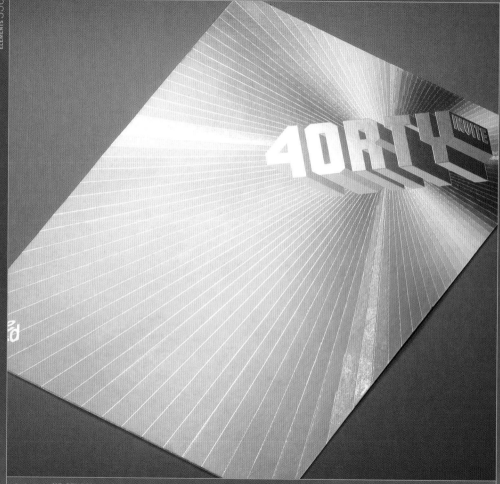

0802 **GIORGIO DAVANZO DESIGN**
USA

0803 **ELMWOOD**
UK

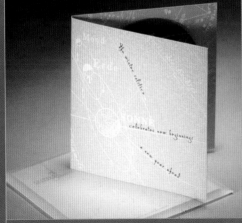

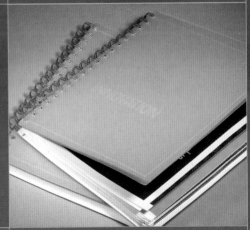

0804 **SELTZER DESIGN**
USA

0805 **WILSON HARVEY**
UK

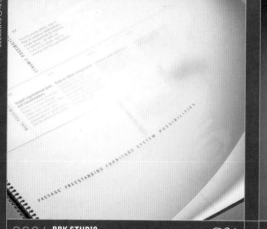

0806 **BBK STUDIO**
USA

0807 **BLOK DESIGN**
MEXICO

0808 **UNTITLED**
UK

0809 **HARRIMANSTEEL**
UK

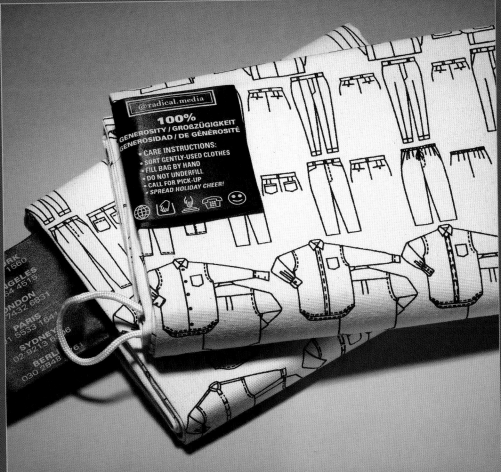

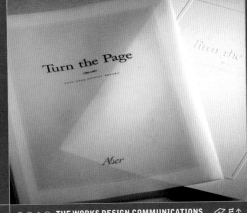

0812 **JADE DESIGN**
UK

0813 **THE WORKS DESIGN COMMUNICATIONS**
CANADA

0814 **ZULVER & CO**
UK

0815 **PH.D**
USA

0816 **HGV FELTON**
UK

0817 **WEBB & WEBB**
UK

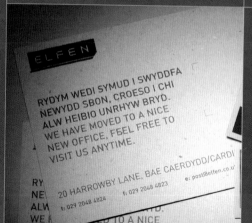

0818 **ELFEN**
WALES

0819 **BISQIT DESIGN**
UK

0821-

0028 0029 0030 0031 0032 0033 0034 0035 0036 0037 0038 0039 0040
0068 0069 0070 0071 0072 0073 0074 0075 0076 0077 0078 0079 0080
0108 0109 0110 0111 0112 0113 0114 0115 0116 0117 0118 0119 0120
0148 0149 0150 0151 0152 0153 0154 0155 0156 0157 0158 0159 0160
0188 0189 0190 0191 0192 0193 0194 0195 0196 0197 0198 0199 0200
0228 0229 0230 0231 0232 0233 0234 0235 0236 0237 0238 0239 0240
0268 0269 0270 0271 0272 0273 0274 0275 0276 0277 0278 0279 0280
0308 0309 0310 0311 0312 0313 0314 0315 0316 0317 0318 0319 0320
0348 0349 0350 0351 0352 0353 0354 0355 0356 0357 0358 0359 0360
0388 0389 0390 0391 0392 0393 0394 0395 0396 0397 0398 0399 0400
0428 0429 0430 0431 0432 0433 0434 0435 0436 0437 0438 0439 0440
0468 0469 0470 0471 0472 0473 0474 0475 0476 0477 0478 0479 0480
0508 0509 0510 0511 0512 0513 0514 0515 0516 0517 0518 0519 0520
0548 0549 0550 0551 0552 0553 0554 0555 0556 0557 0558 0559 0560
0588 0589 0590 0591 0592 0593 0594 0595 0596 0597 0598 0599 0600
0628 0629 0630 0631 0632 0633 0634 0635 0636 0637 0638 0639 0640
0668 0669 0670 0671 0672 0673 0674 0675 0676 0677 0678 0679 0680
0708 0709 0710 0711 0712 0713 0714 0715 0716 0717 0718 0719 0720
0748 0749 0750 0751 0752 0753 0754 0755 0756 0757 0758 0759 0760
0788 0789 0790 0791 0792 0793 0794 0795 0796 0797 0798 0799 0800
0828 0829 0830 0831 0832 0833 0834 0835 0836 0837 0838 0839 0840
0868 0869 0870 0871 0872 0873 0874 0875 0876 0877 0878 0879 0880
0908 0909 0910 0911 0912 0913 0914 0915 0916 0917 0918 0919 0920
0948 0949 0950 0951 0952 0953 0954 0955 0956 0957 0958 0959 0960
0988 0989 0990 0991 0992 0993 0994 0995 0996 0997 0998 0999 1000

06

GRAPHIC DEVICES

TYPE TREATMENT
GRAPHIC ELEMENTS
IMAGE MANIPULATION

0821 **SCANDINAVIAN DESIGN GROUP**
DENMARK T ↑

0822 **ZIP DESIGN**
UK T ✳ ∅ ⬠ ↑

0823 **LCTS**
UK T ✳ ◊ ↑

0824 **CAPSULE**
USA T ✳ ◊ ↑

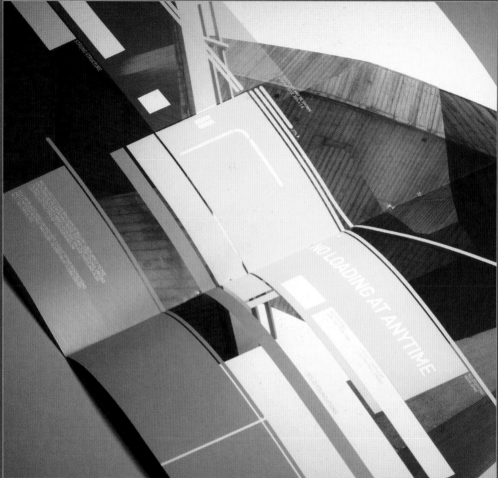

NO LOADING AT ANYTIME

T ✳ ◊ ↑

0827 **MACHINE**
THE NETHERLANDS　T ✱ ↑

0828 **MACHINE**
THE NETHERLANDS　✱ ↑

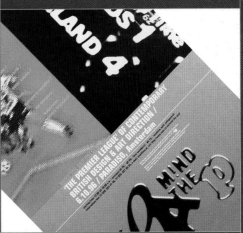

0829 **BASIA KNOBLOCH**
THE NETHERLANDS　T ↑

0830 **KOEWEIDEN POSTMA**
THE NETHERLANDS　T ✱ ◇ ↑

0831 **MACHINE**
THE NETHERLANDS ☀↑

0832 **MACHINE**
THE NETHERLANDS T☀◊↑

0833 **CUCKOOLAND**
UK T☀✍◊+↑

0834 **MACHINE**
THE NETHERLANDS ☀◊↑

b-hive

b-hive

BRONSTEIN & BERMAN **B-HIVE PRODUCTIONS** PHOTOGRAPHERS 38 GREENE STREET NEW YORK, NY 10013

b-hive

MAUREEN M. SMITH MSMITH@B-HIVEPRO.COM

BRONSTEIN & BERMAN **B-HIVE PRODUCTIONS** PHOTOGRAPHERS
38 GREENE STREET NEW YORK, NY 10013
TELEPHONE 212-925-7999 CELLULAR 917.209.8726
FAX 212-925-3799 WWW.B-HIVEPRO.COM

3XWIDE
DOTCOM
NO DEAD ENDS
WAY STREETS

T ☀ ◊ ↑

0837 **KOLEGRAM DESIGN** CANADA   T ✳ ↑

0838 **LIGALUX** GERMANY   T ✳ ↑

0839 **NAVY BLUE** UK   T ✳ ✍ ⊘ ↑

0840 **IE DESIGN** USA   T ◊ ↑

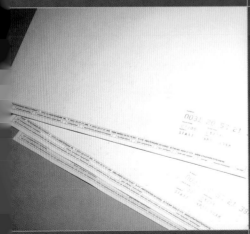

0841 **AUFULDISH & WARINNER**
USA

0842 **FIBRE**
UK

0843 **....STAAT**
THE NETHERLANDS

0844 **TRACY DESIGN**
USA

THURS
DAY
MARCH 13 TH 2 00

AT
LA
NOUVELLE
SCE NE

DAVID
USHER

OTTAWA CANADA
333 KING-EDWARD
819 777-7717

WWW.CU-AUA.CUM

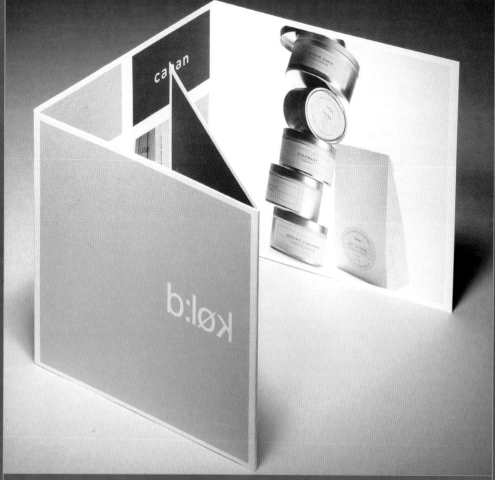

BLOK DESIGN MEXICO

T

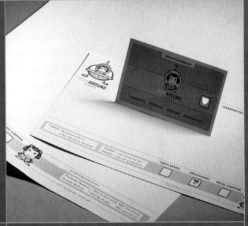

0847 **BLOK DESIGN**
MEXICO   T ✳ ✿ ◊ ↑

0848 **MARIUS FAHRNER DESIGN**
GERMANY   T ✳ ◊ ↑

0849 **STARSHOT**
GERMANY   T ◊ ↑

0850 **GROOTHUIS + MALSY**
UK   T ✿ ✿ ⊘ ↑

ects which play at the margin of booklshness
n and function with the marriage of ideas and
ttenge the viewer to explore both physical an
sensations. There are some which present a
in to its conversational essence, to a bundle
le others in the collection. They perform dif
hay each book in the project functions. The
ogue has one glaring omission, the defin

0851 **SAS**
UK

T ◊ ✄ ↑

0852 **CUCKOOLAND**
UK

T ✳ ↑

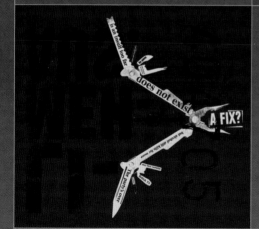

0853 **CUCKOOLAND**
UK

T ✳ ◊ ↑

0854 **AUFULDISH & WARINNER**
USA

✳ ↑

Warum
rasiert sich Simoni a

startalk

052

3

054

T

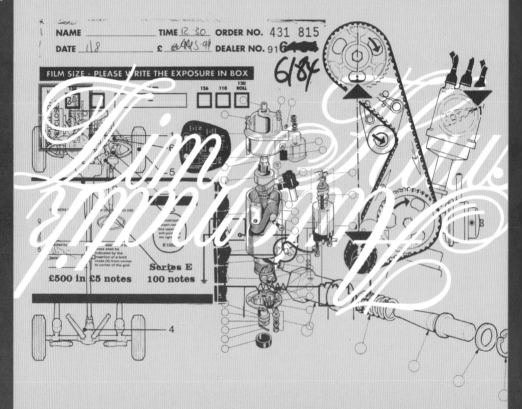

0857 **HGV FELTON** UK ☀↑

0858 **CUCKOOLAND** UK ↑

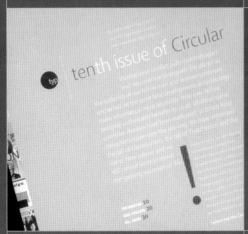

0859 **LIPPA PEARCE DESIGN** UK T↑

0860 **CUCKOOLAND** UK T☀◊↑

0861 **...,STAAT**
THE NETHERLANDS T ☀ ◊ ↑

0862 **GILLESPIE DESIGN**
USA T ☀ ↑

0863 **CUCKOOLAND**
UK T ☀ ◊ ⌀ ↑

0864 **KOLEGRAM DESIGN**
CANADA T ⌀ ⌀ ☀ ◊ ↑

03 10

MÄR · MÄRCH · MARS · MARZO

heartbeat
MOMENT
03 ≙ HEARTFACT NR 3

AT THE HEART OF THE HEART

PUMPLEISTUNG (PRO STUNDE)

normalpuls 300 l/h

T ☀ ⊘ ◊ ⬩ ↑

TWO MIDDLE-AGED AMERICAN DESIGNERS
MISTAKES

T

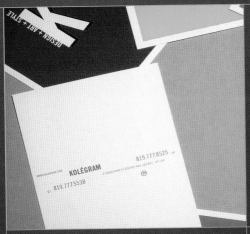

0867 **KOLEGRAM DESIGN**
CANADA

0868 **CDT DESIGN**
UK

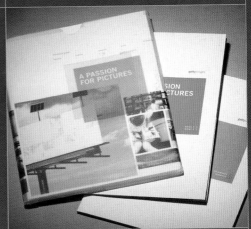

0869 **CDT DESIGN**
UK

0870 **MOTIVE DESIGN RESEARCH**
USA

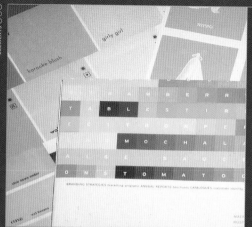

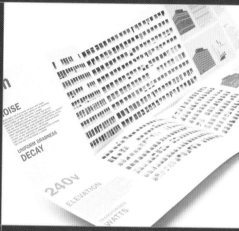

0871 **VIVA DOLAN COMMUNICATIONS & DESIGN**
CANADA ☀↑

0872 **THOMPSON**
UK T☀⌀↑

0873 **STOLTZE DESIGN**
USA ☀◊↑

0874 **SCANDINAVIAN DESIGN GROUP**
DENMARK T⌀↑

.//TRENDSHOW
NIKOLAJS KIRKE . D . 15.05.01

0875 **SCANDINANVIAN DESIGN GROUP**
DENMARK

T ✳ ↑

SPEAK

...laiming freedom to...
speaking what...
...ilenced...

YOUR...
IS NOT...

A COLLECTION OF
10 POSTCARDS

TEN POSTCARDS WITH UNIQUE VISUAL
NARRATIVES THAT PAY TRIBUTE TO THE MOST
POWERFUL METHOD OF COMMUNICATION —
THE HUMAN VOICE

waste not...want not

Don't forget to visit our full
environmental report on-line @

www.emigroup.co

0877 **GREENZWEIG DESIGN**
USA ✳ ☁ ↑

0878 **SALTERBAXTER**
UK T ☁ ↑

0879 **SALTERBAXTER**
UK T ◊ ↑

0880 **WALLACE CHURCH**
USA T ✳ ↑

0881 **CHEN DESIGN ASSOCIATES**
USA
T ✳ ✎ ◊ ↑

0882 **LIPPA PEARCE DESIGN**
UK
T ✇ ↑

0883 **V06**
BRAZIL
T ✇ ✳ ↑

0884 **SCANDINAVIAN DESIGN GROUP**
DENMARK
T ✳ ↑

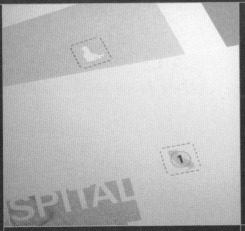

0887 **CHEN DESIGN ASSOCIATES**
USA

T ☀ ⚘ ↑

0888 **GOUTHIER DESIGN**
USA

T ☀ ☰ ↑

0889 **MIRIELLO GRAFICO**
USA

T ☀ ◊ ↑

0890 **CRUSH DESIGN**
UK

☀ ✇ ✎ ↑

0891 **MIRIELLO GRAFICO**
USA

0892 **D-FUSE**
UK

0893 **FAITH**
CANADA

0894 **PLAN-B STUDIO**
UK

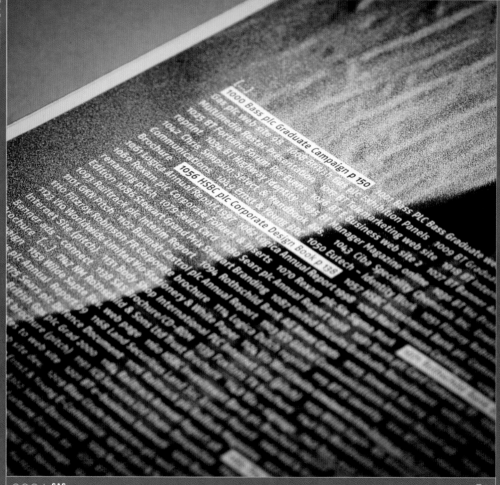

T ↑

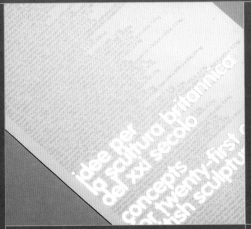

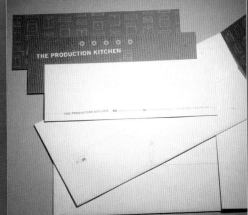

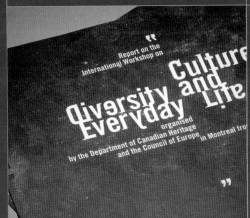

0897 **MADE THOUGHT**
UK
T ◊ ⬩ ↑

0898 **BLOK DESIGN**
MEXICO
T ✳ ⬩ ↑

0899 **KOLEGRAM DESIGN**
CANADA
T ◊ ⬩ ⊘ ↑

0900 **THE DESIGN DELL**
UK
T ↑

Nuclassicdisco
housensoul

paradi
soul

0901 **KOLEGRAM DESIGN**
CANADA

0902 **JONES DESIGN GROUP**
UK

0903 **MACHINE**
THE NETHERLANDS

0904 **METAL**
USA

T ✳ ⚹ ↑

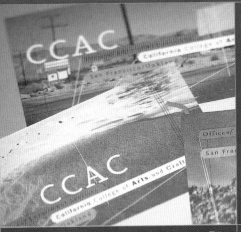

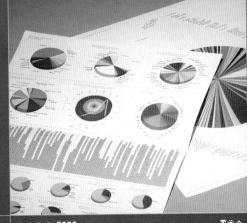

0907 **AUFULDISH & WARINNER**
USA　　　　　　　　　　　　　T ☀ ↑

0908 **EGBG**
THE NETHERLANDS　　　　　　T ☀ ↑

0909 **CUCKOOLAND**
UK　　　　　　　　　　　　　T ☀ ↑

0910 **THE FAMILY**
UK　　　　　　　　　　　　　T ☀ ◊ ↑

0911 **THOMPSON**
UK   T ◇ ✎ ↑

0912 **TYLER MAGAZINE**
FRANCE   T ☀ ↑

0913 **VOICE**
AUSTRALIA   T ☀ ↑

0914 **TYLER MAGAZINE**
FRANCE   T ☀ ↑

T ☀ ✄ ○ ↑

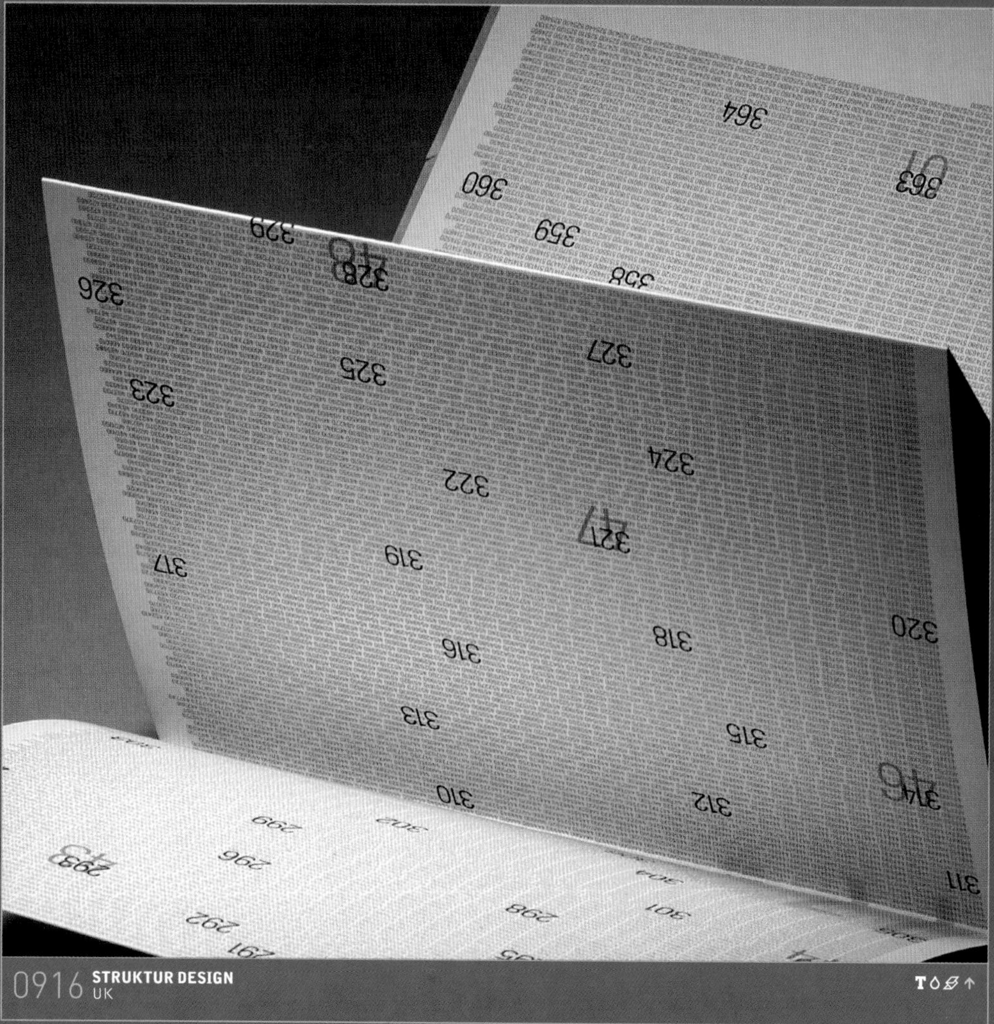

0916 **STRUKTUR DESIGN**
UK

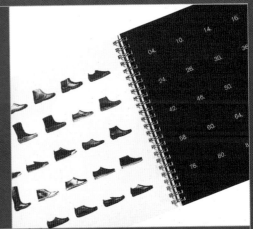

0917 **ROYCROFT DESIGN**
USA   T ✳ ✎ ↑

0918 **TAXI STUDIO**
UK   ✳ T ⊘ ↑

0919 **FOTOGRAFIE & GESTALTUNG**
     CHRISTIAN NIELINGER   ✳ ↑
     GERMANY

0920 **PH.D**
     USA   T ✳ ✎ ↑

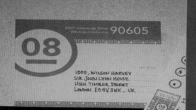

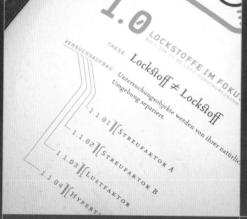

0921 **PHYX DESIGN**
USA

T + ✳ ◿ ↑

0922 **MORLA DESIGN**
USA

T ✳ ↑

0923 **LIGALUX**
GERMANY

T ✳ ◊ ↑

0924 **MADE THOUGHT**
UK

✳ ◊ ↑

INNOVATIVE BUSINESS MODELS HAVE BEEN THE NORM WITH HERMAN MILLER FROM OUR MOVE INTO "MODERN" FURNITURE IN THE 1930S, TO OUR TRANSFORMATION OF THE OFFICE FURNITURE INDUSTRY IN THE 1970S, TO THE "SIMPLE, QUICK, AND AFFORDABLE" SUCCESSES OF THE 1990S. HERMAN MILLER RED IS NOW INTRODUCING US TO A FRESH SET OF CUSTOMERS WITH NEW CHANNELS TO MARKET, HIP NEW PRODUCTS, AND AN ATTITUDE TO MATCH.

T ✳ ↑

T ☀ ↑

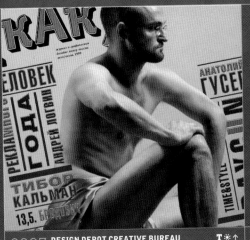

0927 **DESIGN DEPOT CREATIVE BUREAU**
RUSSIA
T ☀ ↑

0928 **DESIGN DEPOT CREATIVE BUREAU**
RUSSIA
T ☀ ↑

0929 **DESIGN DEPOT CREATIVE BUREAU**
RUSSIA
T ☀ ↑

0930 **DESIGN DEPOT CREATIVE BUREAU**
RUSSIA
T ☀ ↑

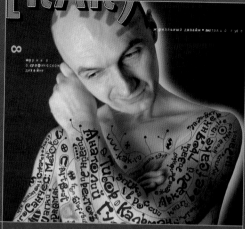

0931 **DESIGN DEPOT CREATIVE BUREAU**
RUSSIA   T ☀ ↑

0932 **DESIGN DEPOT CREATIVE BUREAU**
RUSSIA   T ☀ ↑

0933 **DESIGN DEPOT CREATIVE BUREAU**
RUSSIA   T ☀ ↑

0934 **DESIGN DEPOT CREATIVE BUREAU**
RUSSIA   T ☀ ↑

[RHR] № 18

design magazine

Christoph Niemann
Denise Gonzales
Jenifer Sterling
Rick Valicenti
Sheila de Bretteville
Miller Abbott
Jeff Keedy
Louise Fili
Bill Cahan
Fred Woodward
Chip Kidd

John Bielenberg
Louise Sandhaus
Pentagram
Peter Girardi
Alexander Gelman
Wolfgang Weingart
Warren Lehrer
Scher/Pentagram
Michael Bierut
Mirko Ilić
Paula Scher
Matthias Frere Jones

At the International Art Ex
heralded the be highly decorative
the using a les Wilson fitters on this
Anrison Brochley, is a ration of the
generation was deeply concentration
maximalism and magnificent and a
broadly sophisticated to the common
novies and a taste for excessive and
Minimalism and had had arged in
in design and architectureness

Maximalism returns and magnificent

After years of minimalist rule, gra
more glamorous design cntric mar a
representation on in issue has a comber
color

Maxima one

ars of m
ique Nose
ntroduction

AFTER YEARS OF MINIMALIST RULE, GRA
RETURN TO A MORE DECORATIVE, MAXIMALIST APPROA
ARCHITECTURE IS MORE CURVACEOUS, FASHION MORE
SILHOUETTE AND BOTANICAL MOTIFS AR

0937 **WILSON HARVEY**
UK
T ◊ ↑

01
CHAPTER ONE
Decoration
Ornament, handicraft, technol

0938 **WILSON HARVEY**
UK
T ☀ ↑

Maxima
THE GRAPHIC DESIGN OF D

0939 **WILSON HARVEY**
UK
T ☀ ◊ ↑

Contents 004 *Introduction*

0940 **WILSON HARVEY**
UK
T ☀ ↑

0941 **WILSON HARVEY**
UK
T ☀ ↑

0942 **DESIGN HOCH DREI**
GERMANY
T ☀ ⬿ ↑

0943 **HARRIMANSTEEL**
UK
T ⬿ ↑

0944 **BWA DESIGN**
UK
T ⬿ ◊ ↑

MIKE FAULKNER –DIRECTOR

D-FUSE
PO BOX 39943 LONDON, EC1V 0YZ, UK.
T +44 (0)20 7253 3462   M +44 (0)7973 655 231
W www.dfuse.com   E mike@dfuse.com

T ☀ ✍ ◊↑

T ✳ ◊ ✄ ↑

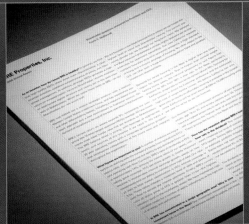

0947 **CAHAN & ASSOCIATES**
USA

T ↑

0948 **UNTITLED**
UK

T ✳ ↑

0949 **CHIMERA DESIGN**
USA

T ✳ ◊ ∅ ↑

0950 **ZIP DESIGN**
UK

T ✳ ◊ ↑

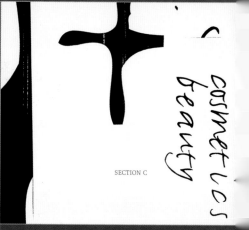

0951 **EMPIRE DESIGN STUDIO**
USA
T ◊ ⬭ ↑

0952 **VOICE**
AUSTRALIA
T ☀ ↑

0953 **IAMALWAYSHUNGRY**
USA
T ☀ + ◊ ↑

0954 **BAUMANN & BAUMANN**
GERMANY
T ☀ ↑

T ✳ ↑

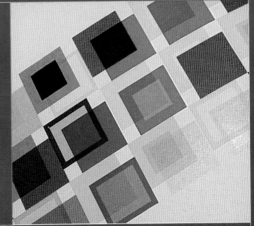

0957 **THE FAMILY**
UK
T☀↑

0958 **THE FAMILY**
UK
☀◌↑

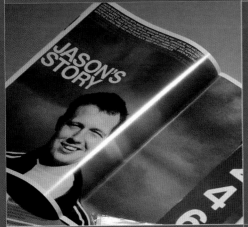

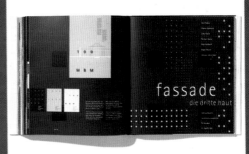

0959 **RADLEY YELDER**
UK
T↑

0960 **BAUMANN & BAUMANN**
GERMANY
T☀↑

RUNNING: 99% MENTAL, 99% PHYSICAL.
AIR MAX

0961 **KOEWEIDEN POSTMA**
THE NETHERLANDS
T ↑

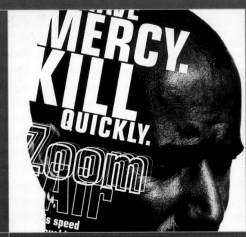

MERCY. KILL QUICKLY.
Zoom AIR
is speed

0962 **KOEWEIDEN POSTMA**
THE NETHERLANDS
T ↑

Jason Kidd
TOO FAST. TOO STRONG. TOO BAD.
Zoom AIR
is speed cushioning

0963 **KOEWEIDEN POSTMA**
THE NETHERLANDS
T ↑

Pippen
EVERYBODY GOTTA LAND sometime
AIR MAX
is maximum cushioning

0964 **KOEWEIDEN POSTMA**
THE NETHERLANDS
T ↑

FICTION TWO

UNDER THE WEATHER
BY JAMES HOPKIN

proof.

vorlesungen zur filmprofessur. hochschule für gestaltung offenbach am main, schlossstraße 31, raum 101
01. 11. 02 freitag:: **stephan sachs** 09:00 uhr **dr. boris penth** 10:45 uhr **h. joachim hofmann** 13:00 uhr **reinhard franz** 14:45 uhr
04. 11. 02 montag:: **philine hofmann** 14:00 uhr **rotraut pape** 15:45 uhr **maike mia höhne** 17:30 uhr

T ✳ ↑

0967 **MODE**
UK   T ✳ ◊ ↑

0968 **MODE**
UK   T ✳ ◊ ↑

0969 **MODE**
UK   T ✳ ◊ ↑

0970 **MODE**
UK   T ✳ ◊ ↑

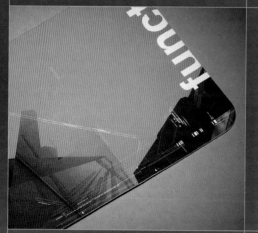

0971 **HESSE DESIGN**
GERMANY
T ◊ ↑

0972 **CHEN DESIGN ASSOCIATES**
USA
T ✳ ☰ ✎ ↑

0973 **TRACY DESIGN**
USA
T ✳ ✿ ↑

0974 **CRUSH DESIGN**
UK
T ✳ ↑

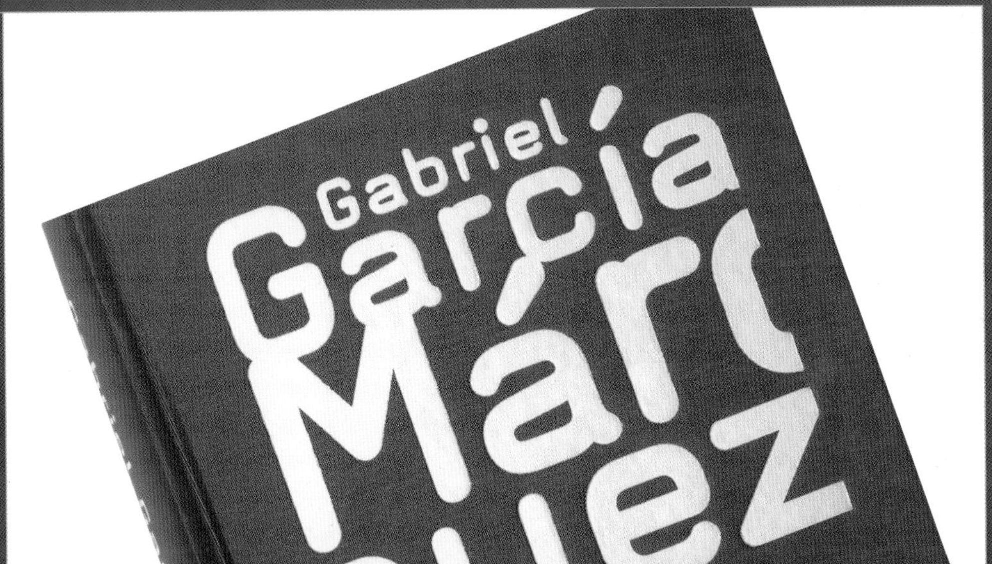

0975 **KOEWEIDEN POSTMA**
THE NETHERLANDS

0977 **TEMPLIN BRINK DESIGN**
USA

0978 **MORLA DESIGN**
USA

0979 **FELDER GRAFIKDESIGN**
AUSTRIA

0980 **IAMALWAYSHUNGRY**
USA

0981 **THIRTEEN**
UK   T ↑

0982 **KOEWEIDEN POSTMA**
THE NETHERLANDS   T ↑

0983 **LIPPA PEARCE DESIGN**
UK   T ✏ ✄ ↑

0984 **SAS**
UK   T ✳ ☙ ↑

Einführung in die politische Philosophie

Massada

WAT
294

WAT
291

Christian Ruby

19.80

Attilio Brilli

22.80

19.80

Iris Origo

WAT
290

26.80

»Im Namen Gottes
und des Geschäfts«

Elsa Morante

Aracoeli

WAT
293

24.80

Kleine Geschichte Italiens von 1943 bis heute

Vergnügen bei Platon

Beunruhigungen

Arturos Insel

Der Schnurrbart

WAT
288

Friederike Hausmann

22.80

Alexandre Koyré

WAT
285

16.80

Erich Fried

WAT
292

15.80

WAT
277

Elsa Morante

24.80

WAT
289

Emmanuel Carrère

17.80

herzb

herzblut

designers

...ism and experiment

Rockport Publishers

Paul Burgess
Wilson Harvey
London

address

designers herzblut alexanderstr. 9b 28203 bremen/germany

project management
alexander boell c/o daniel bastian
phone: + 49 (421) 794 8277
fax: + 49 (421) 70 3774
leo: + 49 (421) 331 96 45
mail: boell@d-herzblut.de

a project
and **ulysses**

in cooperation
verlag hermann s
mainz (germany)

Ennius et sapines
et fortis et alter Homerus, ut critici dicunt, leviter cura
promissa cadant et somnia Pythagorea, Naevius in
sanctum mentibus haeret paene recens? Adeo
poema. Ambigitur quotiens, uter utro sit p
famam senis Accius alti, dicitur Afrani
ad exemplar Siculi properare Epich
theatro spectat Roma potens;
bigitur tempus Livi script
Ennius et sapines et f
curare videtur, qu
manibus non
tum est
Pac

T ↑

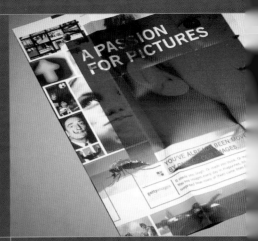

0987 **FROST DESIGN**
UK

T ✳ ↑

0988 **MOTIVE DESIGN RESEARCH**
USA

T ◊ ✐ ↑

0989 **DURSO DESIGN**
USA

T ✳ ◊ ↑

0990 **MODE**
UK

✳ ↑

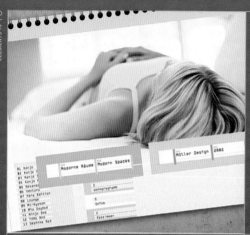

0991 **KEARNEY ROCHOLL**
GERMANY T ✳ ⊘ ↑

0992 **KESSELS KRAMER**
THE NETHERLANDS T ⬦ ↑

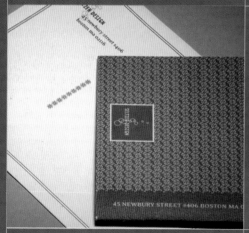

0993 **SELTZER DESIGN**
USA T ✳ ⬦ ↑

0994 **FROST DESIGN**
UK T ✳ ↑

Insiders know more. They have depth and perspective. And they put their expertise to work. In the world of restored muscle cars, Interbrand chief creative officer Courtney Reeser has joined the ranks of the true insiders. Woods Litho celebrates his personal passion, and invites you to join him on the journey inside.

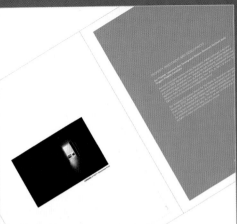

0997 **IRIDIUM, A DESIGN AGENCY**
CANADA   T ◊ ↑

0998 **KINETIC SINGAPORE**
SINGAPORE   T ↑

0999 **KOEWEIDEN POSTMA**
THE NETHERLANDS   T ☀ ↑

1000 **IAMALWAYSHUNGRY**
USA   T ☀ ◊ ↑

INDEX BY AGENCY

@RADICAL.MEDIA

0110
ART DIRECTOR(S): RAPHAEL ESQUER
DESIGNER(S): RAPHAEL ESQUER
CLIENT: @RADICAL.MEDIA
TOOLS: ILLUSTRATOR, PHOTOSHOP, MAC
MATERIALS: ANIMATED 3-D LENTICULAR IMAGE

0738
ART DIRECTOR(S): RAPHAEL ESQUER
DESIGNER(S): WENDY WEN, JONATHAN EVA
CLIENT: OUTPOST DIGITAL
TOOLS: ILLUSTRATOR, QUARK, MAC
MATERIALS: TRANSILWRAP PLASTICS FROSTY CLEAR MATTE, CALENDARERED VINYL

0810
ART DIRECTOR(S): RAPHAEL ESQUER
DESIGNER(S): RAPHAEL ESQUER, WENDY WEN
CLIENT: @RADICAL.MEDIA
TOOLS: ILLUSTRATOR, MAC
MATERIALS: CANVAS, BLACK RIBBON

...STAAT

0081
ART DIRECTOR(S): JOCHEM LEEGSTRA
DESIGNER(S): YOURI KOERS
CLIENT: BARTENDER NETWORK
TOOLS: MAC, ILLUSTRATOR
MATERIALS: PROMINENT 500GSM

0338
ART DIRECTOR(S): JOCHEM LEEGSTRA
DESIGNER(S): YOURI KOERS
CLIENT: CLUB JIMMY WOO
TOOLS: ILLUSTRATOR, PHOTOSHOP, QUARK, MAC
MATERIALS: CHROMOLUX

0719
ART DIRECTOR(S): JOCHEM LEEGSTRA
DESIGNER(S): JARI VERSTEEGEN
CLIENT: MOËT & CHANDON
TOOLS: ILLUSTRATOR, QUARK, MAC
MATERIALS: SILK SCARF AND POCHET, PACKAGING WITH FOILPRINT

0772
ART DIRECTOR(S): JOCHEM LEEGSTRA
DESIGNER(S): YOURI KOERS
CLIENT: CLUB JIMMY WOO
TOOLS: ILLUSTRATOR, PHOTOSHOP, QUARK, MAC
MATERIALS: PENCILS

0843
ART DIRECTOR(S): JOCHEM LEEGSTRA
DESIGNER(S): ...STAAT
CLIENT: ...STAAT
TOOLS: ILLUSTRATOR, QUARK, MAC
MATERIALS: CONQUEROR CX22 PLASTIC

0861
ART DIRECTOR(S): JOCHEM LEEGSTRA, STEF BAKKER
DESIGNER(S): YOURI KOERS
CLIENT: CAFÉ RESTAURANT MAMOUCHE

11D-ELEVEN DESIGN

0150, 0522, 695
ART DIRECTOR(S): OLE LUND, JAN NIELSEN
DESIGNER(S): OLE LUND, JAN NIELSEN
CLIENT: 2GD-2 GRAPHIC DESIGN
TOOLS: ILLUSTRATOR, PHOTOSHOP

0509, 0512
ART DIRECTOR(S): OLE LUND, JAN NIELSEN
DESIGNER(S): OLE LUND, JAN NIELSEN
CLIENT: BRUUNS BAZAAR
TOOLS: ILLUSTRATOR, PHOTOSHOP
MATERIALS: LUMIART SILK 300GSM

0513, 0514
ART DIRECTOR(S): OLE LUND, JAN NIELSEN
DESIGNER(S): OLE LUND, JAN NIELSEN
CLIENT: KØNRÖG
TOOLS: ILLUSTRATOR, PHOTOSHOP

0521
ART DIRECTOR(S): OLE LUND, JAN NIELSEN
DESIGNER(S): OLE LUND, JAN NIELSEN
CLIENT: BLACKBOX MAGAZINE
TOOLS: ILLUSTRATOR, PHOTOSHOP

A2-GRAPHICS/SW/HK

0466
ART DIRECTOR(S): SCOTT WILLIAM, HENRIK KUBEL
DESIGNER(S): SCOTT WILLIAM, HENRIK KUBEL
CLIENT: 1508
MATERIALS: LUMI SILK

0465
ART DIRECTOR(S): SCOTT WILLIAM, HENRIK KUBEL
DESIGNER(S): SCOTT WILLIAM, HENRIK KUBEL
CLIENT: THE INTERNATIONAL SOCIETY OF TYPOGRAPHIC DESIGNERS
TOOLS: MAC
MATERIALS: CONSORT ROYAL

0499
ART DIRECTOR(S): SCOTT WILLIAM, HENRIK KUBEL
DESIGNER(S): SCOTT WILLIAM, HENRIK KUBEL
CLIENT: ARNOLFINI
TOOLS: MAC
MATERIALS: MUNKEN LYNX AND CONSORT ROYAL

0650
ART DIRECTOR(S): SCOTT WILLIAM, HENRIK KUBEL
DESIGNER(S): SCOTT WILLIAM, HENRIK KUBEL
CLIENT: HAYWARD GALLERY/ ARTS COUNCIL COLLECTION
MATERIALS: COLOURPLAN, ARTIC SILK

ABOUD SADANO

ART DIRECTOR(S): ALAN ABOUD
DESIGNER(S): ELLIE RIDSDALE, ALAN ABOUD
CLIENT: PAUL SMITH

ADDUCCI STUDIOS

ART DIRECTOR(S): STEPHEN ADDUCCI
DESIGNER(S): STEPHEN ADDUCCI
CLIENT: ADDUCCI STUDIOS
TOOLS: ILLUSTRATOR, MAC

AFTERHOURS CREATIVE

0174
ART DIRECTOR(S): AFTERHOURS
DESIGNER(S): AFTERHOURS
CLIENT: CLEARDATA.NET
TOOLS: ILLUSTRATOR

0387
ART DIRECTOR(S): AFTERHOURS
DESIGNER(S): AFTERHOURS
CLIENT: BLUESPACE
TOOLS: ILLUSTRATOR

0645
ART DIRECTOR(S): AFTERHOURS
DESIGNER(S): AFTERHOURS
CLIENT: AFTERHOURS
TOOLS: ILLUSTRATOR
MATERIALS: JIFFY POP

0648
ART DIRECTOR(S): AFTERHOURS
DESIGNER(S): AFTERHOURS
CLIENT: ROSIN+BOULE
TOOLS: ILLUSTRATOR

0649, 0794
ART DIRECTOR(S): AFTERHOURS
DESIGNER(S): AFTERHOURS
CLIENT: COTTON CENTER
TOOLS: ILLUSTRATOR
MATERIALS: COTTON

0788
ART DIRECTOR(S): AFTERHOURS
DESIGNER(S): AFTERHOURS
CLIENT: MAX+LUCY
TOOLS: ILLUSTRATOR
MATERIALS: CARDBOARD, RUBBER STAMPS

ALOOF DESIGN

ART DIRECTOR(S): SAM ALOOF
DESIGNER(S): CHRIS BARHAM
CLIENT: GEORGINA GOODMAN
MATERIALS: MACHINE-CODED, 1-SIDED TISSUE PAPER

0260
ART DIRECTOR(S): SAM ALOOF
DESIGNER(S): CHRIS BARHAM
CLIENT: GEORGINA GOODMAN
MATERIALS: G.F. SMITH COLOURPLAN MIST MATT LAM

0271
ART DIRECTOR(S): SAM ALOOF
DESIGNER(S): CHRIS BARHAM
CLIENT: GEORGINA GOODMAN
MATERIALS: CX22

AMANDA HAVEL

0095
DESIGNER(S): AMANDA HAVEL
CLIENT: BREEANNA REILLY
TOOLS: ILLUSTRATOR, MAC
MATERIALS: COLORED WAX, BRASS STAMP

AND PARTNERS

0312
ART DIRECTOR(S): DAVID SCHIMMEL
DESIGNER(S): DAVID SCHIMMEL
CLIENT: AND PARTNERS
TOOLS: ILLUSTRATOR, MAC

0554
ART DIRECTOR(S): DAVID SCHIMMEL
CLIENT: AMEX PUBLISHING
TOOLS: QUARK, MAC
MATERIALS: BIBLE PAPER, SUNDANCE BEET, CRANE'S

0595
ART DIRECTOR(S): DAVID SCHIMMEL
DESIGNER(S): SARAH HOLLOWOOD
CLIENT: AND PARTNERS
TOOLS: PHOTOSHOP, QUARK, MAC

0602
ART DIRECTOR(S): DAVID SCHIMMEL
CLIENT: AND PARTNERS
TOOLS: ILLUSTRATOR, QUARK, MAC
MATERIALS: MOHAWK SUPERFINE, GROMMETS

0723
ART DIRECTOR(S): DAVID SCHIMMEL
CLIENT: BRINSILLITS/NYC
TOOLS: QUARK
MATERIALS: ZANDERS METALLIC AND SAPPI COATED

0835
ART DIRECTOR(S): DAVID SCHIMMEL
DESIGNER(S): TYLER SMALL
CLIENT: B-HIVE STUDIO
TOOLS: ILLUSTRATOR, QUARK, MAC
MATERIALS: MOHAWK OPTIONS SUPERFINE

ANDERSON THOMAS DESIGN

0100
ART DIRECTOR(S): JAY SMITH
DESIGNER(S): JAY SMITH
CLIENT: W DESIGN
TOOLS: QUARK, PHOTOSHOP
MATERIALS: FRENCH BUTCHER COVER AND TEXT

0269
ART DIRECTOR(S): JOEL ANDERSON, ROY ROPER
DESIGNER(S): ROY ROPER
CLIENT: ANDERSON THOMAS DESIGN
TOOLS: PHOTOSHOP, QUARK

0487
ART DIRECTOR(S): JAY SMITH
DESIGNER(S): JAY SMITH
CLIENT: ROCKETOWN YOUTH SERVICES
TOOLS: PHOTOSHOP, QUARK, MAC
MATERIALS: GILBERT ESSE 80LB COVER

AUFULDISH & WARRINER

0841
DESIGNER(S): BOB AUFULDISH
CLIENT: CALIFORNIA COLLEGE OF ARTS AND CRAFTS
TOOLS: ILLUSTRATOR, PHOTOSHOP, MAC
MATERIALS: MOHAWK NAVAJO COVER

0894, 0907
DESIGNER(S): BOB AUFULDISH
CLIENT: CALIFORNIA COLLEGE OF ARTS AND CRAFTS
TOOLS: ILLUSTRATOR, PHOTOSHOP, MAC
MATERIALS: FINCH OPAQUE COVER

AVE DESIGN STUDIO

0119, 0794
ART DIRECTOR(S): MARY ANN AVE
DESIGNER(S): JENNIFER AVE
CLIENT: LUBRIZOL
TOOLS: PHOTOSHOP, QUARK, MAC
MATERIALS: STRATHMORE ELEMENTS, INFLATABLE PLASTIC BAG, REFLECTIVE MIRROR STOCK

BARCELONA

0207
ART DIRECTOR(S): MICHAEL LEONARDINI
DESIGNER(S): ARIS BAJAR
CLIENT: IMAX THEATRE
TOOLS: ILLUSTRATOR, MAC
MATERIALS: STARWHITE

0388
ART DIRECTOR(S): MICHAEL
LEONARDINI
DESIGNER(S): MICHAEL
LEONARDINI
CLIENT: BARCELONA
TOOLS: FREEHAND, MAC
MATERIALS: STARWHITE

BASIA KNOBLOCH

0827
ART DIRECTOR(S): BASIA
KNOBLOCH
DESIGNER(S): BASIA
KNOBLOCH
CLIENT: ART ACADEMY FINAL
PROJECT
TOOLS: ILLUSTRATOR, MAC
MATERIALS: PAPER,
SILKSCREEN PRINT

BAUMANN & BAUMANN

0407
ART DIRECTOR(S): BARBARA
BAUMANN, GIRD BAUMANN
DESIGNER(S): BARBARA
BAUMANN, GIRD BAUMANN
CLIENT: HATJE CANTZ
TOOLS: PHOTOSHOP,
FREEHAND
MATERIALS: PHOENIXMOTION

BBK STUDIO

0363
ART DIRECTOR(S): YANG KIM
DESIGNER(S): YANG KIM
CLIENT: BBK STUDIO
TOOLS: QUARK
MATERIALS: MOHAWK, POLY-
PROPYLENE, TIN

0951
ART DIRECTOR(S): YANG KIM
DESIGNER(S): YANG KIM
CLIENT: BBK STUDIO
TOOLS: ILLUSTRATOR
MATERIALS: PARALUX,
CRANE'S

0351, 0619
ART DIRECTOR(S): YANG KIM
DESIGNER(S): MICHELE
CHARTIER
CLIENT: HAAC
TOOLS: QUARK, PHOTOSHOP
MATERIALS: FINCH

0906
ART DIRECTOR(S): YANG KIM
DESIGNER(S): YANG KIM
CLIENT: BBK STUDIO
TOOLS: QUARK
MATERIALS: MOHAWK, POLY-
PROPYLENE, TIN

0729
ART DIRECTOR(S): SHARON
OLENICZAK
DESIGNER(S): SHARON
OLENICZAK
CLIENT: MANDRIA GAZAL
TOOLS: QUARK

0408
ART DIRECTOR(S): YANG KIM
DESIGNER(S): YANG KIM
CLIENT: JACK RIDL
TOOLS: QUARK
MATERIALS: MONADNOCK
ASTROLITE

0602
ART DIRECTOR(S): SHARON
OLENICZAK
DESIGNER(S): MICHELE
CHARTIER
CLIENT: DYER-IVES
FOUNDATION
TOOLS: QUARK
MATERIALS: BENEFIT/VIA

0896
ART DIRECTOR(S): KEVIN
BUDELMANN
DESIGNER(S): ALISON POPP
CLIENT: HERMAN MILLER
TOOLS: QUARK

0884, 0922
ART DIRECTOR(S): STEVE
FRYKHOLM
DESIGNER(S): YANG KIM,
MICHELE CHARTIER
CLIENT: HERMAN MILLER
TOOLS: QUARK
MATERIALS: GLAMA BECKETT

BBM&D

0286
ART DIRECTOR(S): GILES
BEAULIEU
DESIGNER(S): GILES
BEAULIEU
CLIENT: STYLISMOPTION INC.
TOOLS: ILLUSTRATION,
PHOTOSHOP, MAC
MATERIALS: DOMTAR
PROTERRA: "GRES" AND
"PAILLE"

BECKER DESIGN

0331
ART DIRECTOR(S): NEIL
BECKER
DESIGNER(S): NEIL BECKER
CLIENT: LONDON BY DESIGN
TOOLS: ILLUSTRATOR,
PHOTOSHOP, QUARK, MAC
MATERIALS: DOMTAR
SOLUTIONS SOFT WHITE
SUPER SMOOTH 100LB COVER,
GLAMA VELLUM, BLACK
SATIN RIBBON

BELYEA

0797
ART DIRECTOR(S): PATRICIA
BELYEA
DESIGNER(S): NAOMI
MURPHY
CLIENT: FRASER PAPERS
TOOLS: ILLUSTRATOR, MAC
MATERIALS: FRASER PAPERS
GENESIS AND PASSPORT—
ALL COLORS, WEIGHTS AND
FINISHES, FRASER PAPERS
OUTBACK SYDNEY SURF (COR-
RUGATED PAPER), ELASTIC
CLOSURE BAND

0960
ART DIRECTOR(S): SHARON
OLENICZAK
DESIGNER(S): MICHELE
CHARTIER
CLIENT: DYER-IVES
FOUNDATION
TOOLS: QUARK
MATERIALS: BENEFIT/VIA

0950
ART DIRECTOR(S): PATRICIA
BELYEA
DESIGNER(S): NAOMI
MURPHY
CLIENT: COLORGRAPHICS
SEATTLE
TOOLS: ILLUSTRATOR, MAC
MATERIALS: SPECKLTONE
STARCH VINE BOOK, 80LB
CURIOUS GALVANIZED
BOOK (ENVELOPES), 100LB
SIGNATURE TRUE DULL (INVI-
TATIONS), 100LB SIGNATURE
GLOSS COVER (COVER),
GROMMETS

0804
ART DIRECTOR(S): PATRICIA
BELYEA
DESIGNER(S): RON LARS
HANSEN
CLIENT: COLORGRAPHICS
SEATTLE
TOOLS: ILLUSTRATOR, MAC
MATERIALS: FREEFORM
INVITATION: 80LB GILBERT
OXFORD BLUE COVER, 80LB
GILBERT OXFORD BLACK
COVER, 100LB SIGNATURE
SUEDE BOOK; LYRICAL
AMBIGUITY INVITATION:
100LB CRUSHED LEAF LIME,
100LB CRUSHED LEAF COCOA,
100LB SIGNATURE SUEDE
BOOK; DIVERGENT REALITIES
INVITATIONS.

0756
ART DIRECTOR(S): PATRICIA
BELYEA
DESIGNER(S): NAOMI
MURPHY
CLIENT: FRASER PAPERS
TOOLS: ILLUSTRATOR
MATERIALS: FRASER PAPERS
GENESIS AND PASSPORT—
ALL COLORS, WEIGHTS AND
FINISHES, FRASER PAPERS
OUTBACK SYDNEY SURF (COR-
RUGATED PAPER), ELASTIC
CLOSURE BAND

0770
ART DIRECTOR(S): PATRICIA
BELYEA
DESIGNER(S): NAOMI
MURPHY
CLIENT: IMPERIAL
LITHOGRAPH
TOOLS: ILLUSTRATOR, MAC
MATERIALS: WESTVACO
STERLINE ULTRA DULL 100C
FOR WRAP AND CALENDAR
PAGES

BETH CURTIS

0218
DESIGNER(S): BETH CURTIS
CLIENT: OXFORD CONVERSIS
MATERIALS: NEPTUNE

BIG ACTIVE

0877
ART DIRECTOR(S): GERARD
SAINT, MAT MAITLAND
DESIGNER(S): MAT MAITLAND
CLIENT: SONY MUSIC UK
MATERIALS: BLACK, NATU-
RALLY EXPANDED, FLEXIBLE
PVC

0511
ART DIRECTOR(S): GERARD
SAINT, MAT MAITLAND
DESIGNER(S): MAT MAITLAND
CLIENT: BMG RECORDS
MATERIALS: HEAVYWEIGHT
BLACK, MOLDED, WELDED
AND FOIL-BLOCKED ACRYLIC
(EXTERIOR), HIGH-DENSITY
ROUTED FOAM TRAY (INTE-
RIOR), POLISHED STAINLESS
STEEL

0955
ART DIRECTOR(S): GERARD
SAINT
DESIGNER(S): GERARD SAINT
CLIENT: UNIVERSAL MUSIC
MATERIALS: NYLON ADHE-
SIVE "SECURITY" STICKER

0615
ART DIRECTOR(S): GERARD
SAINT, MAT MAITLAND
DESIGNER(S): MAT MAITLAND
CLIENT: BMG RECORDS
MATERIALS: SILVER MELINEX
BOARD, SILKSCREEN, ROLLED
BANKNOTE MATERIAL

BIRMINGHAM INSTITUTE OF ART & DESIGN

0238
DESIGNER(S): DAPHNE
DIAMANT
CLIENT: HILL & KNOWLTON
TOOLS: FREEHAND, QUARK,
MAC
MATERIALS: 270GSM
SUPERCOL BUFF

BISQIT DESIGN

0188
DESIGNER(S): DAPHNE
DIAMANT
CLIENT: HILL & KNOWLTON
TOOLS: FREEHAND, QUARK,
MAC
MATERIALS: 270GSM
SUPERCOL BUFF

0294
ART DIRECTOR(S): DAPHNE
DIAMANT
DESIGNER(S): ADAM
MITCHINSON
CLIENT: HILL & KNOWLTON
TOOLS: ILLUSTRATOR, MAC
MATERIALS: CHROMOLUX
700GSM AND 350GSM

0643
ART DIRECTOR(S): DAPHNE
DIAMANT
DESIGNER(S): NICOLA TATUM
CLIENT: HILL & KNOWLTON
TOOLS: QUARK, MAC
MATERIALS: BLACK
CHROMOLUX 300, BLCK
SILKSCREEN

0667
DESIGNER(S): DAPHNE
DIAMANT
CLIENT: HILL & KNOWLTON
TOOLS: ILLUSTRATOR,
PHOTOSHOP, QUARK, MAC
MATERIALS: NEPTUNE
UNIQUE

1819
DESIGNER(S): DAPHNE
DIAMANT
CLIENT: WORLD SNOOKER
TOOLS: FREEHAND, QUARK,
MAC
MATERIALS: MEDLEY PURE,
SOFT PVC

BLACKCOFFEE

0429
ART DIRECTOR(S): MARK
GALLAGHER, LAURA SAVARD
DESIGNER(S): MARK
GALLAGHER, LAURA SAVARD
CLIENT: ROCKPORT
PUBLISHERS
TOOLS: ILLUSTRATOR, QUARK,
MAC

0431, 0590
ART DIRECTOR(S): MARK
GALLAGHER
DESIGNER(S): MARK
GALLAGHER, LAURA SAVARD
CLIENT: BLACKCOFFEE
TOOLS: ILLUSTRATOR,
PHOTOSHOP, MAC
MATERIALS: COATED WHITE
COVER (CARD), PLASTIC ENVE-
LOPE WITH HANG TAB

0712
ART DIRECTOR(S): MARK
GALLAGHER, LAURA SAVARD
DESIGNER(S): MARK
GALLAGHER, LAURA SAVARD
CLIENT: BLACKCOFFEE
TOOLS: ILLUSTRATOR, MAC
MATERIALS: BURLAP SACK,
SILVER GROMMETS, TWINE

0724
ART DIRECTOR(S): MARK
GALLAGHER, LAURA SAVARD
DESIGNER(S): MARK
GALLAGHER, LAURA SAVARD
CLIENT: CONVERSE
TOOLS: ILLUSTRATOR
MATERIALS: EMBOSSED AND
1-COLOR SILKSCREEN METAL

0725
ART DIRECTOR(S): MARK
GALLAGHER, LAURA SAVARD
DESIGNER(S): MARK
GALLAGHER, LAURA SAVARD
CLIENT: CONVERSE
TOOLS: ILLUSTRATOR, MAC
MATERIALS: WOOD, VENEER

BLOK DESIGN

0320
ART DIRECTOR(S): VANESSA
ECKSTEIN
DESIGNER(S): VANESSA
ECKSTEIN
CLIENT: EYE CANDY TV.COM
TOOLS: ILLUSTRATOR
MATERIALS: STRATHMORE,
PLASTIC

0925
ART DIRECTOR(S): VANESSA
ECKSTEIN
DESIGNER(S): VANESSA
ECKSTEIN, FRANCES CHEN
CLIENT: RGD/ONTARIO
TOOLS: ILLUSTRATOR

0709
ART DIRECTOR(S): VANESSA
ECKSTEIN
DESIGNER(S): VANESSA
ECKSTEIN, FRANCES CHEN
CLIENT: EL ZANJON
TOOLS: ILLUSTRATOR
MATERIALS: STRATHMORE
ULTIMATE

0807
ART DIRECTOR(S): VANESSA
ECKSTEIN
DESIGNER(S): VANESSA
ECKSTEIN, MARIANA
CONTEGNI
CLIENT: NIKE
TOOLS: ILLUSTRATOR
MATERIALS: STRATHMORE,
CURIOUS COLORS

0846
ART DIRECTOR(S): VANESSA
ECKSTEIN
DESIGNER(S): VANESSA
ECKSTEIN, FRANCES CHEN,
STEPHANIE YOUNG
CLIENT: BLOK DESIGN
TOOLS: ILLUSTRATOR

0847, 0898
ART DIRECTOR(S): VANESSA
ECKSTEIN
DESIGNER(S): VANESSA
ECKSTEIN, FRANCES CHEN,
STEPHANIE YOUNG
CLIENT: THE PRODUCTION
KITCHEN
TOOLS: ILLUSTRATOR
MATERIALS: BECKETT
EXPRESSION

BNIM ARCHITECTS

0232
ART DIRECTOR(S): ERIN
GEHLE, ZACK SHUBKAGEL
DESIGNER(S): ANGIELA
MEYER
CLIENT: BNIM ARCHITECTS
TOOLS: INDESIGN, MAC
MATERIALS: CRANE'S 179LB
COVER WHITE

0236
ART DIRECTOR(S): SHAWN
GEHLE
DESIGNER(S): ZACK
SHUBKAGEL, ERIN GEHLE
CLIENT: BNIM ARCHITECTS
TOOLS: INDESIGN, NEEDLE
MATERIALS: ART BOARD,
THREAD, PUNCH

0920
DESIGNER(S): ZACK
SHUBKAGEL, ERIN GEHLE
CLIENT: BNIM ARCHITECTS
TOOLS: ILLUSTRATOR,
INDESIGN, NEEDLE
MATERIALS: CANVAS,
THREAD, GROMMETS

0599
DESIGNER(S): ERIN GEHLE,
ZACK SHUBKAGEL
CLIENT: BNIM ARCHITECTS
TOOLS: INDESIGN,
PHOTOSHOP, MAC
MATERIALS: VELLUM,
WIRE-O, GROMMETS

BRAD TERRES DESIGN

0620
ART DIRECTOR(S): BRAD
TERRES
DESIGNER(S): BRAD TERRES
CLIENT: TAYLOR ROBERTS
TOOLS: QUARK, MAC G4
MATERIALS: GMUND BIER
PAPIER LUSTRO DULL

BRUKETA & ZINIC

0025, 0006, 0146, 0241, 0745,
0747
ART DIRECTOR(S): DAVOR
BRUKETA, NIKOLA ZINIC
DESIGNER(S): DAVOR
BRUKETA, NIKOLA ZINIC
CLIENT: PRODRAVKA DD
TOOLS: PHOTOSHOP,
FREEHAND, MAC
MATERIALS: AGRIPINA

0084
ART DIRECTOR(S): DAVOR
BRUKETA, NIKOLA ZINIC
DESIGNER(S): DAVOR
BRUKETA, NIKOLA ZINIC
CLIENT: BRUKETA & ZINIC
TOOLS: PHOTOSHOP,
FREEHAND, MAC
MATERIALS: AGRIPINA

0581, 0690, 0740
ART DIRECTOR(S): DAVOR
BRUKETA, NIKOLA ZINIC
DESIGNER(S): DAVOR
BRUKETA, NIKOLA ZINIC
CLIENT: PRODRAVKA DD
TOOLS: PHOTOSHOP,
FREEHAND, MAC
MATERIALS: AGRIPINA,
SCENTED COLOR

BUREAU GRAS

0182
ART DIRECTOR(S): RUUD
WINDER
DESIGNER(S): RUUD WINDER
CLIENT: METIS_NL
TOOLS: ILLUSTRATOR
MATERIALS: FEORIGONI

0544
ART DIRECTOR(S): RUUD
WINDER
DESIGNER(S): RUUD WINDER
CLIENT: BK CORPORATE
TOOLS: ILLUSTRATOR

BWA DESIGN

0210, 0401
ART DIRECTOR(S): BWA
DESIGN
DESIGNER(S): BWA DESIGN
CLIENT: RED CROSS
TOOLS: PHOTOSHOP, QUARK

0212
ART DIRECTOR(S): BWA
DESIGN
DESIGNER(S): BWA DESIGN
CLIENT: RED ROOSTER
TOOLS: ILLUSTRATOR, QUARK
MATERIALS: REVIVE SILK

0347
ART DIRECTOR(S): BWA
DESIGN
DESIGNER(S): BWA DESIGN
CLIENT: GRAN BUTLER
TOOLS: QUARK

0415, 0421, 0944
ART DIRECTOR(S): BWA
DESIGN
DESIGNER(S): BWA DESIGN
CLIENT: THE BIG ISSUE
FOUNDATION
TOOLS: QUARK, PHOTOSHOP
MATERIALS: CYCLUS OFFSET

0423
ART DIRECTOR(S): BWA
DESIGN
DESIGNER(S): BWA DESIGN
CLIENT: STIRLING ACKROYD
TOOLS: ILLUSTRATOR, QUARK
MATERIALS: SILK LAMINATED

0533
ART DIRECTOR(S): BWA
DESIGN
DESIGNER(S): BWA DESIGN
CLIENT: MARKS+SPENCER
TOOLS: ILLUSTRATOR, QUARK
MATERIALS: SILK

BÜRO SCHELS FÜR GESTATUNG

0728
ART DIRECTOR(S): CHRISTINA
SCHELS
DESIGNER(S): CHRISTINA
SCHELS
CLIENT: TOP-CITY-KUTSTEIN
GMBH
TOOLS: QUARK, MAC
MATERIALS: KEAYKOLOUR/
ARJOWIGGINS 300GSM

CAHAN & ASSOCIATES

0492
ART DIRECTOR(S): BILL
CAHAN
DESIGNER(S): TODD SIMMONS
CLIENT: LINEAR TECHNOLOGY
CORP.
TOOLS: ILLUSTRATOR, QUARK
MATERIALS: KROMEKOTE,
UTOPIA 2 DULL

0501
ART DIRECTOR(S): BILL
CAHAN
DESIGNER(S): CRAIG BAILEY
CLIENT: NETOBJECTS
TOOLS: ILLUSTRATOR, QUARK
MATERIALS: KROMEKOTE,
CONCORD MATTE

0506
ART DIRECTOR(S): BILL
CAHAN
DESIGNER(S): BOB DINETZ
CLIENT: GARTNER
TOOLS: ILLUSTRATOR,
PHOTOSHOP, QUARK
MATERIALS: ACCENT OPAQUE

0516
ART DIRECTOR(S): BILL
CAHAN, KEVIN ROBERSON
DESIGNER(S): KEVIN
ROBERSON
CLIENT: COLLATERAL
THERAPEUTICS
TOOLS: ILLUSTRATOR,
PHOTOSHOP, QUARK
MATERIALS: MEAD
SIGNATURE, CHAMPION
CARNIVAL

0517
ART DIRECTOR(S): BILL
CAHAN, KEVIN ROBERSON,
BOB DINETZ
DESIGNER(S): BOB DINETZ,
MARK GIGLIO, KEVIN
ROBERSON
CLIENT: STORA ENSO/
CONSOLIDATED PAPERS
TOOLS: QUARK, ILLUSTRATOR
MATERIALS: REFLECTIONS
SILK

0947
ART DIRECTOR(S): BILL
CAHAN, BOB DINETZ
DESIGNER(S): BOB DINETZ
CLIENT: BRE PROPERTIES
TOOLS: ILLUSTRATOR,
PHOTOSHOP, QUARK
MATERIALS: UTOPIA 2 MATTE
80LB

CAPSULE

0276, 0339, 0489
ART DIRECTOR(S): BRIAN
ADDUCCI
DESIGNER(S): DAN
BAGGENSTOSS, GREG BROSE
CLIENT: CAPSULE
TOOLS: ILLUSTRATOR,
PHOTOSHOP, QUARK, MAC
MATERIALS: STAINLESS
STEEL, FRENCH BUTCHER,
CURIOUS METALICS, FOUND
OBJECTS

0143, 0492, 0824
ART DIRECTOR(S): BRIAN
ADDUCCI
DESIGNER(S): BRIAN ADDUCCI
CLIENT: COMPASS
MARKETING
TOOLS: ILLUSTRATOR,
PHOTOSHOP, QUARK, MAC
MATERIALS: FIBERMARK
TOUCHE, GALVANIZED STEEL

CARTER WONG TOMLIN

0703
ART DIRECTOR(S): PHIL
CARTER
DESIGNER(S): NEIL HEDGER
CLIENT: HOWIES
TOOLS: RUBBER STAMP
MATERIALS: RECYCLED
KRAFT PAPER

CASERTA DESIGN COMPANY

0214
ART DIRECTOR(S): FRED
CASERTA
DESIGNER(S): FRED CASERTA
CLIENT: CASTERA DESIGN
COMPANY
TOOLS: ILLUSTRATOR,
PHOTOSHOP, QUARK, MAC G4
MATERIALS: 100LB
PRODUCTOLITH

CDT DESIGN

0119, 0135, 0649
ART DIRECTOR(S): CHRISTIAN
ALTMANN
DESIGNER(S): ALISTAIR HALL
CLIENT: THE ROYAL COLLEGE
OF ART
TOOLS: QUARK
MATERIALS: STOCK: IMAGINE,
CHROMOLUX

CHEN DESIGN ASSOCIATES

0085, 0923
ART DIRECTOR(S): JOSHUA
C. CHEN
DESIGNER(S): MAX SPECTOR
CLIENT: BARRY AND MAYA
SPECTOR
TOOLS: ILLUSTRATOR, QUARK,
MAC
MATERIALS: BLOTTER PAPER,
JAPANESE PAPER

0300
ART DIRECTOR(S): JOSHUA
C. CHEN
DESIGNER(S): MAX SPECTOR,
JENNIFER TOLO
CLIENT: ADAMO LONDON
TOOLS: ILLUSTRATOR, QUARK,
MAC
MATERIALS: CRANE

0881, 0946
ART DIRECTOR(S): JOSHUA
C. CHEN
DESIGNER(S): MAX SPECTOR,
JENNIFER TOLO
CLIENT: AIGA
TOOLS: QUARK, ILLUSTRATOR,
PHOTOSHOP, MAC
MATERIALS: FOX RIVER
CORONADO, BRIGHT
WHITE VELLUM, GILBERT
CLEARFOLD WHITE LIGHT

0807
ART DIRECTOR(S): JOSHUA
C. CHEN
DESIGNER(S): MAX SPECTOR,
JOSH CHEN
CLIENT: SEQUOIA HOSPITAL
TOOLS: ILLUSTRATOR, QUARK,
MAC
MATERIALS: MOHAWK
SUPERFINE

CHENG DESIGN

0634
DESIGNER(S): JENNIFER
CHENG
CLIENT: SEATTLE ARTS &
LECTURES
TOOLS: PHOTOSHOP, QUARK,
MAC
MATERIALS: DOMTAR
TITANIUM

CHIMERA DESIGN

0382
ART DIRECTOR(S): JOHN
MARGART
DESIGNER(S): KEELIE
TEASDALE
CLIENT: MOMAC
HAIRDRESSING
TOOLS: ILLUSTRATOR,
PHOTOSHOP
MATERIALS: K.W. DOGGETT,
CONQUEROR CONCEPT

0414
ART DIRECTOR(S): JOHN
MARGART
DESIGNER(S): NAOMI MACE
CLIENT: TENNIS VICTORIA
TOOLS: PHOTOSHOP, QUARK
MATERIALS: RALEIGH PAPER,
BOTANY DUPLEX, GRANGE,
RECYCLED TENNIS BALL
TUBES

0949
ART DIRECTOR(S): JOHN MARGART
DESIGNER(S): KEELIE TEASDALE
CLIENT: FALLS CREEK FILM FESTIVAL
TOOLS: 3DS MAX, ILLUSTRATOR, PHOTOSHOP
MATERIALS: K.W.P. DOGGETT, HANNO ART SILK

CHRONICLE BOOKS

0011
ART DIRECTOR(S): HENRY QUIROGA
DESIGNER(S): TOM LEE AND ROB REGER OF COSMIC DEBRIS
CLIENT: CHRONICLE BOOKS
TOOLS: ILLUSTRATOR, MAC
MATERIALS: 350GSM MATTE CIS CARDSTOCK WITH MATTE LAMINATION (CASE), PET-G LENTICULAR WITH WOODFREE (TEXT), 125GSM WHITE ARLIN OVER 10PT CIS ARTBOARD WITH MATTE VARNISH (SPINE), 120GSM WHITE WOODFREE (END SHEETS)

0203
ART DIRECTOR(S): SHAWN HAZEN
DESIGNER(S): SHAWN HAZEN
CLIENT: CHRONICLE BOOKS
TOOLS: QUARK
MATERIALS: 157GSM MATTE ART

0215
ART DIRECTOR(S): AMY ENNIS
DESIGNER(S): NOEL TORENTINO OF COSMIC DEBRIS
CLIENT: CHRONICLE BOOKS
TOOLS: ILLUSTRATOR, MAC
MATERIALS: 1-PIECE CASE COVER'D WITH CONCEALED WIRE-O, 128GSM COATED ART PAPER (COVER), 130GSM WHITE TCF WOODFREE (TEXT), 320GSM COATED WITH TWO-SIDED ARTBOARD WITH MYLAR (TABS)

0216, 0422
ART DIRECTOR(S): AZI RAD
DESIGNER(S): HENRIK DRESCHER
CLIENT: CHRONICLE BOOKS
TOOLS: QUARK
MATERIALS: 157GSM MATTE ART

0610, 0657
ART DIRECTOR(S): ALETHEA MORRISON
DESIGNER(S): VINNY D'ANGELO, ALETHEA MORRISON
CLIENT: CHRONICLE BOOKS
TOOLS: PHOTOSHOP, QUARK
MATERIALS: 157GSM MATTE ART

CINCODEMAYO DESIGN

0252
ART DIRECTOR(S): MAURICIO ALANIS
DESIGNER(S): MAURICIO ALANIS
CLIENT: CINCODEMAYO
TOOLS: FREEHAND, MAC
MATERIALS: FIRENZE OPALINA

CIRCLE K STUDIO

0340
ART DIRECTOR(S): JULIE KEENAN
DESIGNER(S): JULIE KEENAN
CLIENT: CIRCLE K STUDIO
TOOLS: ILLUSTRATOR, MAC
MATERIALS: RIVES BFK

0677
ART DIRECTOR(S): JULIE KEENAN
DESIGNER(S): JULIE KEENAN
CLIENT: CIRCLE K STUDIO
TOOLS: ILLUSTRATOR, MAC
MATERIALS: CRESCENT RAG

CIRCULO SOCIAL

0584
ART DIRECTOR(S): MAURICIO ALANIS
DESIGNER(S): SONIA SALINAS
CLIENT: AIXA & EDUARDO
TOOLS: FREEHAND

COLLEGE DESIGN

0464
ART DIRECTOR(S): TONY KNIGHT
DESIGNER(S): MARK LEVERTON
CLIENT: TENON GROUP PLC
TOOLS: PHOTOSHOP, QUARK
MATERIALS: POLYPROPYLENE TAFFETA IVORY

0732
ART DIRECTOR(S): GUY LANE
DESIGNER(S): MARCUS BENNETT
CLIENT: DELANCEY ESTATES PLC
TOOLS: PHOTOSHOP, QUARK
MATERIALS: STARDREAM, CANSON SATIN TRANSPARENT

CRANHAM ADVERTISING

ART DIRECTOR(S): MARC CRADDOCK
DESIGNER(S): EMMA ROBINSON
CLIENT: ZEON LIMITED
TOOLS: PHOTOSHOP, QUARK, MAC
MATERIALS: SILK ART, PLASTIC

CRUSH DESIGN

0003
ART DIRECTOR(S): CARL RUSH
DESIGNER(S): CARL RUSH
CLIENT: FULL ON FILMS
MATERIALS: GLOSS CORE 130GSM

0038, 0798
ART DIRECTOR(S): CARL RUSH
DESIGNER(S): SIMON SLATER
CLIENT: CRUSH
TOOLS: HANDS
MATERIALS: FOUND WOOD, NAILS, HARDBOARD, RECYCLED BAG, RECYCLED TISSUE PAPER, POSTCARDS PRINTED ON FLORA ANTIQUE

0158
ART DIRECTOR(S): CARL RUSH
DESIGNER(S): CARL RUSH
CLIENT: PALM PICTURES
MATERIALS: BOARD, STICKER

0360, 0786
ART DIRECTOR(S): CARL RUSH
DESIGNER(S): TIM DIACON
CLIENT: SIMULTANE
TOOLS: ILLUSTRATOR, PHOTOSHOP, QUARK
MATERIALS: STORA FINE 115GSM, PATTERNED CUTTING BOARD COVER, RUBBER BAND

0703
ART DIRECTOR(S): CARL RUSH
DESIGNER(S): CARL RUSH
CLIENT: PALM PICTURES
TOOLS: ILLUSTRATOR
MATERIALS: CD PACK, POLYSHIELD STATIC SHIELDING BAG, BURIED METAL TYPE, STICKER

0890
ART DIRECTOR(S): CARL RUSH
DESIGNER(S): CARL RUSH
CLIENT: URBAN THEORY
TOOLS: ILLUSTRATOR, QUARK
MATERIALS: FOLD-OUT DIGIPACK

0924
ART DIRECTOR(S): CARL RUSH
DESIGNER(S): CARL RUSH
CLIENT: CRUSH
MATERIALS: T-SHIRTS, WEB

CUCKOOLAND

0105
ART DIRECTOR(S): ADE WOOD
DESIGNER(S): ADE WOOD
CLIENT: SONNE II
TOOLS: FREEHAND

0833, 0858, 0863
ART DIRECTOR(S): ADE WOOD
DESIGNER(S): DAN LOWE
CLIENT: LIMEHAUS
TOOLS: PHOTOSHOP, FREEHAND, MAC
MATERIALS: JERSEY

0852
ART DIRECTOR(S): ADE WOOD
DESIGNER(S): ADE WOOD
CLIENT: LIMEHAUS
TOOLS: PHOTOSHOP, FREEHAND, MAC
MATERIALS: DENIM, LEATHER

0853, 0856
ART DIRECTOR(S): ADE WOOD
DESIGNER(S): ADE WOOD
CLIENT: LIMEHAUS
TOOLS: PHOTOSHOP, FREEHAND, MAC
MATERIALS: JERSEY

0860
ART DIRECTOR(S): ADE WOOD
DESIGNER(S): ADE WOOD
CLIENT: FULL CIRCLE
TOOLS: PHOTOSHOP, FREEHAND, MAC
MATERIALS: JERSEY, CANVAS

0909
ART DIRECTOR(S): ADE WOOD
DESIGNER(S): ADE WOOD
CLIENT: LIMEHAUS
TOOLS: PHOTOSHOP, FREEHAND, MAC
MATERIALS: CANVAS

DAVID CARTER DESIGN

0559
ART DIRECTOR(S): DONNA ALDRIDGE
DESIGNER(S): DONNA ALDRIDGE
CLIENT: DAVID CARTER DESIGN
TOOLS: ILLUSTRATOR, QUARK

0682
ART DIRECTOR(S): DONNA ALDRIDGE
DESIGNER(S): DONNA ALDRIDGE
CLIENT: LAJITAS: THE ULTIMATE HIDEOUT
TOOLS: ILLUSTRATOR
MATERIALS: FIBERMARK SUEDE TEXT

0733
ART DIRECTOR(S): DONNA ALDRIDGE
DESIGNER(S): DONNA ALDRIDGE
CLIENT: LAJITAS: THE ULTIMATE HIDEOUT
TOOLS: ILLUSTRATOR
MATERIALS: SUEDETEX PAPER, LEATHER

DAWN HOSKINSON

0580, 0581
ART DIRECTOR(S): DAWN HOSKINSON
DESIGNER(S): SEAN CULLEN, SIMON HIGBY
CLIENT: DAWN HOSKINSON
TOOLS: QUARK
MATERIALS: TIN CAN, PAPER

DESIGN 5

0280
ART DIRECTOR(S): RON NIKKEL
DESIGNER(S): DESIGN 5
CLIENT: TIGE BOATS
TOOLS: ILLUSTRATOR, PHOTOSHOP, MAC G4

0302
ART DIRECTOR(S): RON NIKKEL
DESIGNER(S): CHRIS DUBURG
CLIENT: UNITED WAY
TOOLS: ILLUSTRATOR, MAC G4
MATERIALS: M REAL

0307
ART DIRECTOR(S): RON NIKKEL
DESIGNER(S): RON NIKKEL
CLIENT: FRESNO REGIONAL FOUNDATION
TOOLS: ILLUSTRATOR, MAC G4

DESIGN DEPOT CREATIVE BUREAU

0079
ART DIRECTOR(S): PETER BANKOV, KATARINA KOJOUKHOVA
DESIGNER(S): PETER BANKOV
CLIENT: NORILSKY NICKEL
TOOLS: MAC
MATERIALS: KRAFT PAPER, WOODEN STICK

0927, 0928, 0929, 0930, 0931, 0932, 0933, 0934, 0935
ART DIRECTOR(S): PETER BANKOV, KATARINA KOJOUKHOVA
DESIGNER(S): KATARINA KOJOUKHOVA, MIKHAIL LOSKOV
CLIENT: DESIGN DEPOT
TOOLS: MAC
MATERIALS: GALLERY ART

DESIGN HOCH DREI GMBH & CO. KG

0311
ART DIRECTOR(S): SONJA MARTENS
CLIENT: DESIGN HOCH DREI GMBH & CO. KG
MATERIALS: SEWN PAPER

0942
ART DIRECTOR(S): TOBIAS KOLLMANN
CLIENT: DAIMLER CHRYSLER AG
MATERIALS: SILKSCREEN PRINTING ON GLASS

DEW GIBBONS

ART DIRECTOR(S): SHAUN DEW
DESIGNER(S): CHRISTIAN EVES
CLIENT: MAQUIS
MATERIALS: EPISODE 4 (COVER), MUNKEN PURE (TEXT)

D-FUSE

0092, 0945, 0995
ART DIRECTOR(S): MIKE FAULKNER
DESIGNER(S): MIKE FAULKNER
CLIENT: D-FUSE
TOOLS: PHOTOSHOP, FREEHAND

DINNICK & HOWELLS

0056, 0707
ART DIRECTOR(S): JONATHAN HOWELLS
DESIGNER(S): JONATHAN HOWELLS
CLIENT: DAVID DREBIN
TOOLS: PHOTOSHOP, QUARK

0191
ART DIRECTOR(S): JONATHAN HOWELLS, PAUL GARBETT
DESIGNER(S): JONATHAN HOWELLS
CLIENT: IRON DESIGN
TOOLS: ILLUSTRATOR, QUARK
MATERIALS: MOHAWK VELLUM

DOSSIERCREATIVE INC.
0186
ART DIRECTOR(S): DON CHISHOLM
DESIGNER(S): PATRICK SMITH
CLIENT: VINCOR INTERNATIONAL
TOOLS: ILLUSTRATOR
MATERIALS: FASSON

0199
ART DIRECTOR(S): DON CHISHOLM
CLIENT: STEVEN BOLIGER

DURSO DESIGN
0585
ART DIRECTOR(S): ROUANE DURSO
DESIGNER(S): ROUANE DURSO

DYNAMO A&D
0909
ART DIRECTOR(S): NINA WISHNOK
DESIGNER(S): NINA WISHNOK
TOOLS: PHOTOSHOP, QUARK, MAC, RUBBER STAMP
MATERIALS: OLD POSTCARDS, VELLUM, OLD BOOKS, CLOTH, CHAMPION BENEFIT PAPER

EGBG
0027
ART DIRECTOR(S): MARTIJN ENGELBREGT
DESIGNER(S): MARTIJN ENGELBREGT
CLIENT: 7X11
TOOLS: QUARK
MATERIALS: HVO

0135
ART DIRECTOR(S): MARTIJN ENGELBREGT
DESIGNER(S): MARTIJN ENGELBREGT
CLIENT: BOTH ENDS
TOOLS: ILLUSTRATOR, QUARK
MATERIALS: 70GSM

0758
ART DIRECTOR(S): MARTIJN ENGELBREGT
DESIGNER(S): MARTIJN ENGELBREGT
CLIENT: HOOGSTRAATMAKERS
TOOLS: ILLUSTRATOR
MATERIALS: GARBAGE BAG, STICK UP LOGO

0900
ART DIRECTOR(S): MARTIJN ENGELBREGT
DESIGNER(S): MARTIJN ENGELBREGT
CLIENT: 7X11
TOOLS: ILLUSTRATOR, MICROSOFT EXCEL
MATERIALS: HTS 160GSM\

EGGERS & DIAPER
0072
ART DIRECTOR(S): MARK DIAPER
DESIGNER(S): MARK DIAPER
CLIENT: ARTANGEL
TOOLS: QUARK

0748
ART DIRECTOR(S): MARK DIAPER
DESIGNER(S): MARK DIAPER
CLIENT: PHAIDON
TOOLS: QUARK
MATERIALS: PROMICA PRISTINE STEEL

ELFEN
0818
CLIENT: ELFEN
TOOLS: ILLUSTRATOR
MATERIALS: PULPBOARD, 2,000 MICRONS

ELMWOOD
0784
ART DIRECTOR(S): RICHARD SCHOLEY
DESIGNER(S): KEVIN BLACKBURN
CLIENT: BBC
MATERIALS: CARPET

0789
ART DIRECTOR(S): JON STUBLEY
DESIGNER(S): JON STUBLEY, BEN GREENGRASS
CLIENT: MICROBAN
TOOLS: PHOTOSHOP, QUARK, MAC
MATERIALS: SILK ART 400GSM, THERMOCHROMIC INK

0793
ART DIRECTOR(S): RICHARD SCHOLEY
DESIGNER(S): GRAHAM STURZAKER, PAUL SUDRON
CLIENT: REBECCA HOPKINSON AND MICHAEL KITCHING
MATERIALS: ROBERT HORNE STARDREAM SILVER, ACETATE

0797
ART DIRECTOR(S): RICHARD SCHOLEY
DESIGNER(S): RICHARD SCHOLEY, STEVE SHAW, MIKE OWEN
CLIENT: ELMWOOD
MATERIALS: BETTER PAPER COMPANY FLOCKAGE

0803
DESIGNER(S): PAUL SUNDRON, GRAHAM STURZAKER
CLIENT: HOT TIN ROOF PR

0149
ART DIRECTOR(S): ALAN AINSLEY
DESIGNER(S): ALAN AINSLEY, STEVE SHAW, JAYNE WORKHAM
CLIENT: SCHEUFELEN PREMIUM PAPERS
TOOLS: PHOTOSHOP, ILLUSTRATOR, MAC
MATERIALS: LENTICULAR LENS, 464 MICRON, 75LPI

EMERY VINCENT DESIGN
0070
ART DIRECTOR(S): EMERY VINCENT DESIGN
DESIGNER(S): EMERY VINCENT DESIGN
CLIENT: MULTIPLEX
TOOLS: QUARK, MAC

0209
ART DIRECTOR(S): EMERY VINCENT DESIGN
DESIGNER(S): EMERY VINCENT DESIGN
CLIENT: MULTIPLEX
TOOLS: QUARK, MAC
MATERIALS: SILVER INTERSCREWS

0211
ART DIRECTOR(S): EMERY VINCENT DESIGN
DESIGNER(S): EMERY VINCENT DESIGN
CLIENT: MULTIPLEX
TOOLS: QUARK, MAC
MATERIALS: ALUMINUM CASE, LEATHER

0412
ART DIRECTOR(S): EMERY VINCENT DESIGN
DESIGNER(S): EMERY VINCENT DESIGN
CLIENT: CSR
TOOLS: QUARK, MAC

EMPIRE DESIGN STUDIO
0148
ART DIRECTOR(S): GARY TOOTH
CLIENT: SAKS FIFTH AVENUE
TOOLS: QUARK
MATERIALS: FRENCH PAPER CO.

0213
ART DIRECTOR(S): GARY TOOTH
CLIENT: FIT
TOOLS: ILLUSTRATOR
MATERIALS: STRATHMORE

0411, 0568
ART DIRECTOR(S): GARY TOOTH
CLIENT: CHRONICLE BOOKS
TOOLS: QUARK
MATERIALS: SUEDE CLOTH

0951
ART DIRECTOR(S): GARY TOOTH
DESIGNER(S): CARRIE HAMILTON
CLIENT: ABRAMS
TOOLS: ILLUSTRATOR, QUARK

EMSPACE DESIGN GROUP
0213
ART DIRECTOR(S): GAIL SNODGRASS
DESIGNER(S): GAIL SNODGRASS
CLIENT: FIRST NATIONAL MERCHANT SOLUTIONS
TOOLS: QUARK
MATERIALS: SYNERGY RED, CLASSIC COTTON CREAM

ERBE DESIGN
0170
ART DIRECTOR(S): MAUREEN ERBE
DESIGNER(S): MAUREEN ERBE, RITA SOWINS
CLIENT: MOTOROLA LIFE SCIENCES
TOOLS: QUARK, MAC G3
MATERIALS: APPLETON CURIOUS PAPERS

0472
ART DIRECTOR(S): MAUREEN ERBE
DESIGNER(S): MAUREEN ERBE, RITA SOWINS
CLIENT: MOTOROLA LIFE SCIENCES
TOOLS: QUARK, MAC G3
MATERIALS: APPLETON CURIOUS PAPERS

ERIC HESEN GRAPHIC DESIGN
0312
ART DIRECTOR(S): ERIC HESEN
DESIGNER(S): ERIC HESEN, JORIS HULSBOSCH
CLIENT: SINTLUCAS SCHOOL OF COMMUNICATION AND DESIGN
TOOLS: ILLUSTRATOR, PHOTOSHOP, QUARK, MAC
MATERIALS: TOLLIUS, IVERCOTE

FAITH
0201
ART DIRECTOR(S): PAUL SYCH
DESIGNER(S): PAUL SYCH
CLIENT: FAITH
TOOLS: ILLUSTRATOR, MAC
MATERIALS: CURIOUS PAPERS

0778
ART DIRECTOR(S): PAUL SYCH
DESIGNER(S): PAUL SYCH
CLIENT: FAITH
TOOLS: ILLUSTRATOR, MAC
MATERIALS: ZANDERS (CARDS), MIRRI STOCK

0893
ART DIRECTOR(S): PAUL SYCH
DESIGNER(S): PAUL SYCH
CLIENT: FAITH GALLERY
TOOLS: PHOTOSHOP
MATERIALS: CANVAS

FAUXPAS
0266
ART DIRECTOR(S): MARTIN STILLHART
DESIGNER(S): MARTIN STILLHART
CLIENT: SEVERAL ART GALLERIES
TOOLS: ILLUSTRATOR, MAC
MATERIALS: BEER COASTER

FELDER GRAFIKDESIGN
0030, 0042, 0091
ART DIRECTOR(S): PETER FELDER
CLIENT: FELDER GRAFIKDESIGN
TOOLS: QUARK, MAC
MATERIALS: WASTEPAPER, SPOILAGE

0132
ART DIRECTOR(S): PETER FELDER
DESIGNER(S): PETER FELDER, SIGI RAMOSER
CLIENT: NEXT PAGE
TOOLS: QUARK, MAC
MATERIALS: IKONO SILK, 170GSM, FOIL, PLASTIC FILM

0277
ART DIRECTOR(S): PETER FELDER
CLIENT: FELDER GRAFIKDESIGN
TOOLS: QUARK, MAC
MATERIALS: ISKANDAR 115GSM AND 250GSM

0324
ART DIRECTOR(S): RENÉ DALPRA, PETER FELDER
DESIGNER(S): PETER FELDER
CLIENT: OTTO MÜLLER VERLAG/VERLAG DIE QUELLE
TOOLS: QUARK, MAC
MATERIALS: GMUND COLOR 300GSM, WERKDRUCK 100GSM

0377, 0386, 0685
ART DIRECTOR(S): PETER FELDER, JOHANNES RAUCH
DESIGNER(S): PETER FELDER
CLIENT: FELDER GRAFIKDESIGN
TOOLS: QUARK, MAC
MATERIALS: GMUND COLOR 49, 200GSM AND 135GSM

0638, 0640, 0652
ART DIRECTOR(S): PETER FELDER, JOHANNES RAUCH
DESIGNER(S): PETER FELDER
CLIENT: FELDER GRAFIKDESIGN
TOOLS: QUARK, MAC
MATERIALS: GMUND COLOR 49, 200GSM AND 135GSM

0693
ART DIRECTOR(S): PETER FELDER
DESIGNER(S): PETER FELDER
CLIENT: GEBHARD MATHIS
TOOLS: QUARK, MAC
MATERIALS: TRANSPARENT PAPER 115GSM

0905, 0979
ART DIRECTOR(S): PETER FELDER
DESIGNER(S): RENÉ DALPRA, PETER FELDER
CLIENT: TELEFONSEELSORGE VORARLBERG
TOOLS: QUARK, MAC
MATERIALS: ELK MUNKEN OFFSET 150GSM

FELTON COMMUNICATION
0483
ART DIRECTOR(S): BRION FURNELL
CLIENT: TERRENCE HIGGINS TRUST
TOOLS: PHOTOSHOP, QUARK
MATERIALS: CHALLENGER OFFSET, VINYL

FIBRE
0183
ART DIRECTOR(S): DAVID RAINBIRD
DESIGNER(S): GARY BUTCHER
CLIENT: MOTOROLA
MATERIALS: DIE-CUT CARTON BOARD

0381
ART DIRECTOR(S): NATHAN LANDER
DESIGNER(S): GARY BUTCHER
CLIENT: NIKE
MATERIALS: POLYPROPYLENE, HIGH-DENSITY FOAM, TRIPLE SILK, CD

0389, 0795
ART DIRECTOR(S): NATHAN LANDER
DESIGNER(S): NATHAN LANDER, TOMMY MILLER
CLIENT: NIKE
MATERIALS: FILM TIN, FRISBEE, HIGH-DENSITY FOAM, TRIPLE SILK, CD

0395
ART DIRECTOR(S): NATHAN LANDER
DESIGNER(S): NATHAN LANDER
CLIENT: NIKE

0639, 0790
ART DIRECTOR(S): NATHAN LANDER
DESIGNER(S): NATHAN LANDER
CLIENT: NIKE
MATERIALS: NCR PAPER, FILE MASTER, X-RAY FILM, LUSTRELUX, TREASURY TAGS

0651
ART DIRECTOR(S): NATHAN LANDER
DESIGNER(S): TOMMY MILLER
CLIENT: NIKE
MATERIALS: BOX BOARD, TISSUE PAPER, TRIPLE SILK

0842
ART DIRECTOR(S): DAVID RAINBIRD
DESIGNER(S): TOMMY MILLER
CLIENT: MOTOROLA
MATERIALS: SCREWPAK, PLASTIC TUBE, CHROMOLUX SILVER AND RED

FIELD DESIGN CONSULTANTS
0033
ART DIRECTOR(S): SARAH PATERSON
DESIGNER(S): SARAH PATERSON
CLIENT: GROUNDWORK EAST LONDON
TOOLS: PHOTOSHOP, QUARK
MATERIALS: EVOLUTION SATIN, GREYBACK 100

0654
ART DIRECTOR(S): NIGEL ROBERTS
DESIGNER(S): NIGEL ROBERTS
CLIENT: FIELD
TOOLS: PHOTOSHOP, QUARK

FLIGHT CREATIVE
0001, 0182, 0275
ART DIRECTOR(S): LISA NANKERVIS
DESIGNER(S): LISA NANKERVIS
CLIENT: FLIGHT CREATIVE
TOOLS: ILLUSTRATOR
MATERIALS: SUMO 200GSM, 250GSM, 300GSM; CYBERSTAR 90GSM AND 110GSM

FORM
0112
ART DIRECTOR(S): PAULA BENSON
DESIGNER(S): PAULA BENSON
CLIENT: INDOOR GARDEN DESIGN
TOOLS: PHOTOSHOP, FREEHAND, MAC
MATERIALS: CONSORT ROYAL SILK

0117
ART DIRECTOR(S): PAULA BENSON, PAUL WEST
DESIGNER(S): PAULA BENSON, PAUL WEST, NICK HARD
CLIENT: FORM
TOOLS: FREEHAND, MAC
MATERIALS: COURIER SUPERWOVE, HARD-ROLLED STAINLESS STEEL

0407
ART DIRECTOR(S): PAUL WEST, PAULA BENSON
DESIGNER(S): PAUL WEST
CLIENT: THE MOVING PICTURE COMPANY
TOOLS: FREEHAND, MAC
MATERIALS: CHROMOLUX

0413
ART DIRECTOR(S): PAUL WEST
DESIGNER(S): NICK HARD
CLIENT: DAZED AND CONFUSED/TOP SHOP
TOOLS: PHOTOSHOP, FREEHAND, MAC

0490
ART DIRECTOR(S): PAUL WEST
DESIGNER(S): PAUL WEST
CLIENT: VISION ON
TOOLS: QUARK, MAC
MATERIALS: BALACRON BOOKBINDING FABRIC, PAPER BELLY BAND

0494
ART DIRECTOR(S): PAULA BENSON
DESIGNER(S): PAULA BENSON, CRAIG ROBINSON, CLAIRE WARNER
CLIENT: DESIGN COUNCIL
TOOLS: FREEHAND
MATERIALS: MUNKEN LYNX

0608
ART DIRECTOR(S): PAULA BENSON, PAUL WEST
DESIGNER(S): NICK HARD
CLIENT: UNIFORM
TOOLS: FREEHAND, MAC
MATERIALS: SELF-ADHESIVE STICKER SHEET, COURIER BLANK SHEET

0696
ART DIRECTOR(S): PAULA BENSON, PAUL WEST
DESIGNER(S): PAULA BENSON, PAUL WEST, NICK HARD
CLIENT: FORM
TOOLS: FREEHAND, MAC
MATERIALS: BEER MAT, TRACING PAPER ENVELOPES

0703
ART DIRECTOR(S): PAULA BENSON, PAUL WEST
DESIGNER(S): NICK HARD
CLIENT: UNIFORM
TOOLS: FREEHAND, MAC
MATERIALS: GREEN GLOW-EDGE POLYCARBONATE

0743
ART DIRECTOR(S): PAULA BENSON, PAUL WEST
DESIGNER(S): CLAIRE WARNER
CLIENT: UNIFORM
TOOLS: FREEHAND, MAC
MATERIALS: PLASTIC AIR BAG

0749
ART DIRECTOR(S): PAUL WEST
DESIGNER(S): PAUL WEST
CLIENT: VISION ON
TOOLS: QUARK, MAC
MATERIALS: DEBOSSED LOGO ON VELVET

0820
ART DIRECTOR(S): PAUL WEST
DESIGNER(S): PAUL WEST, CHRIS HILTON
CLIENT: MUSIC WEEK/CMP
TOOLS: PHOTOSHOP, FREEHAND, QUARK, MAC
MATERIALS: SCREEN-PRINTED FROMACONE COVER

FORM FÜNF
0520
ART DIRECTOR(S): ECKHARD JUNG, DANIEL BASTIAN
DESIGNER(S): DAVID LINDEMANN, RASMUS GIESEL, ISABELL ZIRBECK
CLIENT: GOHRSHUHLE BANKPOST
TOOLS: FREEHAND
MATERIALS: STÜRKEN DRUCK

0980
ART DIRECTOR(S): DANIEL BASTIAN, ULYSSES VOE
CLIENT: QUARK
TOOLS: GOHRS MÜHLE

FORTYFOUR DESIGN
0049, 0066, 0200, 0214, 0779
ART DIRECTOR(S): LISA MINICHIELLO, DEAN GORISSEN
DESIGNER(S): LISA MINICHIELLO
CLIENT: CFC FOR FCS
TOOLS: ILLUSTRATOR, PHOTOSHOP, QUARK, MAC
MATERIALS: SPICERS IMPRESS SATIN, CURIOUS

FOTOGRAFIE & GESTALTUNG CHRISTIAN NIELINGER
0919
ART DIRECTOR(S): CHRISTIAN NIELINGER
DESIGNER(S): CHRISTIAN NIELINGER
CLIENT: CHRISTIAN NIELINGER
TOOLS: PHOTOSHOP, QUARK, MAC
MATERIALS: ARJOWIGGINS CURIOUS METALLICS OXYGEN WHITE 240GSM

FOUR-LETTER WORD
0229
ART DIRECTOR(S): PETER WARD
DESIGNER(S): NEIL QUIDDINGTON
CLIENT: YI-BAN RESTAURANT
TOOLS: ILLUSTRATOR, PHOTOSHOP, QUARK, MAC

FOXINABOX
0436, 0726
TOOLS: ILLUSTRATOR, PHOTOSHOP, QUARK

FROST DESIGN, LONDON
0956, 0965, 0971, 0974
ART DIRECTOR(S): VINCE FROST
DESIGNER(S): VINCE FROST, MATT WILLEY
CLIENT: SIMON FINCH RARE BOOKS
MATERIALS: WOODFREE GLOSS PAPER 250GSM, OPP MATT LAMINATE PAGES (COVER), GALERIE FINE PAPER 90GSM (TEXT)

GEE & CHUNG DESIGN
0230
ART DIRECTOR(S): EARL GEE
DESIGNER(S): EARL GEE, FANI CHUNG
CLIENT: COMVENTURES
TOOLS: PHOTOSHOP, QUARK, MAC G4
MATERIALS: POTLATCH MCCOY SILK COVER 80LB AND 120LB

0259, 0243
ART DIRECTOR(S): EARL GEE
DESIGNER(S): EARL GEE, FANI CHUNG
CLIENT: XINET INC.
TOOLS: ILLUSTRATOR, PHOTOSHOP, QUARK
MATERIALS: POTLATCH MCCOY UNCOATED 80LB COVER, MOHAWK SUPERFINE SMOOTH 65LB COVER

GILLESPIE DESIGN
0392
ART DIRECTOR(S): MAUREEN GILLESPIE
DESIGNER(S): LIZ SCHENKEL
CLIENT: WENDY AND AMY
TOOLS: ILLUSTRATOR, QUARK, MAC
MATERIALS: NEENAH ENVIRONMENT

0491
ART DIRECTOR(S): MAUREEN GILLESPIE
DESIGNER(S): LIZ SCHENKEL
CLIENT: GILLESPIE DESIGN
TOOLS: ILLUSTRATOR, QUARK, MAC

0497, 0862
ART DIRECTOR(S): MAUREEN GILLESPIE
DESIGNER(S): LIZ SCHENKEL
CLIENT: GILLESPIE DESIGN
TOOLS: PHOTOSHOP, QUARK, MAC
MATERIALS: CHAMPION BENEFIT

0701
ART DIRECTOR(S): MAUREEN GILLESPIE
DESIGNER(S): MAUREEN GILLESPIE
CLIENT: AMERICA ONLINE
TOOLS: ILLUSTRATOR, QUARK, MAC
MATERIALS: HONEYCOMB ORANGE, VINYL

GIORGIO DAVANZO DESIGN
0016
DESIGNER(S): GIORGIO DAVANZO
CLIENT: LOOPWORX
TOOLS: PHOTOSHOP, QUARK, MAC
MATERIALS: CRANE'S CREST 100% COTTON

0121
DESIGNER(S): GIORGIO DAVANZO
CLIENT: SENOK TEA
TOOLS: PHOTOSHOP, QUARK, MAC
MATERIALS: STRATHMORE CLASSIC

0130
DESIGNER(S): GIORGIO DAVANZO
CLIENT: GIORGIO DAVANZO
TOOLS: PHOTOSHOP, QUARK, MAC
MATERIALS: METAL

0634
DESIGNER(S): GIORGIO DAVANZO
CLIENT: GIORGIO DAVANZO
TOOLS: PHOTOSHOP, QUARK, MAC
MATERIALS: STRATHMORE SCRIPT

0902
DESIGNER(S): GIORGIO DAVANZO
CLIENT: GIORGIO DAVANZO
TOOLS: ILLUSTRATOR, MAC
MATERIALS: LEXAN

GOUTHIER DESIGN INC.

ART DIRECTOR(S): JONATHAN
GOUTHIER
DESIGNER(S): JONATHAN
GOUTHIER
CLIENT: AIGA MIAMI, XPEDX,
MOHAWK
TOOLS: ILLUSTRATOR,
PHOTOSHOP, QUARK, MAC
MATERIALS: MOHAWK
SUPERFINE

ART DIRECTOR(S): JONATHAN
GOUTHIER
DESIGNER(S): JONATHAN
GOUTHIER, KILEY DEL VALLE
CLIENT: GOUTHIER DESIGN
INC.
TOOLS: ILLUSTRATOR,
PHOTOSHOP, QUARK, MAC
MATERIALS: FRENCH CON-
STRUCTION, STORA ENZO
CENTRALE

ART DIRECTOR(S): JONATHAN
GOUTHIER
DESIGNER(S): JONATHAN
GOUTHIER, KILEY DEL VALLE
CLIENT: ADVERTISING
FEDERATION OF GREATER
FORT LAUDERDALE
TOOLS: ILLUSTRATOR, QUARK,
MAC
MATERIALS: EPSON HIGH
QUALITY INKJET, FRENCH
CONSTRUCTION

ART DIRECTOR(S): JONATHAN
GOUTHIER
DESIGNER(S): JONATHAN
GOUTHIER, KILEY DEL VALLE
CLIENT: SAMANTHA SCOTT
PHOTOGRAPHY
TOOLS: ILLUSTRATOR,
PHOTOSHOP, QUARK, MAC
MATERIALS: FRENCH PAPER
SMART WHITE

ART DIRECTOR(S): JONATHAN
GOUTHIER
DESIGNER(S): JONATHAN
GOUTHIER
CLIENT: GOUTHIER DESIGN
INC.
TOOLS: ILLUSTRATOR,
PHOTOSHOP, QUARK, MAC
MATERIALS: PORCELIN,
GLASS

ART DIRECTOR(S): JONATHAN
GOUTHIER
DESIGNER(S): JONATHAN
GOUTHIER, KILEY DEL VALLE
CLIENT: GOUTHIER DESIGN
INC.
TOOLS: ILLUSTRATOR, QUARK,
MAC
MATERIALS: MOHAWK
SUPERFINE

GRAPEFRUIT DESIGN

ART DIRECTOR(S): MARIUS
URSACHE
DESIGNER(S): MARIUS
URSACHE
CLIENT: GRAPEFRUIT DESIGN
TOOLS: ILLUSTRATOR,
PHOTOSHOP
MATERIALS: GARDA MATT

GRAPHISCHE FORMGEBUNG

ART DIRECTOR(S): HERBERT
ROHSIEPE
DESIGNER(S): HERBERT
ROHSIEPE
CLIENT: GRAPHISCHE
FORMGEBUNG
TOOLS: PHOTOSHOP,
FREEHAND, MAC
MATERIALS: ARJOWIGGINS
IMPRESSIONS RIVES ARTIST
SENSATION NATUR 250GSM

ART DIRECTOR(S): HERBERT
ROHSIEPE
DESIGNER(S): HERBERT
ROHSIEPE
CLIENT: SORADIOSO/CYRUS
KARGAR
TOOLS: PHOTOSHOP,
FREEHAND, MAC

ART DIRECTOR(S): HERBERT
ROHSIEPE
DESIGNER(S): HERBERT
ROHSIEPE
CLIENT: W.P. DATA, RAINER
SCHUMACHER & JÜRGEN
SEIFERT
TOOLS: PHOTOSHOP,
FREEHAND, MAC
MATERIALS:
SCHNEIDERSOEHNE,
LUXOSAMTOFFSET

GREENEWEIG DESIGN

ART DIRECTOR(S): TIM
GREENEWEIG
DESIGNER(S): TIM
GREENEWEIG
CLIENT: GREENEWEIG
DESIGN
TOOLS: PHOTOSHOP, QUARK,
MAC
MATERIALS: 120LB REPLY

GREENFIELD/BELSER

ART DIRECTOR(S): BURKEY
BELSER
DESIGNER(S): BURKEY
BELSER, LIZA CORBETT
CLIENT: WEIL GOTSHAL AND
MANGES
TOOLS: PHOTOSHOP, QUARK
MATERIALS: MCCOY 120LB
SILK COVER, MCCOY 100LB
SILK TEXT

GRETEMAN GROUP

ART DIRECTOR(S): SONIA
GRETEMAN
DESIGNER(S): JAMES
STRANGE, CRAIG TOMSON
CLIENT: GRETEMAN GROUP
TOOLS: FREEHAND

GROOTHIUS + MALSY

ART DIRECTOR(S): RAINER
GOOTHIUS, GILMAR WENDT
DESIGNER(S): RAINER
GOOTHIUS, GILMAR WENDT
CLIENT: VERLAG KLAUS
WAGENBACH
TOOLS: QUARK, MAC

HAND MADE GROUP

ART DIRECTOR(S):
ALESSANDRO ESTERI
DESIGNER(S): GIOMA
MAIARECCI
CLIENT: LANIFICIO F. LLI
CERROTII
TOOLS: QUARK
MATERIALS: PLIKE
CORDEMONS

ART DIRECTOR(S):
ALESSANDRO ESTERI
DESIGNER(S): GIOMA
MAIARECCI
CLIENT: LANIFICIO F. LLI
CERROTII
TOOLS: PHOTOSHOP, QUARK
MATERIALS: ZANDERS

ART DIRECTOR(S):
ALESSANDRO ESTERI
DESIGNER(S): GIOMA
MAIARECCI
CLIENT: LANIFICIO F. LLI
CERROTII
TOOLS: QUARK
MATERIALS: GSK ZANDERS

ART DIRECTOR(S):
ALESSANDRO ESTERI
DESIGNER(S): GIOMA
MAIARECCI
CLIENT: LANIFICIO F. LLI
CERROTII
TOOLS: QUARK

HANS DESIGN

ART DIRECTOR(S): BILL HANS,
T. MARTI
DESIGNER(S): KRISTIN MIASO
CLIENT: SALON GIA
TOOLS: ILLUSTRATOR, QUARK
MATERIALS: FRASER

HARRIMANSTEEL

ART DIRECTOR(S):
HARRIMANSTEEL
DESIGNER(S):
HARRIMANSTEEL
CLIENT: NIKE
MATERIALS: RETREEVE

ART DIRECTOR(S):
HARRIMANSTEEL
DESIGNER(S):
HARRIMANSTEEL
CLIENT: HARRIMANSTEEL
MATERIALS: KRAFT PAPER

ART DIRECTOR(S):
HARRIMANSTEEL
DESIGNER(S):
HARRIMANSTEEL
CLIENT: NIKE
MATERIALS: TESLIN 305
MICRONS (WATERPROOF
PAPER), PVC POUCH, MUD,
CLEAR GEL (TO LOOK LIKE
WATER)

ART DIRECTOR(S):
HARRIMANSTEEL
DESIGNER(S):
HARRIMANSTEEL
CLIENT: NIKE
MATERIALS:
POLYPROPYLENE

ART DIRECTOR(S):
HARRIMANSTEEL
DESIGNER(S):
HARRIMANSTEEL
CLIENT: HARRIMANSTEEL
TOOLS: FEDRIGONI
SPLENDOURLUX

HEATHER BIANCHI DESIGN

DESIGNER(S): HEATHER
BIANCHI
CLIENT: HEATHER BIANCHI
TOOLS: PHOTOSHOP, QUARK
MATERIALS: RIBBON, CLEAR
PHOTOCORNERS

HEESE DESIGN

ART DIRECTOR(S): KLAUS
HESSE
DESIGNER(S): KLAUS HESSE
CLIENT: ACADEMY OF ART
AND DESIGN OFFENBACH/
MAIN

HENRI LUCAS/MARTIN ENGELBREGT

ART DIRECTOR(S): HENRI
LUCAS, MARTIN ENGELBREGT
DESIGNER(S): HENRI LUCAS,
MARTIN ENGELBREGT
CLIENT: CENTRAAL MUSEUM
TOOLS: QUARK
MATERIALS: CHROMOLUX
PRINTING, CMYK PLUS 2 PMS

HGV FELTON

ART DIRECTOR(S): PIERRE
VERMEIR
DESIGNER(S): PIERRE
VERMEIR
CLIENT: HGV
MATERIALS: 300GSM
MODIGLIANNI NOTTURNO
(COVER), CHROMOLUX GLASS
ART (TEXT)

ART DIRECTOR(S): PIERRE
VERMEIR
DESIGNER(S): PIERRE
VERMEIR
CLIENT: ROYAL MAIL
MATERIALS:
THERMOCHROMIC INK,
EMBOSSING, HOLOGRAPHIC
FOIL, INTAGIO

ART DIRECTOR(S): PIERRE
VERMEIR
DESIGNER(S): FARRAH
GUDGEON
CLIENT: HGV
MATERIALS: 1,000 MICRONS
GREYBOARD

ART DIRECTOR(S): PIERRE
VERMEIR
DESIGNER(S): TOMMY TAYLOR
CLIENT: VANILLA

ART DIRECTOR(S): PIERRE
VERMEIR
DESIGNER(S): DAMAIN
NOWELL
CLIENT: BAILHACHE LABESSE
MATERIALS: CONSORT ROYAL

ART DIRECTOR(S): PIERRE
VERMEIR
DESIGNER(S): PIERRE
VERMEIR
CLIENT: BAILHACHE LABESSE

ART DIRECTOR(S): PIERRE
VERMEIR
DESIGNER(S): DAMAIN
NOWELL
CLIENT: HGV FELTON
MATERIALS: LIVE EDGE

ART DIRECTOR(S): PIERRE
VERMEIR
DESIGNER(S): TOMMY
TAYLOR, DAMIAN NOWELL
CLIENT: SCOPE
TOOLS: PHOTOSHOP
MATERIALS: 70GSM
PRINTSPEED

HORNALL ANDERSON DESIGN WORKS

ART DIRECTOR(S): JACK
ANICKER
DESIGNER(S): KATHY SAITO,
HENRY YIU, SONJA MAX
CLIENT: INSITE WORKS
ARCHITECTS

ART DIRECTOR(S): JACK
ANDERSON
DESIGNER(S): JACK
ANDERSON, HENRY YIU
CLIENT: BOEING

0450
ART DIRECTOR(S): JACK ANDERSON, KATHA DALTON
DESIGNER(S): KATHA DALTON, GRETCHEN COOK, SONJA MAX, HENRY YIU
CLIENT: LINCOLN SQUARE

0471
ART DIRECTOR(S): JACK ANDERSON, JOHN ANICKER
DESIGNER(S): JACK ANDERSON, JOHN ANICKER, ANDREW SMITH, ANDREW WICKLUND, MARY HERMES, JOHN ANDERLE
CLIENT: ONEWORLD CHALLENGE
TOOLS: FREEHAND
MATERIALS: 80LB GOLDESSE TEXTURE (COVER), 70LB RECYCLED WHITE MOHAWK SUPERFINE TEXT SMOOTH (TEXT)

0716
ART DIRECTOR(S): JACK ANDERSON
DESIGNER(S): JULIE LOCK, JANA WILSON ESSER
CLIENT: OKAMOTO CORPORATION

IAMALWAYSHUNGRY

0085
ART DIRECTOR(S): NESSIM HIGSON
DESIGNER(S): NESSIM HIGSON
TOOLS: ILLUSTRATOR, QUARK

0103
ART DIRECTOR(S): NESSIM HIGSON
DESIGNER(S): NESSIM HIGSON
CLIENT: IAMALWAYSHUNGRY
TOOLS: PHOTOSHOP, TRANSFERS
MATERIALS: HANDMADE PAPER

0384
ART DIRECTOR(S): NESSIM HIGSON
DESIGNER(S): NESSIM HIGSON
CLIENT: IAMALWAYSHUNGRY
TOOLS: PHOTOSHOP, PHOTO-COPY MACHINE
MATERIALS: ACETATE, PLEXIGLAS

0953
ART DIRECTOR(S): NESSIM HIGSON
DESIGNER(S): NESSIM HIGSON
CLIENT: CITY STYLES
TOOLS: ILLUSTRATOR, TRANSFERS
MATERIALS: T-SHIRT

0980
ART DIRECTOR(S): NESSIM HIGSON
DESIGNER(S): NESSIM HIGSON
CLIENT: VULCAN CORP.
TOOLS: PHOTOSHOP
MATERIALS: STORA ENSO 100LB

1000
ART DIRECTOR(S): NESSIM HIGSON
DESIGNER(S): NESSIM HIGSON
CLIENT: SHIFT
TOOLS: PHOTOSHOP

IE DESIGN

0181
ART DIRECTOR(S): MARCIE CARSON
CLIENT: IE DESIGN

0322
ART DIRECTOR(S): MARCIE CARSON
CLIENT: EL CAMINO RESOURCES INTERNATIONAL
TOOLS: PHOTOSHOP, QUARK

0325
ART DIRECTOR(S): MARCIE CARSON
DESIGNER(S): RICHARD HAYNIE
CLIENT: CREATIVE DESIGN GROUP
TOOLS: ILLUSTRATOR

0394
ART DIRECTOR(S): MARCIE CARSON
CLIENT: GOOD GRACIOUS! CATERING

0564
ART DIRECTOR(S): MARCIE CARSON
CLIENT: JENNIFER NICHOLSON
TOOLS: ILLUSTRATOR

0625
ART DIRECTOR(S): CAROL KUMMER
CLIENT: USCF COMPREHENSIVE CANCER CENTERS

0840
ART DIRECTOR(S): MARCIE CARSON
CLIENT: USC SCHOOL OF ENGINEERING

IMAGINATION (GIC)

0400
ART DIRECTOR(S): CHRIS HAMMOND
DESIGNER(S): STEPHANE HARRISON
CLIENT: E.A. SHAW

0532
ART DIRECTOR(S): CHRIS HAMMOND
DESIGNER(S): STEPHANE HARRISON
CLIENT: E.A. SHAW
MATERIALS: CONSORT

IRBE DESIGN

0211
ART DIRECTOR(S): IGORS IRBE
CLIENT: IRBE DESIGN
TOOLS: PHOTOSHOP, QUARK, MAC
MATERIALS: GILBERT CLEAR VELLUM

IRIDIUM, A DESIGN AGENCY

0083
ART DIRECTOR(S): JEAN-LUC DENAT, GAËTAN ALBERT
DESIGNER(S): GAËTAN ALBERT
CLIENT: OTTAWA KNIGHTS
TOOLS: ILLUSTRATOR, QUARK, MAC
MATERIALS: DOMTAR FUSION (FIVE COLORS)

0123
ART DIRECTOR(S): JEAN-LUC DENAT, MARIO L'ÉCUYER
DESIGNER(S): MARIO L'ÉCUYER
CLIENT: MITEL CORPORATION
TOOLS: PHOTOSHOP, QUARK, MAC
MATERIALS: GRAPHIKA LINEAL, POTLATCH MCCOY GLOSS, FRENCH PAPERS CONSTRUCTION

0223
ART DIRECTOR(S): MARIO L'ÉCUYER
DESIGNER(S): MARIO L'ÉCUYER
CLIENT: NYGEM CORPORATION
TOOLS: ILLUSTRATOR, PHOTOSHOP, QUARK, MAC
MATERIALS: MOHAWK SUPERFINE

0225
ART DIRECTOR(S): JEAN-LUC DENAT, ETIENNE BESSETTE
DESIGNER(S): ETIENNE BESSETTE
CLIENT: SERVICE PLUS
TOOLS: ILLUSTRATOR, QUARK, MAC
MATERIALS: CONDAT SUPREME GLOSS

0226
ART DIRECTOR(S): MARIO L'ÉCUYER, JEAN-LUC DENAT
DESIGNER(S): MARIO L'ÉCUYER
CLIENT: SCHOELER+HEATON ARCHITECTS
TOOLS: PHOTOSHOP, ILLUSTRATOR, QUARK, MAC
MATERIALS: FOX RIVER STARWHITE

0292
ART DIRECTOR(S): MARIO L'ÉCUYER, JEAN-LUC DENAT
DESIGNER(S): MARIO L'ÉCUYER
CLIENT: TETHER CAM SYSTEMS
TOOLS: ILLUSTRATOR, PHOTOSHOP, QUARK, MAC
MATERIALS: MOHAWK SUPERFINE, FRENCH PAPERS CONSTRUCTION

0311
ART DIRECTOR(S): MARIO L'ÉCUYER, JEAN-LUC DENAT
DESIGNER(S): MARIO L'ÉCUYER, MARY KOCH
CLIENT: MYTEL CORPORATION
TOOLS: ILLUSTRATOR, PHOTOSHOP, QUARK, MAC
MATERIALS: BECKETT CAMBRIC, SAPPI HORIZON SILK

0315
ART DIRECTOR(S): MARIO L'ÉCUYER, JEAN-LUC DENAT
DESIGNER(S): MARIO L'ÉCUYER, DAVID DAIGLE
CLIENT: SSHRC
TOOLS: ILLUSTRATOR, PHOTOSHOP, QUARK, MAC
MATERIALS: SAPPI LUSTRO DULL, DOMTAR CORNWALL PINWEAVE CIS, ROLAND OPAQUE

0323
ART DIRECTOR(S): MARIO L'ÉCUYER
DESIGNER(S): MARIO L'ÉCUYER
CLIENT: NEXWARE CORPORATION
TOOLS: QUARK, ILLUSTRATOR, PHOTOSHOP, MAC
MATERIALS: BECKETT EXPRESSION, GILBERT GILCLEAR

0355, 0628
ART DIRECTOR(S): MARIO L'ÉCUYER, JEAN-LUC DENAT
DESIGNER(S): MARIO L'ÉCUYER
CLIENT: COCREATIONS LIGHTING DESIGN
TOOLS: PHOTOSHOP, QUARK, MAC G3
MATERIALS: GEORGIA-PACIFIC PROTERRA, FOX RIVER CONFETTI

0483, 0576
ART DIRECTOR(S): JEAN-LUC DENAT, MARIO L'ÉCUYER, DAVID DAIGLE
DESIGNER(S): MARIO L'ÉCUYER
CLIENT: GENOME CANADA
TOOLS: ILLUSTRATOR, PHOTOSHOP, QUARK, MAC
MATERIALS: DOMTAR PLAINFIELD HOMESPUN, DOMTAR SKYTONE, GLAMA NATURAL

0507
ART DIRECTOR(S): MARIO L'ÉCUYER
DESIGNER(S): MARIO L'ÉCUYER
CLIENT: CANADA DANCE FESTIVAL
TOOLS: PHOTOSHOP, QUARK, MAC
MATERIALS: CURTIS TUSCAN ANTIQUE, FOX RIVER CONFETTI AND CIRCA

0510
ART DIRECTOR(S): JEAN-LUC DENAT, MARIO L'ÉCUYER
DESIGNER(S): MARIO L'ÉCUYER
CLIENT: COCREATIONS LIGHTING DESIGN
TOOLS: ILLUSTRATOR, PHOTOSHOP, QUARK, MAC
MATERIALS: GEORGIA-PACIFIC PROTERRA, FOX RIVER CIRCA, CHICAGO SCREWS

0557
ART DIRECTOR(S): MARIO L'ÉCUYER, JEAN-LUC DENAT
DESIGNER(S): MARIO L'ÉCUYER
CLIENT: CANADIAN INSTITUTES OF HEALTH RESEARCH
TOOLS: ILLUSTRATOR, PHOTOSHOP, QUARK, MAC
MATERIALS: MOHAWK SUPERFINE EGGSHELL, GLAMA NATURAL, RIVETS

0628
ART DIRECTOR(S): JEAN-LUC DENAT
DESIGNER(S): MARIO L'ÉCUYER
CLIENT: CANADIAN INDEPENDENT FILM AND VIDEO FUND
TOOLS: PHOTOSHOP, QUARK, MAC
MATERIALS: STRATHMORE ELEMENTS, SHREDDED PAPER, FILM CAN

0997
ART DIRECTOR(S): ETIENNE BESSETTE
DESIGNER(S): ETIENNE BESSETTE
CLIENT: EPSILON
TOOLS: ILLUSTRATOR, PHOTOSHOP, QUARK
MATERIALS: SAPPI HORIZON SILK

JADE DESIGN

0424
ART DIRECTOR(S): JAMES ALEXANDER
DESIGNER(S): JAMES ALEXANDER
CLIENT: TYPOGRAPHIC CIRCLE
TOOLS: ILLUSTRATOR, QUARK, MAC
MATERIALS: COLORPLAN

0705
ART DIRECTOR(S): JAMES ALEXANDER
DESIGNER(S): JAMES ALEXANDER
CLIENT: TYPOGRAPHIC CIRCLE
TOOLS: ILLUSTRATOR, QUARK, MAC
MATERIALS: PLASMA POLYCOAT (CLEAR)

0812
ART DIRECTOR(S): JAMES ALEXANDER
CLIENT: RGL
TOOLS: ILLUSTRATOR, QUARK, MAC
MATERIALS: ENCAPSULATED OILS

JASON & JASON

0059
ART DIRECTOR(S): JONATHAN JASON
DESIGNER(S): DALIA INBAR
CLIENT: ESRA
TOOLS: PHOTOSHOP, FREEHAND
MATERIALS: 300GSM CHROME PAPER

0166
ART DIRECTOR(S): JONATHAN JASON
DESIGNER(S): DALIA INBAR
CLIENT: TELRAD
TOOLS: PHOTOSHOP, FREEHAND
MATERIALS: 300GSM CHROME PAPER

0228, 0445
ART DIRECTOR(S): JONATHAN JASON
DESIGNER(S): TAMAR LOURIE
CLIENT: NUR MACROPRINTERS
TOOLS: PHOTOSHOP, FREEHAND
MATERIALS: 300GSM CHROME

0255, 0441
ART DIRECTOR(S): JONATHAN JASON
DESIGNER(S): DALIA INBAR
CLIENT: KERYX BIOPHARMACEUTICALS INC.
TOOLS: PHOTOSHOP, FREEHAND
MATERIALS: 300GSM CHROME (COVER), 250GSM CHROME (INTERIOR)

0274
ART DIRECTOR(S): JONATHAN JASON
DESIGNER(S): TAMAR LOURIE
CLIENT: RR DONNELLY
TOOLS: PHOTOSHOP, FREEHAND
MATERIALS: 300GSM CHROME

0299
ART DIRECTOR(S): JONATHAN JASON
DESIGNER(S): DALIA INBAR
CLIENT: GILON
TOOLS: PHOTOSHOP, FREEHAND
MATERIALS: 300GSM CHROME PAPER

0305
ART DIRECTOR(S): DOMENIC LIPPA
DESIGNER(S): DALIA INBAR
CLIENT: ACTIMIZE
TOOLS: PHOTOSHOP, FREEHAND
MATERIALS: 300GSM CHROME PAPER

0363
ART DIRECTOR(S): JONATHAN JASON
DESIGNER(S): DALIA INBAR, TAMAR LOURIE
CLIENT: RR DONNELLY
TOOLS: PHOTOSHOP, FREEHAND
MATERIALS: 300GSM CHROME PAPER (COVER), 225GSM CHROMO (INTERIOR)

JOHNSON BANKS

0307
ART DIRECTOR(S): MICHAEL JOHNSON
DESIGNER(S): MICHAEL JOHNSON
CLIENT: CAMPAIGN FOR CLIMATE CHANGE
TOOLS: FREEHAND
MATERIALS: MAP PAPER

0536
ART DIRECTOR(S): MICHAEL JOHNSON
DESIGNER(S): SARAH FULLERTON
CLIENT: JOHNSON BANKS
TOOLS: QUARK
MATERIALS: THIN UNCOATED

0540
ART DIRECTOR(S): MICHAEL JOHNSON
DESIGNER(S): SARAH FULLERTON
CLIENT: DESIGN COUNCIL
TOOLS: QUARK
MATERIALS: NEPTUNE UNIQUE

0552
ART DIRECTOR(S): MICHAEL JOHNSON
DESIGNER(S): SARAH FULLERTON
CLIENT: JOHNSON BANKS
TOOLS: QUARK
MATERIALS: THIN UNCOATED

0730
ART DIRECTOR(S): MICHAEL JOHNSON
DESIGNER(S): JULIA WOOLLAMS, KATE TUDSALL
CLIENT: CONRAN OCTOPUS
TOOLS: QUARK
MATERIALS: CLOTH, MACHINE EMBROIDERY

JONES DESIGN GROUP

0173
ART DIRECTOR(S): VICKY JONES
DESIGNER(S): BETSY PEREZ
CLIENT: COCA-COLA
TOOLS: QUARK
MATERIALS: DOMTAR FELTWEAVE 100LB COVER

0344
ART DIRECTOR(S): VICKY JONES
DESIGNER(S): HOLLEY SILIRIE
CLIENT: DEVIN PROPERTIES
TOOLS: PHOTOSHOP, QUARK
MATERIALS: 100LB COUGAR OPAQUE NATURAL COVER

0619, 0631
ART DIRECTOR(S): VICKY JONES
DESIGNER(S): BRODY BOYER
CLIENT: JONES DESIGN GROUP
TOOLS: ILLUSTRATOR, QUARK
MATERIALS: AIR FRESHENER

0762
ART DIRECTOR(S): VICKY JONES
DESIGNER(S): HOLLEY SILIRIE
CLIENT: COCA-COLA
TOOLS: ILLUSTRATOR, QUARK
MATERIALS: CARDBOARD, MYLAR

0902
ART DIRECTOR(S): VICKY JONES
DESIGNER(S): KATHERINE STAGGS, BRODY BOYER
CLIENT: JONES DESIGN GROUP
TOOLS: ILLUSTRATOR, QUARK
MATERIALS: TATTOOS

JULIA TAM DESIGN

0208
ART DIRECTOR(S): JULIA CHONG TAM
DESIGNER(S): JULIA CHONG TAM
CLIENT: JULIA TAM DESIGN
TOOLS: ILLUSTRATOR, QUARK, MAC

KBDA

0098
ART DIRECTOR(S): KIM BAER
DESIGNER(S): KATE RIVINOUS
CLIENT: THE JEWISH COMMUNITY FOUNDATION
TOOLS: MAC

0110, 0627
ART DIRECTOR(S): KIM BAER
DESIGNER(S): JAMIE DIERSING
CLIENT: KBDA
TOOLS: QUARK, MAC

0531
ART DIRECTOR(S): KIM BAER
DESIGNER(S): BARBARA COOPER
CLIENT: LEE BURKHARDT LIU
TOOLS: MAC

0537, 0736
ART DIRECTOR(S): KIM BAER
DESIGNER(S): MAGGIE VAN OPPEN
CLIENT: ARMORY CENTER FOR THE ARTS
TOOLS: MAC

KEARNEY ROCHOLL

0017, 0024
ART DIRECTOR(S): FRANK ROCHOLL
DESIGNER(S): DIMITRI LAVROW
CLIENT: MÖLLER DESIGN
TOOLS: QUARK, MAC
MATERIALS: ZANDERS GALAXY KERA

0782
ART DIRECTOR(S): FRANK ROCHOLL
CLIENT: KEARNEY ROCHOLL
TOOLS: QUARK
MATERIALS: ZANDERS GALAXY 200GSM, PLEXIGLAS

KESSELS KRAMER

0252, 0453, 0457, 0458, 0670
ART DIRECTOR(S): ERIK KESSELS

0436
ART DIRECTOR(S): ERIK KESSELS, KAREN HEUTER
CLIENT: DO FUTURE

0443
ART DIRECTOR(S): ERIK KESSELS, KRISTA ROZEMA
CLIENT: 55 DSL—CHRISTINA CLERICI, ANDREA ROSSO, JEAN-LUC BATTAGLIA

0446
ART DIRECTOR(S): ERIK KESSELS
CLIENT: 55 DSL—CHRISTINA CLERICI, ANDREA ROSSO, JEAN-LUC BATTAGLIA

0447
ART DIRECTOR(S): ERIK KESSELS, PIM VAN NUENEN

0460, 0800
ART DIRECTOR(S): ERIK KESSELS
CLIENT: DIESEL SPA

0654
ART DIRECTOR(S): ERIK KESSELS, PIM VAN NUENEN
CLIENT: ONVZ

0791
ART DIRECTOR(S): ERIK KESSELS, KRISTA ROZEMA

0992
ART DIRECTOR(S): ERIK KESSELS, KRISTA ROZEMA
CLIENT: HANS BRINKER

KINETIC SINGAPORE

0157, 0331
ART DIRECTOR(S): PANN LIM, LENG SOH, ROY POH
DESIGNER(S): PANN LIM, LENG SOH, ROY POH
CLIENT: KINETIC SINGAPORE
TOOLS: FREEHAND
MATERIALS: WOODFREE PAPER

0242, 0245, 0246
ART DIRECTOR(S): PANN LIM, ROY POH
DESIGNER(S): PANN LIM, ROY POH
CLIENT: SINGLE TREK CYCLE
TOOLS: PHOTOSHOP, FREEHAND
MATERIALS: ART PAPER

0278, 0998
ART DIRECTOR(S): PANN LIM, LENG SOH, ROY POH
DESIGNER(S): PANN LIM, LENG SOH, ROY POH
CLIENT: AMARA HOLDINGS LTD.
TOOLS: PHOTOSHOP, FREEHAND
MATERIALS: ART CARD, ART PAPER

KOEWEIDEN POSTMA

0004
ART DIRECTOR(S): JACQUES KOEWEIDEN, PAUL POSTMA
DESIGNER(S): JACQUES KOEWEIDEN
CLIENT: BOOK INDUSTRY PUBLISHERS

0580
ART DIRECTOR(S): JACQUES KOEWEIDEN, PAUL POSTMA
DESIGNER(S): JACQUES KOEWEIDEN, PAUL POSTMA
CLIENT: PHOTOGRAPHY ASSOCIATION OF THE NETHERLANDS

0030
ART DIRECTOR(S): JACQUES KOEWEIDEN, PAUL POSTMA, ALVIN CHAN
DESIGNER(S): JACQUES KOEWEIDEN, PAUL POSTMA, ALVIN CHAN
CLIENT: MIND THE GAP

0975
ART DIRECTOR(S): JACQUES KOEWEIDEN
DESIGNER(S): JACQUES KOEWEIDEN
CLIENT: MEULENHOFF

0982
ART DIRECTOR(S): JACQUES KOEWEIDEN, PAUL POSTMA, ALVIN CHAN
DESIGNER(S): JACQUES KOEWEIDEN, PAUL POSTMA, ALVIN CHAN
CLIENT: MINISTRY OF EDUCATION, CULTURE & SCIENCE

0961, 0962, 0963, 0964
ART DIRECTOR(S): JACQUES KOEWEIDEN, PAUL POSTMA
DESIGNER(S): JACQUES KOEWEIDEN, PAUL POSTMA
CLIENT: NIKE EUROPE

0999
ART DIRECTOR(S): ALVIN CHAN
DESIGNER(S): ALVIN CHAN
CLIENT: LEINE & ROEBANA

KOLEGRAM DESIGN

0076
ART DIRECTOR(S): JEAN-FRANCOIS PLANTE
DESIGNER(S): JEAN-FRANCOIS PLANTE
CLIENT: ISFI CANADA
TOOLS: ILLUSTRATOR, QUARK

ART DIRECTOR(S): MIKE TEIXEIRA
DESIGNER(S): ANNIE TANGUAY
CLIENT: BAYSHORE SHOPPING CENTRE
TOOLS: ILLUSTRATOR, QUARK, MAC

ART DIRECTOR(S): GOWTRAN BLAIS
DESIGNER(S): GOWTRAN BLAIS
CLIENT: LE GARAGE
TOOLS: ILLUSTRATOR, QUARK, MAC

ART DIRECTOR(S): MIKE TEIXEIRA
DESIGNER(S): GOWTRAN BLAIS
CLIENT: DU PROGRÈS
TOOLS: ILLUSTRATOR, QUARK, MAC

ART DIRECTOR(S): MIKE TEIXEIRA
DESIGNER(S): MIKE TEIXEIRA
CLIENT: KOLEGRAM DESIGN
TOOLS: ILLUSTRATOR, QUARK, MAC

ART DIRECTOR(S): GOWTRAN BLAIS
DESIGNER(S): GOWTRAN BLAIS
CLIENT: CANADIAN COMMISSION FOR UNESCO
TOOLS: ILLUSTRATOR, QUARK
MATERIALS: TEXTURED PAPER

ART DIRECTOR(S): MIKE TEIXEIRA
DESIGNER(S): MIKE TEIXEIRA
CLIENT: UNISOURCE
TOOLS: ILLUSTRATOR, PHOTOSHOP, QUARK

ART DIRECTOR(S): MIKE TEIXEIRA
DESIGNER(S): MIKE TEIXEIRA
CLIENT: KOLEGRAM AND HEADLIGHT IMAGERY
TOOLS: ILLUSTRATOR, PHOTOSHOP, QUARK
MATERIALS: PAPER AND CO CUPS, BUBBLE BAG

ART DIRECTOR(S): MIKE TEIXEIRA
DESIGNER(S): MIKE TEIXEIRA
CLIENT: CENTRE D'ARTISTES AXENÉ07
TOOLS: ILLUSTRATOR, QUARK
MATERIALS: PAPER, STICKER, PLASTIC BAG

ART DIRECTOR(S): JEAN-FRANCOIS PLANTE
DESIGNER(S): JEAN-FRANCOIS PLANTE
CLIENT: PORTRAIT GALLERY OF CANADA
TOOLS: ILLUSTRATOR, QUARK

ART DIRECTOR(S): MIKE TEIXEIRA
DESIGNER(S): ANDRÉ MITCHELL
CLIENT: KOLEGRAM
TOOLS: ILLUSTRATOR, QUARK
MATERIALS: PAPER, PLASTIC BAG

ART DIRECTOR(S): MIKE TEIXEIRA
DESIGNER(S): MIKE TEIXEIRA
CLIENT: ADVERTISING AND DESIGN ASSOCIATION OF OTTAWA
TOOLS: ILLUSTRATOR, PHOTOSHOP, QUARK

ART DIRECTOR(S): MIKE TEIXEIRA
DESIGNER(S): MIKE TEIXEIRA
CLIENT: KOLEGRAM DESIGN
TOOLS: QUARK, MAC

ART DIRECTOR(S): FRANCOIS BOUCHER
DESIGNER(S): FRANCOIS BOUCHER
CLIENT: CANADIAN HERITAGE
TOOLS: PHOTOSHOP, QUARK, MAC

ART DIRECTOR(S): MIKE TEIXEIRA
DESIGNER(S): MIKE TEIXEIRA
CLIENT: CENTRE D'ARTISTES AXENÉ07
TOOLS: PHOTOSHOP, QUARK
MATERIALS: NEWSPAPER AND SEWING IMPLEMENTS

KONTRAPUNKT

ART DIRECTOR(S): EDUARD CEHOVIN
DESIGNER(S): EDUARD CEHOVIN
CLIENT: IVANA WINGHAM
MATERIALS: PAPER

ART DIRECTOR(S): EDUARD CEHOVIN
DESIGNER(S): EDUARD CEHOVIN
CLIENT: KONRAPUNKT
MATERIALS: RUBBER BAND

LAVA

CLIENT: STUDIO STALLINGA

CLIENT: IBM NEDERLAND/ VSLP

CLIENT: AALSMEER FLOWER AUCTION

CLIENT: ART DIRECTORS CLUB OF NEW YORK

CLIENT: VAN HOEKEN/THOES ARCHITECTS
TOOLS: PHOTOSHOP, PHOTOCOPY MACHINE

LAYFIELD

ART DIRECTOR(S): STEPHEN LAYFIELD
DESIGNER(S): STEPHEN LAYFIELD
CLIENT: STEVEN AND JULIE SWIRES
TOOLS: ILLUSTRATOR
MATERIALS: RALEIGH SUPERFINE ULTRA WHITE SMOOTH 352GSM

ART DIRECTOR(S): STEPHEN LAYFIELD
DESIGNER(S): STEPHEN LAYFIELD
CLIENT: THE CATS' HOME
TOOLS: ILLUSTRATOR
MATERIALS: RALEIGH SUPERFINE ULTRA WHITE SMOOTH 352GSM

ART DIRECTOR(S): STEPHEN LAYFIELD
DESIGNER(S): STEPHEN LAYFIELD
CLIENT: THE SHIRT COMPANY
TOOLS: ILLUSTRATOR
MATERIALS: RALEIGH SUPERFINE ULTRA WHITE SMOOTH 352GSM

LCTS

ART DIRECTOR(S): STEPHANE HARRISON
CLIENT: LCTS

LEWIS COMMUNICATIONS

ART DIRECTOR(S): ROBERT FROEDGE
CLIENT: LEWIS COMMUNICATIONS
TOOLS: PHOTOSHOP, QUARK

ART DIRECTOR(S): ROBERT FROEDGE
CLIENT: NASHVILLE SOUNDS BASEBALL
TOOLS: PHOTOSHOP, QUARK

ART DIRECTOR(S): ROBERT FROEDGE
CLIENT: NEXTLINK
TOOLS: PHOTOSHOP, QUARK
MATERIALS: CLASSIC CREST

LIGALUX GMBH

ART DIRECTOR(S): CLAUDIA FISCHER-APPELT
DESIGNER(S): CLAUDIA FISCHER-APPELT, LARS NIEBUHR
CLIENT: LIGALUX GMBH
TOOLS: FREEHAND, MAC
MATERIALS: MUNKEN LUXOMAG

ART DIRECTOR(S): CLAUDIA FISCHER-APPELT
DESIGNER(S): FLORIAN SCHOFFRO
CLIENT: LIGALUX GMBH
TOOLS: FREEHAND
MATERIALS: 100GSM ATTRACTION

ART DIRECTOR(S): CLAUDIA FISCHER-APPELT
DESIGNER(S): FLORIAN SCHOFFRO
CLIENT: LIGALUX GMBH
TOOLS: FREEHAND
MATERIALS: 410GSM INVERCOTE DUO

ART DIRECTOR(S): CLAUDIA FISCHER-APPELT
DESIGNER(S): ISABELLA HAENDLER, LARS NIEBUHR
CLIENT: LIGALUX GMBH

ART DIRECTOR(S): PETRA MATOUSCHEK, MARTINA MASSONG
DESIGNER(S): ISABELLA MAENOLER
CLIENT: FISCHER-APPELT KOMMUNIKATION, LIGALUX
TOOLS: FREEHAND
MATERIALS: 135GSM MUNKEN PRINT

ART DIRECTOR(S): CLAUDIA FISCHER-APPELT
DESIGNER(S): LARS NIEBUHR
CLIENT: FISCHER-APPELT KOMMUNIKATION, LIGALUX
TOOLS: FREEHAND, MAC
MATERIALS: 135GSM PROFI SILK

ART DIRECTOR(S): CLAUDIA FISCHER-APPELT
DESIGNER(S): FLORIAN SCHOFFRO
CLIENT: LIGALUX GMBH
TOOLS: FREEHAND
MATERIALS: 300GSM TAURO

LIPPA PEARCE DESIGN

ART DIRECTOR(S): HARRY PEARCE
DESIGNER(S): DOMENIC LIPPA, JEREMY ROO
CLIENT: BEN KELLY DESIGN

ART DIRECTOR(S): HARRY PEARCE
DESIGNER(S): HARRY PEARCE
CLIENT: "26"

ART DIRECTOR(S): HARRY PEARCE
DESIGNER(S): HARRY PEARCE
CLIENT: LIPPA PEARCE

ART DIRECTOR(S): DOMENIC LIPPA
DESIGNER(S): DOMENIC LIPPA, MARK DIAPER
CLIENT: CULTURAL INDUSTRIES

ART DIRECTOR(S): DOMENIC LIPPA
DESIGNER(S): DOMENIC LIPPA
CLIENT: D+AD

ART DIRECTOR(S): DOMENIC LIPPA
DESIGNER(S): RACHAEL DINNIS
CLIENT: SOUP OPERA

ART DIRECTOR(S): DOMENIC LIPPA
DESIGNER(S): DOMENIC LIPPA, MUKESH PALMER
CLIENT: ARTHUR ANDERSEN

ART DIRECTOR(S): HARRY PEARCE
DESIGNER(S): HARRY PEARCE
CLIENT: LIPPA PEARCE DESIGN

ART DIRECTOR(S): HARRY PEARCE
DESIGNER(S): HARRY PEARCE
CLIENT: KENNETH GRANGE

ART DIRECTOR(S): DOMENIC LIPPA
DESIGNER(S): MARK DIAPER
CLIENT: TERRENCE HIGGINS TRUST

ART DIRECTOR(S): DOMENIC LIPPA
DESIGNER(S): DOMENIC LIPPA
CLIENT: TORZO MCARONIA

ART DIRECTOR(S): DOMENIC LIPPA
DESIGNER(S): DOMENIC LIPPA, MUKESH PALMER
CLIENT: THE TYPOGRAPHIC CIRCLE

LIQUID AGENCY INC.

0075
ART DIRECTOR(S): JOSHUA SWANBECK
DESIGNER(S): JOSHUA SWANBECK
CLIENT: ICA
TOOLS: MAC
MATERIALS: STRATHMORE GRANDEE

0281
ART DIRECTOR(S): JOSHUA SWANBECK
DESIGNER(S): JOSHUA SWANBECK
CLIENT: LIQUID AGENCY INC.
TOOLS: MAC
MATERIALS: CHROME KOTE

0364
ART DIRECTOR(S): JOSHUA SWANBECK
DESIGNER(S): JOSHUA SWANBECK
CLIENT: BUSINESS OBJECTS
TOOLS: MAC
MATERIALS: RUBBER BAND BINDING

LISKA + ASSOCIATES

0108
ART DIRECTOR(S): STEVE LISKA
DESIGNER(S): KIM FRY
CLIENT: LISKA + ASSOCIATES
TOOLS: PHOTOSHOP, QUARK, MAC
MATERIALS: SAPPI STROBE GLOSS PRINTING: 4-COLOR PROCESS

LLOYDS GRAPHIC DESIGN AND COMMUNICATION

0012
ART DIRECTOR(S): ALEXANDER LLOYD
DESIGNER(S): ALEXANDER LLOYD
CLIENT: PRENZEL DISTILLING COMPANY
TOOLS: FREEHAND, MAC
MATERIALS: MATT ARTBOARD 300GSM, GRANDEE BLACK 216GSM

0177
ART DIRECTOR(S): ALEXANDER LLOYD
DESIGNER(S): ALEXANDER LLOYD
CLIENT: CPR DISTRIBUTORS LTD. (COFFEE PREMIUM ROAST)
TOOLS: FREEHAND, MAC
MATERIALS: MATT ARTBOARD 300GSM

0199
ART DIRECTOR(S): ALEXANDER LLOYD
DESIGNER(S): ALEXANDER LLOYD
CLIENT: JASON TRIPE CONTRACTING LTD.
TOOLS: FREEHAND, MAC
MATERIALS: MATT ARTBOARD 300GSM

0417
ART DIRECTOR(S): ALEXANDER LLOYD
DESIGNER(S): ALEXANDER LLOYD
CLIENT: LLOYDS GRAPHIC DESIGN AND COMMUNICATION
TOOLS: FREEHAND, QUARK, MAC
MATERIALS: VIA PURE WHITE ULTRA SMOOTH 216GSM

MACHINE

0827, 0803
ART DIRECTOR(S): MACHINE
DESIGNER(S): MACHINE
CLIENT: CLUB PARADISO
TOOLS: ILLUSTRATOR
MATERIALS: HVO 300GSM

0820, 0831, 0832
ART DIRECTOR(S): MACHINE
DESIGNER(S): MACHINE
CLIENT: RUSHHOUR
TOOLS: ILLUSTRATOR, PHOTOSHOP, MAC
MATERIALS: HVO 300GSM

0834
ART DIRECTOR(S): MACHINE
DESIGNER(S): MACHINE
CLIENT: MACHINE
TOOLS: ILLUSTRATOR, MAC
MATERIALS: SILKSCREEN ON COTTON

MADE THOUGHT

0006, 0081, 0094
ART DIRECTOR(S): BEN PARKER, PAUL AUSTIN
CLIENT: THE MILL

0015, 0924
ART DIRECTOR(S): BEN PARKER, PAUL AUSTIN
CLIENT: VIADUCT

0029
ART DIRECTOR(S): BEN PARKER, PAUL AUSTIN
CLIENT: SUZY HOODLESS

0160
ART DIRECTOR(S): BEN PARKER, PAUL AUSTIN
CLIENT: JUMP

0231
ART DIRECTOR(S): BEN PARKER, PAUL AUSTIN
CLIENT: ESTHER FRANKLIN

0897
ART DIRECTOR(S): BEN PARKER, PAUL AUSTIN
CLIENT: SCULPTURE AT GOODWOOD/PEGGY GUGGENHEIM COLLECTION

MAGMA

0679
ART DIRECTOR(S): LARS HARMSEN
DESIGNER(S): CHRIS STEURER
CLIENT: PT AG
TOOLS: PHOTOSHOP, QUARK, MAC

0773
ART DIRECTOR(S): LARS HARMSEN
CLIENT: MAGMA
TOOLS: FREEHAND, QUARK, MAC
MATERIALS: METAL BOX

MAIOW CREATIVE BRANDING

0148
ART DIRECTOR(S): PAUL RAPACIOLI
DESIGNER(S): PAUL RAPACIOLI, DAVE WORTHINGTON
CLIENT: WOODHOUSE HUGHES
TOOLS: FREEHAND
MATERIALS: 350GSM NEPTUNE UNIQUE

0154
ART DIRECTOR(S): PAUL RAPACIOLI, MAI IKUZANA
DESIGNER(S): PAUL RAPACIOLI
CLIENT: MAIOW CREATIVE BRANDING
TOOLS: QUARK, FREEHAND DESIGN
MATERIALS: 118GSM AND 325GSM MONADNOCK ASTRALITE SMOOTH

0523
ART DIRECTOR(S): MAI IKUZANA
DESIGNER(S): MAI IKUZANA
CLIENT: MAIOW CREATIVE BRANDING
TOOLS: ILLUSTRATOR, QUARK
MATERIALS: TOGSM CRUSADE OFFSET (BIBLE PAPER)

0706
ART DIRECTOR(S): PAUL RAPACIOLI
DESIGNER(S): PAUL RAPACIOLI
CLIENT: MAIOW CREATIVE BRANDING
TOOLS: FREEHAND, QUARK
MATERIALS: TOGSM CRUSADE OFFSET

MARIUS FAHRNER DESIGN

0020
ART DIRECTOR(S): MARIUS FAHRNER
DESIGNER(S): MARIUS FAHRNER
CLIENT: RESET PRINTERY
TOOLS: FREEHAND
MATERIALS: IVERCOTE, IGEPA 300GSM

0142
ART DIRECTOR(S): MARIUS FAHRNER
DESIGNER(S): MARIUS FAHRNER
CLIENT: LIA STAEHLIN JEWELERS
TOOLS: FREEHAND
MATERIALS: ROEMERTURM CURTIS ESPARTO

0169
ART DIRECTOR(S): MARIUS FAHRNER
DESIGNER(S): MARIUS FAHRNER
CLIENT: DERMATOLOGIUUM FOUNDATION
TOOLS: FREEHAND
MATERIALS: IGEPA EXTRA 120-250GSM

0296, 0994
ART DIRECTOR(S): MARIUS FAHRNER
DESIGNER(S): MARIUS FAHRNER
CLIENT: SBC, PROFESSOR STENKRAUS
TOOLS: FREEHAND
MATERIALS: ROEMERTURN PRECIOSO

0327
ART DIRECTOR(S): MARIUS FAHRNER
DESIGNER(S): MARIUS FAHRNER
CLIENT: FRITZEN MOETTER
TOOLS: FREEHAND

0442
ART DIRECTOR(S): MARIUS FAHRNER
DESIGNER(S): MARIUS FAHRNER
CLIENT: DAHLER+COMPANY REAL ESTATE
TOOLS: FREEHAND
MATERIALS: IGEPA AGRIPINA 170-250GSM

0617
ART DIRECTOR(S): MARIUS FAHRNER
DESIGNER(S): MARIUS FAHRNER
CLIENT: RESET PRINTER
TOOLS: FREEHAND
MATERIALS: MUNKEN PURE 240GSM

0848
ART DIRECTOR(S): MARIUS FAHRNER
DESIGNER(S): MARIUS FAHRNER
CLIENT: ASIA AROUND
TOOLS: FREEHAND

METAL

0297
ART DIRECTOR(S): PEAT JARIYA
DESIGNER(S): PEAT JARIYA, GABE SCHREIBER
CLIENT: CAMDEN
TOOLS: ILLUSTRATOR, PAGEMAKER, PHOTOSHOP, MAC G4
MATERIALS: POLYPROPYLENE COVER .8 POINT

0466
ART DIRECTOR(S): PEAT JARIYA
DESIGNER(S): PEAT JARIYA, SHAD LINDO
CLIENT: BIRDVIEW
TOOLS: ILLUSTRATOR, PAGEMAKER, PHOTOSHOP, MAC G4
MATERIALS: POTLATCH MCCOY

0479
ART DIRECTOR(S): PEAT JARIYA
DESIGNER(S): SHAD LINDO
CLIENT: CAMDEN
TOOLS: ILLUSTRATOR, PAGEMAKER, PHOTOSHOP, MAC G4
MATERIALS: CURIOUS

0792
ART DIRECTOR(S): PEAT JARIYA
DESIGNER(S): SHAD LINDO, PEAT JARIYA
CLIENT: GCA
TOOLS: ILLUSTRATOR, PAGEMAKER, PHOTOSHOP
MATERIALS: TRANSLUCENT

0904
ART DIRECTOR(S): PEAT JARIYA
DESIGNER(S): PEAT JARIYA
CLIENT: RELIANCE

MIASO DESIGN

0119
ART DIRECTOR(S): KRISTIN MIASO
DESIGNER(S): KRISTIN MIASO
CLIENT: MIASO DESIGN
TOOLS: ILLUSTRATOR
MATERIALS: FRENCH CONSTRUCTION SLATE BLUE

MINGZHAN HUANG

0569
ART DIRECTOR(S):
DESIGNER(S): MINGZHAN HUANG
CLIENT: VISUAL WORK FOR MASTER'S IN VISUAL COMMUNICATION
TOOLS: ILLUSTRATOR, PHOTOSHOP, MAC, PC
MATERIALS: CONQUEROR PAPER, MISCELLANEOUS MATERIALS

MIRES

0277
ART DIRECTOR(S): JOSÉ SERRANO
DESIGNER(S): MIGUEL PEREZ, GALE SPITZLEY, JOY PRICE
CLIENT: QUALCOMM

0773
ART DIRECTOR(S): JOSÉ SERRANO
DESIGNER(S): GALE SPITZLEY, JOY PRICE
CLIENT: J.F. SHEA COMPANY
MATERIALS: SUNDANCE FELT (COVER), GILBERT RELM (INSIDE)

0203
ART DIRECTOR(S): JOHN BALL
DESIGNER(S): TAVO GALINDO
CLIENT: J.F. LUX ART INSTITUTE
MATERIALS: MCCOY KARMA NATURAL 100% TEXT

0495
ART DIRECTOR(S): JOHN BALL
DESIGNER(S): PAM MEIERDENG
CLIENT: MIRES

0796
ART DIRECTOR(S): SCOTT MIRES
DESIGNER(S): JEN CADEM
CLIENT: WOODS LITHOGRAPHICS
MATERIALS: 600-LINE ULTRA DOT PRINTING WITH SPECIAL QUETONE COLOR INTEGRATION

MIRIELLO GRAFICO INC.
0121, 0191, 0743
ART DIRECTOR(S): RON MIRIELLO
DESIGNER(S): CHRIS KEENEY
CLIENT: FOX RIVER PAPER
TOOLS: ILLUSTRATOR, PHOTOSHOP
MATERIALS: STARWHITE VICKSBURG

0538, 0876, 0889
ART DIRECTOR(S): DENNIS GARCIA
DESIGNER(S): DENNIS GARCIA
CLIENT: MIRIELLO GRAFICO INC.
TOOLS: ILLUSTRATOR, PHOTOSHOP
MATERIALS: STARWHITE

0663
ART DIRECTOR(S): RON MIRIELLO
DESIGNER(S): TRACEY MEINERS
CLIENT: ISIS PHARMACEUTICALS
TOOLS: ILLUSTRATOR
MATERIALS: MCCOY SILK COVER AND BOOK

MIRKO ILIC
0008
ART DIRECTOR(S): MIRKO ILIC
DESIGNER(S): MIRKO ILIC, HEATH HINEGARDNER
CLIENT: VICTOR CALDERONE
TOOLS: MAYA, QUARK

0316
ART DIRECTOR(S): MIRKO ILIC
DESIGNER(S): MIRKO ILIC
CLIENT: SARI LEVI, LEVI CREATIVE
TOOLS: QUARK

0328
ART DIRECTOR(S): MIRKO ILIC
DESIGNER(S): MIRKO ILIC
CLIENT: 5K MEDIA
TOOLS: PHOTOSHOP, QUARK

0366
ART DIRECTOR(S): MIRKO ILIC
DESIGNER(S): MIRKO ILIC
CLIENT: SLM
TOOLS: PHOTOSHOP, QUARK

0524
ART DIRECTOR(S): MIRKO ILIC
DESIGNER(S): MIRKO ILIC
CLIENT: AMERICAN FRIENDS OF TEL AVIV MUSEUM OF ART AND MARNIE AND ADAM D. TIHANY
TOOLS: ILLUSTRATOR, QUARK

MODE
0009, 0231, 0990
ART DIRECTOR(S): PHIL COSTINI, IAN STYLES
DESIGNER(S): DARRELL GIBBONS
CLIENT: LOST ROBOT
TOOLS: ILLUSTRATOR, PHOTOSHOP, EMAIL EFFECT, FONTOGRAPHER, QUARK
MATERIALS: 3M RADIANT LIGHT FILM

0097, 0955
ART DIRECTOR(S): PHIL COSTINI, IAN STYLES
DESIGNER(S): PHIL COSTINI, IAN STYLES
CLIENT: DALTON MAAG
TOOLS: ILLUSTRATOR, PHOTOSHOP, QUARK

0138
ART DIRECTOR(S): PHIL COSTINI, IAN STYLES
DESIGNER(S): DARRELL GIBBONS
CLIENT: MODE
TOOLS: ILLUSTRATOR, QUARK
MATERIALS: IKONO GLOSS

0967, 0968, 0969, 0970
ART DIRECTOR(S): PHIL COSTINI, IAN STYLES
DESIGNER(S): DARRELL GIBBONS
CLIENT: DALTON MAAG
TOOLS: ILLUSTRATOR, QUARK
MATERIALS: CHALLENGER OFFSET

MONA MCDONALD DESIGN
0151
DESIGNER(S): MONA MCDONALD
CLIENT: MARK BOLSTER
TOOLS: QUARK, MAC
MATERIALS: WHITE FOIL STAMP WITH HALFTONE

MONDERER DESIGN
0508
ART DIRECTOR(S): STEWART MONDERER
DESIGNER(S): JASON CK MILLER
CLIENT: MONDERER DESIGN
TOOLS: QUARK, MAC
MATERIALS: ASTROLITE 120LB COVER

0811
ART DIRECTOR(S): JASON CK MILLER
DESIGNER(S): JASON CK MILLER
CLIENT: UNIVERSITY OF MASSACHUSETTS MEDICAL SCHOOL
TOOLS: QUARK, MAC
MATERIALS: UTOPIA, GILCLEAR, FRENCH

MONSTER DESIGN
0051
ART DIRECTOR(S): HANNAH WYGAL, THERESA MONICA
DESIGNER(S): DENISE SAKAKI
CLIENT: XTENSIVE MEDIA SOLUTIONS
TOOLS: PHOTOSHOP, FREEHAND, MAC

0630
DESIGNER(S): HANNAH WYGAL, THERESA MONICA
CLIENT: MONSTER DESIGN
TOOLS: FREEHAND, MAC

MORLA DESIGN
0180
ART DIRECTOR(S): JENNIFER MORLA
DESIGNER(S): JENNIFER MORLA, BRIAN SINGER
CLIENT: MERVYN'S CALIFORNIA
TOOLS: ILLUSTRATOR

0978
ART DIRECTOR(S): JENNIFER MORLA
DESIGNER(S): JENNIFER MORLA, HIZAM HARON
CLIENT: AGI
TOOLS: ILLUSTRATOR, PHOTOSHOP
MATERIALS: ROLLAND OPAQUE BRIGHT WHITE 80LB TEXT

MORTENSEN DESIGN INC.
0292
ART DIRECTOR(S): GORDON MORTENSEN
DESIGNER(S): ANN JORDAN
CLIENT: CPP INC.
TOOLS: ILLUSTRATOR
MATERIALS: STARWHITE STRIUS SMOOTH 130LB DOUBLE THICK COVER

0295
ART DIRECTOR(S): GORDON MORTENSEN
DESIGNER(S): HELENA SEA
CLIENT: MORTENSEN DESIGN INC.
TOOLS: ILLUSTRATOR
MATERIALS: CRANE'S FLUORESCENT WHITE, KID FINISH 134LB (COVER), IMAGING FINISH 70LB TEXT (LETTERHEAD, AND ENVELOPE)

MOTIVE DESIGN RESEARCH
0073
ART DIRECTOR(S): KARI STRAND, MICHAEL CONNORS
DESIGNER(S): PETER ANDERSON
CLIENT: SUPREME
TOOLS: PHOTOSHOP, QUARK, MAC
MATERIALS: MOHAWK NAVAJO, THERMOGRAPHY

0260
ART DIRECTOR(S): KARI STRAND, MICHAEL CONNORS
DESIGNER(S): KARI STRAND
CLIENT: MOTIVE DESIGN RESEARCH
TOOLS: FREEHAND, QUARK, MAC
MATERIALS: MOHAWK SUPERFINE, BLOTTER PAPER (BUSINESS CARDS)

0264
ART DIRECTOR(S): MICHAEL CONNORS, KARI STRAND
DESIGNER(S): HEATHER HEFLIN
CLIENT: GETTY IMAGES
TOOLS: ILLUSTRATOR, PHOTOSHOP, QUARK, MAC
MATERIALS: SAPPI MCCOY SILK

0546
ART DIRECTOR(S): MICHAEL CONNORS, KARI STRAND
DESIGNER(S): PETER ANDERSON
CLIENT: N21+2
TOOLS: PHOTOSHOP, QUARK, MAC
MATERIALS: FOX RIVER STARWHITE VICKSBURG, BUBBLEWRAP, CUSTOM-PRINTED MASKING TAPE

0653
ART DIRECTOR(S): MICHAEL CONNORS, KARI STRAND
DESIGNER(S): DAVID COX
CLIENT: GETTY IMAGES
TOOLS: ILLUSTRATOR, PHOTOSHOP, QUARK, MAC
MATERIALS: SAPPI MCCOY SILK

0659
ART DIRECTOR(S): MICHAEL CONNORS, KARI STRAND
DESIGNER(S): PETER ANDERSON
CLIENT: MOTIVE DESIGN RESEARCH
TOOLS: ILLUSTRATOR, PHOTOSHOP, QUARK, MAC
MATERIALS: FRENCH CONSTRUCTION CLASSIC CREST LABLE, GLASSINE BAG, WILDFLOWERS

0870, 0988
ART DIRECTOR(S): MICHAEL CONNORS, KARI STRAND
DESIGNER(S): KRIS DELANEY
CLIENT: GETTY IMAGES
TOOLS: PHOTOSHOP, FREEHAND, QUARK, MAC
MATERIALS: STARWHITE VICKSBURG, GILCLEAR

NASSER DESIGN
0195
ART DIRECTOR(S): NELINDA NASSER
DESIGNER(S): NELINDA NASSER, MARGARITA ENCOMIENDA
CLIENT: LOUISE WEGMAN SCHOOL
TOOLS: ILLUSTRATOR, QUARK
MATERIALS: SPENDORGEL 300LB, FABRIANO COLORE PERLA 200LB (FOR POP-OUTS)

0337
ART DIRECTOR(S): NELINDA NASSER
DESIGNER(S): NELINDA NASSER, MARGARITA ENCOMIENDA
CLIENT: WEIDLINGER ASSOCIATES INC., CONSULTING ENGINEERS
TOOLS: ILLUSTRATOR PHOTOSHOP, QUARK
MATERIALS: ZANDERS IKONO GLOSS 80LB COVER

0574
ART DIRECTOR(S): NELINDA NASSER
DESIGNER(S): MARGARITA ENCOMIENDA, NELINDA NASSER
CLIENT: NASSER DESIGN
TOOLS: QUARK
MATERIALS: CHARTHAM TRANSLUCENTS PLATINUM 30LB, THIBIERGE ET COMAR CROMATICA (INSERT AND ENVELOPES)

NAVY BLUE
0104, 0386
ART DIRECTOR(S): CLARE LUNDY
DESIGNER(S): CLARE LUNDY
CLIENT: ZANDERS
TOOLS: QUARK
MATERIALS: ZANDERS ZETA SMOOTH BRILLIANT 850GSM

0624, 0839
DESIGNER(S): CLARE LUNDY
CLIENT: ROBERT HORNE
TOOLS: QUARK
MATERIALS: PARILUX GLASS 170GSM, IMAGINE 150 GSM, HOLOPRISM BOARD 717GSM

NB:STUDIO
0116
ART DIRECTOR(S): BEN STOTT, ALAN DYE, NICK FINNEY
DESIGNER(S): NICK VINCENT
CLIENT: D&AD
TOOLS: QUARK

0329
ART DIRECTOR(S): ALAN DYE, BEN STOTT, NICK FINNEY
DESIGNER(S): NICK VINCENT, CHARLIE SMITH
CLIENT: NB:STUDIO
TOOLS: ILLUSTRATOR, QUARK

0373
ART DIRECTOR(S): ALAN DYE, NICK FINNEY, BEN STOTT
DESIGNER(S): NICK FINNEY
CLIENT: MERCHANT
TOOLS: QUARK

0526
ART DIRECTOR(S): ALAN DYE, NICK FINNEY, BEN STOTT
DESIGNER(S): CHARLIE SMITH
CLIENT: CRAFTS COUNCIL
TOOLS: DUTCH GREYBOARD

0542
ART DIRECTOR(S): BEN STOTT, NICK FINNEY, ALAN DYE
DESIGNER(S): NICK VINCENT
CLIENT: SPEEDY HIRE
TOOLS: ILLUSTRATOR, QUARK, PEN
MATERIALS: MANILLA ENVELOPES

0533
ART DIRECTOR(S): ALAN DYE, BEN STOTT, NICK FINNEY
DESIGNER(S): NICK VINCENT
CLIENT: ROYAL SOCIETY OF ARTS
TOOLS: QUARK

0545
ART DIRECTOR(S): ALAN DYE, NICK FINNEY, BEN STOTT
DESIGNER(S): NICK VINCENT, CHARLIE SMITH
CLIENT: MERCHANT
MATERIALS: FENMER PAPER 7X STOCKS

0609
ART DIRECTOR(S): NICK FINNEY, BEN STOTT, ALAN DYE
DESIGNER(S): IAN PIERCE
CLIENT: CRAFTS COUNCIL
TOOLS: QUARK
MATERIALS: FLY WEIGHT

0718
ART DIRECTOR(S): ALAN DYE, BENN STOTT, NICK FINNEY
DESIGNER(S): JODIE WIGHTMAN
CLIENT: THE HUB
TOOLS: ILLUSTRATOR, QUARK
MATERIALS: MEED CUSTOM NOTE

0801
ART DIRECTOR(S): ALAN DYE, NICK FINNEY, BEN STOTT
DESIGNER(S): NICK VINCENT
CLIENT: D&AD
TOOLS: ILLUSTRATOR, QUARK
MATERIALS: DUFEX

NBBJ GRAPHIC DESIGN

0534
ART DIRECTOR(S): LEO RAYMUNDO
DESIGNER(S): LEO RAYMUNDO
CLIENT: FOUR SEASONS RESIDENTIAL PROPERTIES
TOOLS: FREEHAND, MAC G4
MATERIALS: CLASSIC CREST COVER, 110LB AVON BRILLIANT WHITE (ENVELOPE), 100LB CENTURY GLOSS (POSTCARDS), 60LB CENTURA DULL (BROCHURE)

NET#WORK BBDO

0229
ART DIRECTOR(S): GLENDA VENN
DESIGNER(S): RENATO SABBIONI
CLIENT: THE MIN INSTITUTE OF ART AND MATERIAL CULTURE
TOOLS: FREEHAND, MAC
MATERIALS: CONQUEROR WOVE

0572, 0575
ART DIRECTOR(S): GLENDA VENN
DESIGNER(S): CHRIS GOUGH PALMER
CLIENT: THE INDEPENDENT NEWSPAPER GROUP
TOOLS: FREEHAND

0588
ART DIRECTOR(S): CHRIS GOUGH PALMER
DESIGNER(S): CHRIS GOUGH PALMER
CLIENT: SAS INSTITUTE
TOOLS: FREEHAND, MAC
MATERIALS: CUSTOM-MADE STEEL CAPSULE, BUBBLEWRAP, MAGNOMAT, WING NUT

NETSUCCESS

0306
ART DIRECTOR(S): ANNIS LEUNG
DESIGNER(S): ANNIS LEUNG
CLIENT: THOMPSON ADVISORY GROUP
TOOLS: ILLUSTRATOR, MAC
MATERIALS: NEENAH CLASSIC CREST

NIELINGER & ROHSIEPE

0539
ART DIRECTOR(S): CHRISTIAN NIELINGER, HERBERT ROHSIEPE
DESIGNER(S): HERBERT ROHSIEPE
CLIENT: NIELINGER & ROHSIEPE
TOOLS: PHOTOSHOP, FREEHAND, MAC
MATERIALS: ARJOWIGGINS SENSATION 270GSM

NIKLAUS TROXLER DESIGN

0056
ART DIRECTOR(S): NIKLAUS TROXLER
DESIGNER(S): NIKLAUS TROXLER
CLIENT: JAZZ IN WILLISAU
TOOLS: HANDMADE STAMP LETTER
MATERIALS: POSTER PAPER, WRAP PAPER

0057
ART DIRECTOR(S): NIKLAUS TROXLER
DESIGNER(S): NIKLAUS TROXLER
CLIENT: JAZZ IN WILLISAU
TOOLS: HANDMADE STAMP LETTER
MATERIALS: POSTER PAPER

NO PARKING

0082
ART DIRECTOR(S): SABINE LERCHER
DESIGNER(S): ELISA DELL'ANGELO
CLIENT: BURGDENTAL
TOOLS: ILLUSTRATOR, QUARK
MATERIALS: MAGNOMATT PAPER 120GSM, TRANSPARENT SHEETS, TRANSPARENT PAPER CLIP

0422
ART DIRECTOR(S): CATERINA ROMIO
DESIGNER(S): CATERINA ROMIO
CLIENT: NO PARKING
TOOLS: ILLUSTRATOR
MATERIALS: PLASTIC CLIP

0729
ART DIRECTOR(S): CATERINA ROMIO, SABINE LERCHER
DESIGNER(S): CATERINA ROMIO, SABINE LERCHER
CLIENT: J. MISHRA
TOOLS: ILLUSTRATOR, PHOTOSHOP
MATERIALS: HOLOGRAPHIC PAPER, NATURAL PAPER

NYC COLLEGE OF TECHNOLOGY

0152
ART DIRECTOR(S): DOMINICK SARICA
DESIGNER(S): JAMIE SNOW MARKOWITZ
CLIENT: BROOKLYN BOROUGH PRESIDENT
TOOLS: ILLUSTRATOR, PHOTOSHOP, MAC
MATERIALS: BECKETT DUPLEX BLUE AND WHITE (COVER)

0690
ART DIRECTOR(S): DOMINICK SARICA
DESIGNER(S): DOMINICK SARICA
CLIENT: NEW YORK CITY COLLEGE OF TECHNOLOGY
TOOLS: QUARK, MAC G4
MATERIALS: BASEBALL, ASTROTURF, CORRUGATED BOX

OCTAVO DESIGN

0587
ART DIRECTOR(S): GARY DOMENY
CLIENT: OCTAVO DESIGN
TOOLS: ILLUSTRATOR, MAC
MATERIALS: TWINE, HANDMADE PAPER

ONE O'CLOCK GUN DESIGN CONSULTANTS

0002
ART DIRECTOR(S): MARK HOSKER
DESIGNER(S): MICHAEL DUNLOP
CLIENT: ONE O'CLOCK GUN DESIGN CONSULTANTS
TOOLS: ILLUSTRATOR
MATERIALS: FLUORESCENT INK

ORANGESEED DESIGN

0137
ART DIRECTOR(S): DAMIEN WOLF
DESIGNER(S): DAMIEN WOLF
CLIENT: WILD MEADOWS
TOOLS: PHOTOSHOP, QUARK, G4
MATERIALS: 80LB BRIGHT WHITE CORONADO VELLUM COVER

ORIGIN

0459
ART DIRECTOR(S): MARK BOTTOMLEY
CLIENT: MAT WRIGHT PHOTOGRAPHY
MATERIALS: CURTIS MALTS

PH.D.

0043, 0190, 0197, 0334, 0401, 0637, 0635
ART DIRECTOR(S): CLIVE PIERCY, MICHAEL HODGSON
DESIGNER(S): CAROL CONO-NOBLE
CLIENT: DICKSON'S
TOOLS: ILLUSTRATOR, PHOTOSHOP, QUARK
MATERIALS: NEENAH CLASSIC CREST

0178
ART DIRECTOR(S): CLIVE PIERCY
DESIGNER(S): CLIVE PIERCY
CLIENT: THE FAD GALLERY
TOOLS: ILLUSTRATOR, QUARK
MATERIALS: MOHAWK NAVAJO COVER BRILLIANT WHITE 160LB (BUSINESS CARDS), MOHAWK NAVAJO WRITING BRILLIANT WHITE 28LB (LETTERHEAD), MOHAWK NAVAJO WRITING BRILLIANT WHITE 24LB (ENVELOPE), ULTRABAK MATTE LITHO LABEL (LABEL), MOHAWK SUPERFINE SMOOTH COVER ULTRAWHITE 160LB

0196, 0621
ART DIRECTOR(S): CLIVE PIERCY
DESIGNER(S): CLIVE PIERCY
CLIENT: QUIKSILVER
TOOLS: PHOTOSHOP, QUARK, MAC

0402
ART DIRECTOR(S): CLIVE PIERCY
DESIGNER(S): CLIVE PIERCY
CLIENT: AIGA
TOOLS: QUARK, ILLUSTRATOR
MATERIALS: NEW LEAF 70LB REINCARNATION (POSTER), NEW LEAF 80LB REINCARNATION (BROCHURE)

0769, 0815
CLIENT: DEVELOPMENTOR

0920
CLIENT: FOUNDATION PRESS
MATERIALS: REIANCE 140LB WHITE HALFTONE PRINTABLE BLOTTER (BUSINESS CARDS), CONVERTED DOR-O-TONE TEXT 60LB BUTCHER (ENVELOPES), MACTAC STARLINER NOVELTY UNCOATED 60LB WHITE (LABELS), CONSTRUCTION WRITING 70LB WHITEWASH (LETTERHEAD, SECOND SHEETS, NOTEPAD), DUR-O-TON

PHILLIPS

0123
ART DIRECTOR(S): PETER PHILLIPS
CLIENT: BERG

0258
ART DIRECTOR(S): PETER PHILLIPS
CLIENT: BEBOP

0262
ART DIRECTOR(S): PETER PHILLIPS
CLIENT: TSL

0267
ART DIRECTOR(S): PETER PHILLIPS
CLIENT: REDIDOSE

0455
ART DIRECTOR(S): PETER PHILLIPS
CLIENT: PHILLIPS

0720
ART DIRECTOR(S): PETER PHILLIPS
CLIENT: B+H

0741
ART DIRECTOR(S): PETER PHILLIPS

0755
ART DIRECTOR(S): PETER PHILLIPS
CLIENT: VIRTUALL

0766
ART DIRECTOR(S): PETER PHILLIPS
CLIENT: SONY

PHYX DESIGN

0921
ART DIRECTOR(S): MASAKI KOIKE
DESIGNER(S): MASAKI KOIKE
CLIENT: PHYX DESIGN
TOOLS: MAC, SCREEN PRINT, HANDS
MATERIALS: FRENCH PAPER COMPANY CONSTRUCTION

PLAN-B STUDIO

0894
ART DIRECTOR(S): STEVE PRICE
DESIGNER(S): STEVE PRICE
CLIENT: ROTOVISION
TOOLS: PHOTOGRAPHIC DARKROOM, SCALPEL
MATERIALS: 150GSM UNCOATED, ACETATE

0926
ART DIRECTOR(S): STEVE PRICE
CLIENT: WALL OF SOUND RECORDINGS
MATERIALS: DOUBLE WHITE BOARD

PLUS DESIGN INC.

0273
ART DIRECTOR(S): ANITA MEYER
DESIGNER(S): ANITA MEYER
CLIENT: THE EDMOND-HOWARD NETWORK
TOOLS: QUARK, MAC
MATERIALS: FRENCH CONSTRUCTION WHITEWASH 24LB TEXT (LETTERHEAD, SECOND SHEET AND ENVELOPE), FRENCH CONSTRUCTION WHITEWASH 100LB COVER (BUSINESS CARDS)

0319
ART DIRECTOR(S): ANITA MEYER
DESIGNER(S): ANITA MEYER
CLIENT: THE INSTITUTE OF CONTEMPORARY ART
TOOLS: PHOTOSHOP, QUARK
MATERIALS: PLATINUM TRANSLUCENT (ENVELOPE), BECKETT EXPRESSION RADIANCE 100LB COVER (SLEEVE), CONSORT ROYAL SILK 80LB COVER (BROCHURE)

0666
ART DIRECTOR(S): ANITA MEYER, KAREN FICKETT
DESIGNER(S): ANITA MEYER, KAREN FICKETT, DINA ZACCAGNINI, MATT NICOLE JUEN, CAROLINA SENIOR, VERONICA MAJIL
CLIENT: PLUS DESIGN INC.
MATERIALS: FRENCH BUTCHER WHITE 60LB TEXT (MEMO SHEET), FRENCH NEWSPRINT 70LB TEXT (LETTERHEAD), FRENCH PRIMER 60LB 60LB TEXT (ENVELOPE), CHIPBOARD (BUSINESS CARD AND FOLDER)

POINT BLANK DESIGN

0147
ART DIRECTOR(S): PETER OWEN
CLIENT: UNIVERSAL
TOOLS: ILLUSTRATOR, PHOTOSHOP, QUARK

0349, 0368
ART DIRECTOR(S): STEVE WALLINGTON, NICK FOLEY
DESIGNER(S): STEVE WALLINGTON, NICK FOLEY
CLIENT: DOCKERS
TOOLS: QUARK

0374
DESIGNER(S): JAMES KELLEY
CLIENT: UNIVERSAL
TOOLS: FREEHAND, QUARK

0742
DESIGNER(S): PETER OWEN
CLIENT: BBC
TOOLS: ILLUSTRATOR, QUARK
MATERIALS: FOIL RECOVERY BLANKET

0765
DESIGNER(S): POINT BLANK DESIGN
CLIENT: AS WORN BY
TOOLS: ILLUSTRATOR, QUARK
MATERIALS: T-SHIRT, BOX

POPCORN INITIATIVE

0361
ART DIRECTOR(S): CHRIS JONES
DESIGNER(S): CHRIS JONES
CLIENT: KISSIMMEE UTILITY AUTHORITY
TOOLS: ILLUSTRATOR, PHOTOSHOP, QUARK, MAC
MATERIALS: MOHAWK NAVAJO, CHIPBOARD

0601
ART DIRECTOR(S): CHRIS JONES
DESIGNER(S): CHRIS JONES, ROGER WOOD
CLIENT: POPCORN INITIATIVE
TOOLS: ILLUSTRATOR, PHOTOSHOP, MAC
MATERIALS: MOHAWK NAVAJO 120LB COVER

PRECURSOR

0008, 0124, 0686
ART DIRECTOR(S): PRECURSOR
DESIGNER(S): PRECURSOR
CLIENT: WOODHEAD CALLIVA
TOOLS: ILLUSTRATOR, MAC
MATERIALS: CURIOUS TOUCH, FAULKNERS FINE PAPERS (BOOKCLOTH)

0010, 0746
DESIGNER(S): PRECURSOR
CLIENT: WOODHEAD CALLIVA
TOOLS: ILLUSTRATOR, MAC
MATERIALS: FLOCKAGE, PERSPEX

0035, 0140
DESIGNER(S): PRECURSOR
CLIENT: PRECURSOR
TOOLS: ILLUSTRATOR, MAC
MATERIALS: CURIOUS TOUCH, FAULKNERS FINE PAPERS (BOOKCLOTH)

0294
ART DIRECTOR(S): PRECURSOR
DESIGNER(S): PRECURSOR
CLIENT: WOODHEAD CALLIVA
TOOLS: ILLUSTRATOR, MAC
MATERIALS: FOCKAGE, COLORPLAN COLTSKIN, STAINLESS STEEL

0498
ART DIRECTOR(S): PRECURSOR
DESIGNER(S): PRECURSOR
CLIENT: WOODHEAD CALLIVA
TOOLS: ILLUSTRATOR, MAC
MATERIALS: COLORPLAN, TYVEK

PROGRESS

0107
CLIENT: CREATIVE REVIEW

0118
CLIENT: THIRTEEN (BRISTOL)

0243
CLIENT: UNICHEM
MATERIALS: PAPER, BOARD

0248
DESIGNER(S): MILLER SEALE
CLIENT: PRO-DG
MATERIALS: METAL TIN

0473
CLIENT: REFLECTIVE TECHNOLOGIES
MATERIALS: RIGID POLYPROPYLENE

0482
DESIGNER(S): BDW
CLIENT: ALFA ROMEO
MATERIALS: PVC

0566
CLIENT: TEQUILA

0687
ART DIRECTOR(S):
DESIGNER(S): MCCANN ERICKSON
CLIENT: MCCANN ERICKSON
MATERIALS: PVC, THEATRICAL BLOOD

0688
CLIENT: MOLTEN TV

0704
CLIENT: THE PAINT FACTORY

0713
CLIENT: LIFFE

0753
CLIENT: MOON ESTATES
MATERIALS: ANTISTATIC FILM

0754
CLIENT: PDP MOMENTUM
MATERIALS: TOUCH PVC, ALUMINUM

0757
CLIENT: ETNIES

PROJECTOR

0202, 0682, 0775
ART DIRECTOR(S): OLIVER HALL, GRAHAM SPILLER, ALED WILLIAMS
DESIGNER(S): OLIVER HALL, GRAHAM SPILLER, ALED WILLIAMS
CLIENT: FIERCE PANDA RECORDINGS
TOOLS: ILLUSTRATOR, PHOTOSHOP, MAC G4
MATERIALS: 180GSM, XPACE TRANSLUCENT PAPER, FILEMASTER LAMINATED MANILLA BUFF 180GSM

Q

0475, 0480
ART DIRECTOR(S): LAURENZ NIELBOCK
CLIENT: ARJOWIGGINS GERMANY
TOOLS: PHOTOSHOP, QUARK, MAC
MATERIALS: VARIOUS

QUESTION DESIGN

0157
ART DIRECTOR(S): CHARLOTTE NORUZI
DESIGNER(S): CHARLOTTE NORUZI
CLIENT: STEVEN MADDEN INC.
TOOLS: QUARK, MAC
MATERIALS: COTTON FABRIC, STITCHING

0582
ART DIRECTOR(S): CHARLOTTE NORUZI
DESIGNER(S): CHARLOTTE NORUZI
CLIENT: QUESTION DESIGN
TOOLS: QUARK, MAC
MATERIALS: WOOD, PAPER, ROPE

0613
ART DIRECTOR(S): CHARLOTTE NORUZI
DESIGNER(S): CHARLOTTE NORUZI
CLIENT: QUESTION DESIGN
TOOLS: QUARK, MAC
MATERIALS: WOOD, PAPER, YARN

R2 DESIGN

0025, 0074, 0212
ART DIRECTOR(S): LIZA RAMALHO, ARTUR REBELO
DESIGNER(S): LIZA RAMALHO, ARTUR REBELO
CLIENT: TEATRO BRUTO
TOOLS: FREEHAND, MAC
MATERIALS: MUNKEN COUCHE

0369, 0370, 0410
ART DIRECTOR(S): LIZA RAMALHO, ARTUR REBELO
DESIGNER(S): LIZA RAMALHO, ARTUR REBELO
CLIENT: CASSIOPEIA
TOOLS: FREEHAND, MAC
MATERIALS: MUNKEN COUCHE, CLK

0573
ART DIRECTOR(S): LIZA RAMALHO, ARTUR REBELO
DESIGNER(S): LIZA RAMALHO, ARTUR REBELO
CLIENT: MARTA + GIL
TOOLS: FREEHAND, MAC
MATERIALS: COUCHE CLK

RADFORD WALLIS

0451, 0730
ART DIRECTOR(S): STUART RADFORD, ANDREW WALLIS
DESIGNER(S): STUART RADFORD, LEE WILSON
CLIENT: ARTS & BUSINESS
TOOLS: QUARK
MATERIALS: NEPTUNE UNIQUE 200GSM, LUC PRINT PVC

RADLEY YELDAR

0437, 0959
ART DIRECTOR(S): ROB RICHE
DESIGNER(S): ROB RICHE, NEIL LATMORE
CLIENT: COMIC RELIEF
TOOLS: PHOTOSHOP, QUARK

0515
ART DIRECTOR(S): ROB RICHE
DESIGNER(S): DARREN BARBER
CLIENT: MCNAUGHTON PAPER
TOOLS: PHOTOSHOP, QUARK
MATERIALS: COLOR IT

0518
ART DIRECTOR(S): ANDREW GORMAN
DESIGNER(S): KEITH CULLEN
CLIENT: RADLEY YELDAR
TOOLS: ILLUSTRATOR, PHOTOSHOP, QUARK

0519, 0085
ART DIRECTOR(S): ANDREW GORMAN
DESIGNER(S): JAMIE NEALE, KEITH CULLEN
CLIENT: DIAGO
TOOLS: PHOTOSHOP, QUARK

0549
ART DIRECTOR(S): ADAM MILLS
DESIGNER(S): ADAM MILLS
CLIENT: MINERVA PLC
TOOLS: PHOTOSHOP, QUARK

0664
ART DIRECTOR(S): ANDREW GORMAN
DESIGNER(S): KEITH CULLEN
CLIENT: RADLEY YELDAR
TOOLS: QUARK, NEEDLE

0671
ART DIRECTOR(S): ROB RICHE
DESIGNER(S): DARREN BARBER
CLIENT: MCNAUGHTON PAPER
TOOLS: ILLUSTRATOR, PHOTOSHOP, QUARK
MATERIALS: COLOR IT

0675
ART DIRECTOR(S): PHIL METSON
DESIGNER(S): CHRISTIAN BATES
CLIENT: UNIVERSITY OF PORTSMOUTH
TOOLS: PHOTOSHOP, QUARK

ART DIRECTOR(S): ANDREW
GORMAN
DESIGNER(S): ROB RICHE
CLIENT: MCNAUGHTON PAPER
TOOLS: PHOTOSHOP, QUARK
MATERIALS: T2500, HANNO
ART

REEBOK DESIGN SERVICES

ART DIRECTOR(S): ELENI
CHRONOPOULOS
DESIGNER(S): ELENI
CHRONOPOULOS, VILISLAVA
PETROVA
CLIENT: REEBOK
TOOLS: ILLUSTRATOR,
PHOTOSHOP, QUARK, MAC
MATERIALS: 3M REFLECTIVE
MATERIAL, FIBERMARK
TOUCHE, CURIOUS METALLICS

RICK JOHNSON & COMPANY

ART DIRECTOR(S): TIM
MCGRATH
DESIGNER(S): RICK JOHNSON &
COMPANY
TOOLS: ILLUSTRATOR, MAC
MATERIALS: TAGS, RUBBER
STAMP

RICKABAUGH GRAPHICS

ART DIRECTOR(S): ERIC
RICKABAUGH
DESIGNER(S): ERIC
RICKABAUGH
CLIENT: THE COLUMBUS
CREW, MLS
TOOLS: FREEHAND, MAC
MATERIALS: CENTURA GLOSS
BLACK CORRUGATED

RINZEN

CLIENT: FAMILY (CLUB)
TOOLS: FREEHAND, MAC

CLIENT: EDWARDS DUNLOP
PAPER
TOOLS: FREEHAND, MAC

RIORDON DESIGN

ART DIRECTOR(S): RIC
RIORDON, DAN WHEATON
DESIGNER(S): SHIRLEY
RIORDON
CLIENT: SCOTIA CAPITAL
TOOLS: QUARK, ILLUSTRATOR
MATERIALS: SILK FABRIC,
VELLUM

ART DIRECTOR(S): RIC
RIORDON
DESIGNER(S): DAN WHEATON,
ALAN KAPLAN
CLIENT: RIORDON DESIGN
TOOLS: ILLUSTRATOR, QUARK
MATERIALS: BENEFIT TEXT
AND COVER

ART DIRECTOR(S): RIC
RIORDON
DESIGNER(S): SHARON PELE,
AMY MONTGOMERY
CLIENT: RIORDON DESIGN
TOOLS: ILLUSTRATOR, QUARK
MATERIALS: NEENAH
ENVIRONMENT

ART DIRECTOR(S): SHIRLEY
RIORDON
DESIGNER(S): ALAN KAPAN
CLIENT: RIORDON DESIGN
TOOLS: ILLUSTRATOR,
PHOTOSHOP, QUARK
MATERIALS: CLASSIC LINEN
VELVET SYNERGY

**RIPE IN ASSOCIATION WITH
ALCAN PRINT FINISHING**

ROBIN RAYNO

ART DIRECTOR(S): ROBIN
RAYNO
DESIGNER(S): ROBIN RAYNO
CLIENT: CHRISTABEL
ROMANLIER
TOOLS: ILLUSTRATOR, PC
MATERIALS: WOOD,
STARDREAM 150GSM,
CONQUEROR 150GSM

ROSE DESIGN

ART DIRECTOR(S): SIMON
ELLIOTT
DESIGNER(S): ESTHER
KIRKPATRICK
CLIENT: SPINE PUBLISHING
TOOLS: ILLUSTRATOR,
PHOTOSHOP, QUARK, MAC

ART DIRECTOR(S): SIMON
ELLIOTT
DESIGNER(S): SIMON ELLIOTT
CLIENT: WESTZONE
PUBLISHING
TOOLS: ILLUSTRATOR,
PHOTOSHOP, QUARK, MAC
MATERIALS: 350 NEPTUNE
UNIQUE, 250 CHROMOMAT

ART DIRECTOR(S): SIMON
ELLIOTT
DESIGNER(S): SIMON ELLIOTT
CLIENT: WESTZONE
PUBLISHING
TOOLS: ILLUSTRATOR,
PHOTOSHOP, QUARK, MAC
MATERIALS: 250 CYCLUS, 120
FRENCH LEAVES HELLO SILK

ROUNDEL

ART DIRECTOR(S): JOHN
BATESON
DESIGNER(S): PAUL INGLE
CLIENT: ZANDERS FINEPAPER
TOOLS: MAC
MATERIALS: IKONO PAPER

ART DIRECTOR(S): JOHN
BATESON
DESIGNER(S): KEELAN ROSS
CLIENT: ZANDERS FINEPAPER
TOOLS: MAC
MATERIALS: SPECTRAL
PAPER

ROYCROFT DESIGN

ART DIRECTOR(S): JENNIFER
ROYCROFT
DESIGNER(S): JENNIFER
ROYCROFT
CLIENT: MOHAWK PAPERMILL
TOOLS: QUARK, MAC
MATERIALS: MOHAWK 50/10

ART DIRECTOR(S): JENNIFER
ROYCROFT
DESIGNER(S): JENNIFER
ROYCROFT
CLIENT: MOHAWK PAPERMILL
TOOLS: ILLUSTRATOR, QUARK,
MAC
MATERIALS: MOHAWK
SUPERFINE

ART DIRECTOR(S): JENNIFER
ROYCROFT
DESIGNER(S): JENNIFER
ROYCROFT
CLIENT: MOHAWK PAPERMILL
TOOLS: QUARK
MATERIALS: FINCH FINE

SAGE COMMUNICATION

ART DIRECTOR(S): KELSEY
MCLACHLAN
DESIGNER(S): CHRISTOPHER
MCLACHLAN
CLIENT: BRIAN SHARPE
TOOLS: MAC
MATERIALS: FOX RIVER

SALTERBAXTER

ART DIRECTOR(S): PENNY
BAXTER
DESIGNER(S): ALAN DELGADO
CLIENT: SALTBAXTER &
CONTEXT
TOOLS: ILLUSTRATOR, QUARK,
MAC
MATERIALS: FLOCKAGE

ART DIRECTOR(S): ALAN
DELGADO
DESIGNER(S): ROSE
MCMULLAN
CLIENT: DISCOVERY
NETWORKS EUROPE
TOOLS: ILLUSTRATOR, MAC
MATERIALS: TYVEK

ART DIRECTOR(S): ALAN
DELGADO
DESIGNER(S): ALAN DELGADO
CLIENT: DISCOVERY
NETWORKS EUROPE
TOOLS: QUARK, MAC
MATERIALS: PLASMA
POLYCOAT CLEAR NATURAL

ART DIRECTOR(S): PENNY
BAXTER
DESIGNER(S): PENNY BAXTER
CLIENT: THE EMI GROUP
TOOLS: QUARK, MAC
MATERIALS: DISCARDED
WASTE SHEETS

ART DIRECTOR(S): ALAN
DELGADO
DESIGNER(S): ALAN DELGADO,
LINDSEY KALMAN
CLIENT: DISCOVERY
NETWORKS EUROPE
TOOLS: QUARK, MAC
MATERIALS: PRIPLACK CLEAR
AND TRANSLUCENT RED SILK
SCREEN

SAMPSONMAY

ART DIRECTOR(S): RICKY
SAMPSON
DESIGNER(S): KATE
MESSENGER
CLIENT: SAMPSONMAY
TOOLS: WOOD BLOCK
MATERIALS: G.F. SMITH
COLOURPLAN

ART DIRECTOR(S): RICKY
SAMPSON
DESIGNER(S): RICKY
SAMPSON
CLIENT: SAMPSONMAY
MATERIALS: G.F. SMITH
COLOURPLAN

ART DIRECTOR(S): RICKY
SAMPSON
DESIGNER(S): KATE
MESSENGER
CLIENT: ROLLS-ROYCE PLC

ART DIRECTOR(S): RICKY
SAMPSON
DESIGNER(S): KATE
MESSENGER
CLIENT: SAMPSONMAY
TOOLS: NOVA SPACE INK
TECHNIQUE

SAS

ART DIRECTOR(S): DAVID
STOCKS
DESIGNER(S): MIKE HALL
CLIENT: BBA
TOOLS: QUARK, MAC
MATERIALS: ZANDERS MEGA
MATT

ART DIRECTOR(S): DAVID
STOCKS
DESIGNER(S): MAREK
GWLAZDA
CLIENT: RADIO TAXIS
TOOLS: ILLUSTRATOR, MAC
MATERIALS: G.F. SMITH
COLOURPLAN

ART DIRECTOR(S): GILMAR
WENDT
DESIGNER(S): CHRISTINE
FENT, JOE MADEIRA, ANDY
ROBINSON, BEN TOMLINSON
CLIENT: BT
TOOLS: QUARK, MAC
MATERIALS: CONSORT
ROYAL SILK, CONSORT ROYAL
COMPLEMENT, HOWARD
SMITH UNCOATED

ART DIRECTOR(S): DAVID
STOCKS, GILMAR WENDT
DESIGNER(S): GILMAR WENDT
CLIENT: SAS
TOOLS: INDESIGN, MAC
MATERIALS:
PHOENIXMOTION, GLOW-EDGE
POLYCARBONATE

ART DIRECTOR(S): DAVID
STOCKS
DESIGNER(S): JAMES
PARSONS
CLIENT: HSBC
TOOLS: QUARK, ILLUSTRATOR,
MAC
MATERIALS: JOB PARILUX
MATT

ART DIRECTOR(S): CHRISTINE
FENT, GILMAR WENDT
DESIGNER(S): CHRISTINE
FENT, GILMAR WENDT
CLIENT: SAS
TOOLS: ILLUSTRATOR, QUARK,
MAC
MATERIALS: PLANO PAK
DÜNNDRUCK, SURBALIN
MOIRÉ, CABRA

ART DIRECTOR(S): GILMAR
WENDT
DESIGNER(S): GILMAR
WENDT, FRANKIE GOODWIN,
MATT TOMLIN
CLIENT: MAKINGSPACE
PUBLISHERS
TOOLS: MAC, ILLUSTRATOR
MATERIALS:
PHOENIXMOTION, VELBEC

ART DIRECTOR(S): DAVID
STOCKS
DESIGNER(S): ALAN DELGADO
CLIENT: BBA
TOOLS: QUARK, MAC
MATERIALS: ZANDERS MEGA
MATT, MATERIAL FROM BBA
NONVOWENS

ART DIRECTOR(S): PENNY
BAXTER
DESIGNER(S): MIKE HALL
CLIENT: NM ROTHSCHILD
TOOLS: QUARK, MAC
MATERIALS: G.F. SMITH
COLOURPLAN, MUNKEDALS
MUNKEN, FEDRIGONI
PERGAMENATA

SCANDINAVIAN DESIGN GROUP
0004, 0060, 0102, 0821
ART DIRECTOR(S): MUGGIE RAMADANI
DESIGNER(S): MUGGIE RAMADANI
CLIENT: PRICEWATER-HOUSECOOPERS
TOOLS: ILLUSTRATOR, PHOTOSHOP, QUARK, MAC

0007, 0342, 0343, 0469, 0702
ART DIRECTOR(S): MUGGIE RAMADANI, PER MADSEN
DESIGNER(S): PER MADSEN, MUGGIE RAMADANI
CLIENT: MUNTHE PLUS SIMONSEN
TOOLS: ILLUSTRATOR, PHOTOSHOP, QUARK, MAC

0021, 0089, 0136, 0141, 0874
ART DIRECTOR(S): MUGGIE RAMADANI, PER MADSEN
DESIGNER(S): PER MADSEN, MUGGIE RAMADANI
CLIENT: CREATIVE CIRCLE
TOOLS: ILLUSTRATOR, PHOTOSHOP, QUARK, MAC

0244, 0261, 0279, 0477, 0478
ART DIRECTOR(S): MUGGIE RAMADANI, PER MADSEN
DESIGNER(S): PER MADSEN, MUGGIE RAMADANI
CLIENT: PORTFOLIO--CPH
TOOLS: ILLUSTRATOR, PHOTOSHOP, QUARK, MAC

0367, 0875
ART DIRECTOR(S): MUGGIE RAMADANI
DESIGNER(S): MUGGIE RAMADANI
CLIENT: PORTFOLIO--CPH/ STYLE COUNSEL/UNIQUE LOOK
TOOLS: ILLUSTRATOR, PHOTOSHOP, QUARK, MAC

0468, 0484, 0505, 0884
ART DIRECTOR(S): MUGGIE RAMADANI, PER MADSEN
DESIGNER(S): PER MADSEN, MUGGIE RAMADANI
CLIENT: 6 AGENCY
TOOLS: ILLUSTRATOR, PHOTOSHOP, QUARK, MAC

0505, 0708
ART DIRECTOR(S): PER MADSEN
DESIGNER(S): PER MADSEN
CLIENT: NIGHTCLUB X-RAY
TOOLS: ILLUSTRATOR, PHOTOSHOP, QUARK, MAC

SEA DESIGN
0063
ART DIRECTOR(S): BRYAN GOMONOSON
DESIGNER(S): CARSTEN KLEIN
CLIENT: IDENTITY
TOOLS: ILLUSTRATOR, PHOTOSHOP, QUARK, MAC G4
MATERIALS: ACCENT SMOOTH 115GSM

SELTZER DESIGN
0439
ART DIRECTOR(S): ROCHELLE SELTZER
DESIGNER(S): MEAGHAN O'KEEFE
CLIENT: PARTNERS HEALTHCARE SYSTEM
TOOLS: ILLUSTRATOR, QUARK, MAC
MATERIALS: ROLAND MOTIF SCREENED, FRASER PEGASUS, FINCH OPAQUE

0680
ART DIRECTOR(S): ROCHELLE SELTZER
DESIGNER(S): MEAGHAN O'KEEFE
CLIENT: ANIMATION MD
TOOLS: ILLUSTRATOR, QUARK, MAC
MATERIALS: GILCLEAR WHITE HEAVY, CANSON SATIN 75LB CLEAR, MCCOY VELVET 180LB COVER, BUBBLEOPE, LION LABELS

0804
ART DIRECTOR(S): ROCHELLE SELTZER
DESIGNER(S): MEAGHAN O'KEEFE
CLIENT: SELTZER DESIGN
TOOLS: QUARK, MAC
MATERIALS: CURIOUS METALLIC ANODIZED

0993
ART DIRECTOR(S): ROCHELLE SELTZER
DESIGNER(S): ANNIE SMIDT
CLIENT: SELTZER DESIGN
TOOLS: ILLUSTRATOR, INDESIGN
MATERIALS: MAC

SHARP COMMUNICATIONS
0409
ART DIRECTOR(S): ANRI SEKI
DESIGNER(S): ANRI SEKI
CLIENT: NORDIC PARTNERS
TOOLS: ILLUSTRATOR, QUARK

SHIH DESIGN
0031
ART DIRECTOR(S): GING-HUNG SHIH
DESIGNER(S): GING-HUNG SHIH
CLIENT: AUSPICE PAPER CO. LTD.
TOOLS: ILLUSTRATOR, PHOTOSHOP
MATERIALS: PHOENIXMOTION

SK VISUAL
0027, 0152
ART DIRECTOR(S): KATYA LYUMKIS, SPENCER LUM
DESIGNER(S): KATYA LYUMKIS, SPENCER LUM
CLIENT: SK VISUAL
TOOLS: ILLUSTRATOR
MATERIALS: VELLUM, LABEL TABS, METAL CLIPS, STAMP

STARSHOT
0155
ART DIRECTOR(S): LARS HARMSEN
DESIGNER(S): LARS HARMSEN, TINA WEISSER
CLIENT: STARSHOP BYKE STYLE MAGAZINE
TOOLS: PHOTOSHOP, FREEHAND, QUARK
MATERIALS: GMUND BUTENPAPIER (COVER), VIBE GENTLE ROSE (COLLECTION), HOT FOIL

0017, 0251, 0855
ART DIRECTOR(S): LARS HARMSEN
DESIGNER(S): LARS HARMSEN
CLIENT: STARSHOP BYKE STYLE MAGAZINE
TOOLS: PHOTOSHOP, FREEHAND, QUARK
MATERIALS: REFLECTING IMAGE

0167
ART DIRECTOR(S): LARS HARMSEN
DESIGNER(S): LARS HARMSEN, AXEL BRINKMANN, TINA WEISSER
CLIENT: BERGWERK BIKES
TOOLS: PHOTOSHOP, FREEHAND, QUARK
MATERIALS: IVERCOTE

0751, 0849
ART DIRECTOR(S): LARS HARMSEN
DESIGNER(S): LARS HARMSEN, TINA WEISSER, CLAUDIA KLEIN
CLIENT: STARSHOT
TOOLS: PHOTOSHOP, FREEHAND, QUARK
MATERIALS: GMUND BÜTENPAPIER, COLLECTION TREASURY

STEERSMCGILLAN
0091, 0121
ART DIRECTOR(S): RICHARD MCGILLAN
DESIGNER(S): CHLOE STEERS
CLIENT: SPIKE ISLAND, BRISTOL
TOOLS: QUARK, MAC

0155
ART DIRECTOR(S): RICHARD MCGILLAN
DESIGNER(S): CHLOE STEERS
CLIENT: CLORE DUFFED FOUNDATION
TOOLS: QUARK, MAC
MATERIALS: TRUCARD 1-COLOR PLUS FOIL

0633
ART DIRECTOR(S): CHLOE STEERS
DESIGNER(S): RICHARD MCGILLAN
CLIENT: DULWICH PICTURE GALLERY
TOOLS: QUARK, MAC
MATERIALS: ARCTIC VOLUME

0714
ART DIRECTOR(S): RICHARD MCGILLAN
DESIGNER(S): CHLOE STEERS
CLIENT: THE STUDY GALLERY, POOLE
TOOLS: QUARK, MAC
MATERIALS: TINTED PRIPLAK, SCREEN PRINT

0717
ART DIRECTOR(S): RICHARD MCGILLAN
DESIGNER(S): PETER THOMPSON
CLIENT: INSANELY GREAT
TOOLS: MAC
MATERIALS: PRIPLAK

STOLTZE DESIGN
0308
ART DIRECTOR(S): CLIFFORD STOLTZE, ROY BURNS
DESIGNER(S): ROY BURNS
CLIENT: STOLTZE DESIGN

0359, 0873
ART DIRECTOR(S): CLIFFORD STOLTZE
DESIGNER(S): CLIFFORD STOLTZE
CLIENT: DOROTHEA VAN CAMP

0493
ART DIRECTOR(S): CLIFFORD STOLTZE
DESIGNER(S): BRANDON BLANGGER, CINDY PATTEN
CLIENT: SIX RED MARBLES

STRICHPUNKT
0087
ART DIRECTOR(S): KIRSTEN DIETZ, JOCHEN RADEKER
DESIGNER(S): KIRSTEN DIETZ, FELIX WIDMAIER, TANJA GÜNTHER
CLIENT: PAPIER-FABRIK SCHEUFELEN
TOOLS: QUARK, MAC
MATERIALS: PHOENIXMOTION/ SCHEUFELEN

0090, 0065
ART DIRECTOR(S): KIRSTEN DIETZ, JOCHEN RADEKER
DESIGNER(S): KIRSTEN DIETZ, TANJA GÜNTHER
CLIENT: PAPIERFABRIK SCHEUFELEN
TOOLS: QUARK, MAC
MATERIALS: PHOENIXMOTION/ SCHEUFELEN

0265
ART DIRECTOR(S): KIRSTEN DIETZ, JOCHEN RADEKER
DESIGNER(S): KIRSTEN DIETZ
CLIENT: 4MBO INTERNATIONAL ELECTRONIC AG
TOOLS: QUARK, MAC
MATERIALS: LUXOR STAIN (SCHNEIDER & SÖHNE), SHOPPING BAG

STRUKTUR DESIGN
0171, 0356, 0918
ART DIRECTOR(S): ROGER FAWCETT-TANG
CLIENT: STRUKTUR DESIGN
TOOLS: QUARK, MAC
MATERIALS: STORA FINE

0386
ART DIRECTOR(S): ROGER FAWCETT-TANG
DESIGNER(S): ROGER FAWCETT-TANG, SANNE FAWCETT-TANG
CLIENT: STRUKTUR DESIGN
TOOLS: QUARK, MAC
MATERIALS: STORA FINE

SUM DESIGN
0116
ART DIRECTOR(S): SIMON WOOLFORD
DESIGNER(S): CAMERON LEADBETTER
CLIENT: RIVER ISLAND
TOOLS: PHOTOSHOP, QUARK
MATERIALS: MIRROR BOARD

0131
ART DIRECTOR(S): SIMON WOOLFORD
DESIGNER(S): LORINDA SMITH
CLIENT: INCA PRODUCTIONS
TOOLS: ILLUSTRATOR
MATERIALS: CX22

0558
ART DIRECTOR(S): SIMON WOOLFORD
DESIGNER(S): LORINDA SMITH
CLIENT: BILLY BAG
TOOLS: ILLUSTRATOR, PHOTOSHOP, QUARK
MATERIALS: ESSENTIAL SILK

SUSSNER DESIGN COMPANY
0096, 0800
ART DIRECTOR(S): DEREK SUSSNER
DESIGNER(S): DEREK SUSSNER, RALPH SCHRADER, BRENT GALE, RYAN CARLSON
CLIENT: SUSSNER DESIGN
TOOLS: ILLUSTRATOR, PHOTOSHOP, QUARK, MAC
MATERIALS: 100LB NEKOOSA SOUTIONS CARRARA WHITE SMOOTH COVER, 80LB FOX RIVER EVERGREEN HICKORY COVER, 80LB MCCOY SILK TEXT, 80LB NEKOOSA SOLUTIONS RECYCLED WHITE SMOOTH TEXT

TAXI STUDIO
0018
ART DIRECTOR(S): RYAN WILLS
DESIGNER(S): RYAN WILLS
CLIENT: CLARKS
TOOLS: PHOTOSHOP, QUARK
MATERIALS: CHALLENGER OFFSET

0127
ART DIRECTOR(S): RYAN WILLS
DESIGNER(S): OLLY GUISE
CLIENT: CLARKS
TOOLS: PHOTOSHOP, QUARK
MATERIALS: ARCTIC VOLUME

0352
ART DIRECTOR(S): SPENCER BUCK, RYAN WILLS
DESIGNER(S): ALEX BANE
CLIENT: INTEGRALIS
TOOLS: PHOTOSHOP, QUARK

0357
ART DIRECTOR(S): OLLY GUISE
DESIGNER(S): OLLY GUISE
CLIENT: CLARKS
MATERIALS: CHALLENGER OFFSET

TEMPLIN BRINK DESIGN
0001
ART DIRECTOR(S): GABY BRINK, JOEL TEMPLIN
DESIGNER(S): BRIAN GUNDERSON, GABY BRINK
CLIENT: JANUS CAPITAL GROUP
TOOLS: ILLUSTRATOR, PHOTOSHOP, QUARK, MAC

0016
ART DIRECTOR(S): GABY BRINK, JOEL TEMPLIN
DESIGNER(S): BRIAN GUNDERSON, GABY BRINK
CLIENT: ORACLE
TOOLS: ILLUSTRATOR, PHOTOSHOP, QUARK, MAC

0018, 0589
ART DIRECTOR(S): GABY BRINK, JOEL TEMPLIN
DESIGNER(S): BRIAN GUNDERSON
CLIENT: LEVI STRAUSS
TOOLS: ILLUSTRATOR, PHOTOSHOP, QUARK, MAC

0039
ART DIRECTOR(S): GABY BRINK, JOEL TEMPLIN
DESIGNER(S): BRIAN GUNDERSON
CLIENT: OAKLAND A'S
TOOLS: ILLUSTRATOR, PHOTOSHOP, QUARK, MAC

0040
ART DIRECTOR(S): GABY BRINK, JOEL TEMPLIN
DESIGNER(S): MARIUS GEDGAUDUS, GABY BRINK
CLIENT: EDAW
TOOLS: ILLUSTRATOR, PHOTOSHOP, QUARK, MAC

0161
ART DIRECTOR(S): JOEL TEMPLIN
DESIGNER(S): JOEL TEMPLIN
CLIENT: SHARPE + ASSOCIATES
TOOLS: ILLUSTRATOR, PHOTOSHOP, QUARK, MAC

0164
ART DIRECTOR(S): GABY BRINK, JOEL TEMPLIN
DESIGNER(S): GABY BRINK
CLIENT: KELHAM MACLEAN
TOOLS: ILLUSTRATOR, PHOTOSHOP, QUARK, MAC

0308, 0354, 0371, 0597
ART DIRECTOR(S): GABY BRINK, JOEL TEMPLIN
DESIGNER(S): BRIAN GUNDERSON, GABY BRINK
CLIENT: TARGET
TOOLS: ILLUSTRATOR, PHOTOSHOP, QUARK, MAC

0691
ART DIRECTOR(S): GABY BRINK, JOEL TEMPLIN
DESIGNER(S): BRIAN GUNDERSON, GABY BRINK
CLIENT: SAND STUDIO
TOOLS: ILLUSTRATOR, PHOTOSHOP, QUARK, MAC

0927
ART DIRECTOR(S): GABY BRINK, JOEL TEMPLIN
DESIGNER(S): BRIAN GUNDERSON, GABY BRINK
CLIENT: LEO BURNETT
TOOLS: ILLUSTRATOR, PHOTOSHOP, QUARK, MAC

THAT'S NICE LLC
0555
ART DIRECTOR(S): SCOTT ROBERTSON
DESIGNER(S): ELAN HARRIS
CLIENT: THAT'S NICE LLC
TOOLS: ILLUSTRATOR
MATERIALS: 128LB STROBE COVER

THE DESIGN DELL
0623, 0900
ART DIRECTOR(S): DAN DONOVAN
DESIGNER(S): DAN DONOVAN
CLIENT: THE DESIGN DELL
TOOLS: QUARK
MATERIALS: CYCLUS OFFSET

THE FAMILY
0122
ART DIRECTOR(S): ANDREW ROBINSON
DESIGNER(S): GRAHAM NUTTALL, ANDREW KING
CLIENT: LAUREUS WORLD SPORTS AWARDS
TOOLS: ILLUSTRATOR, MAC
MATERIALS: CHELSEA CLOTH LAMINATED TO BOARD AND BOILED

0249
ART DIRECTOR(S): ANDREW ROBINSON
DESIGNER(S): ANDREW KING
CLIENT: AKEBONO
TOOLS: ILLUSTRATOR, PHOTOSHOP, QUARK
MATERIALS: SKY SILK

0275
ART DIRECTOR(S): ANDREW ROBINSON
DESIGNER(S): ANDREW KING, DOUGLAS MAIN
CLIENT: ALFRED DUNHILL
TOOLS: ILLUSTRATOR, QUARK, MAC
MATERIALS: ZERKALL BÜTTEN WITH DECAL EDGE

0579
ART DIRECTOR(S): ANDREW ROBINSON
DESIGNER(S): GRAHAM NUTTALL, ANDREW KING
CLIENT: LAUREUS WORLD SPORTS AWARDS
TOOLS: ILLUSTRATOR, MAC
MATERIALS: LEATHER LAMINATED TO BOARD

0592
ART DIRECTOR(S): ANDREW ROBINSON
DESIGNER(S): ANDREW KING, DOUGLAS MAIN
CLIENT: GRENADA MEDIA
TOOLS: ILLUSTRATOR, PHOTOSHOP, QUARK, MAC
MATERIALS: FAULKNERS HANDMADE PAPER, FOIL RUBDOWNS, FEATHER

0710
ART DIRECTOR(S): ANDREW ROBINSON
CLIENT: DONSIDE PAPER
TOOLS: ILLUSTRATOR, QUARK, MAC
MATERIALS: DONSIDE LABEL PAPER, 10-COLOR PLUS FOILS

0957
ART DIRECTOR(S): ANDREW ROBINSON
CLIENT: DONSIDE PAPER
TOOLS: ILLUSTRATOR, QUARK, MAC
MATERIALS: DONSIDE LABEL PAPER, 10-COLOR PLUS FOILS

0958
ART DIRECTOR(S): ANDREW ROBINSON
CLIENT: DONSIDE PAPER
TOOLS: ILLUSTRATOR, QUARK, MAC
MATERIALS: DONSIDE LABEL PAPER, 10-COLOR PLUS FOILS

THE FORMATION
ART DIRECTOR(S): ADRIAN KILBY
DESIGNER(S): ADRIAN KILBY, AIMEE MARTEN
CLIENT: THE FORMATION
MATERIALS: G.F. SMITH COLOURPLAN, CURTISS SUPERWOVE

THE PHOENIX STUDIO
0014
ART DIRECTOR(S): KIM FRANCISCO
DESIGNER(S): KIM FRANCISCO
CLIENT: THE PHOENIX STUDIO
TOOLS: FREEHAND
MATERIALS: STARDREAM TEXT AND COVER, CURIOUS TEXT AND COVER

THE WORKS DESIGN COMMUNICATIONS
0036, 0590
ART DIRECTOR(S): SCOTT MCFARLAND
DESIGNER(S): MIKE REHDER
CLIENT: UNISOURCE
TOOLS: ILLUSTRATOR, PHOTOSHOP, MAC
MATERIALS: NEENAH CLASSIC LINEN DUPLEX

0131
ART DIRECTOR(S): SCOTT MCFARLAND
DESIGNER(S): MIKE REHDER
CLIENT: THE WORKS DESIGN
TOOLS: ILLUSTRATOR, PHOTOSHOP, MAC
MATERIALS: BLACK KEAY KOLOUR HOPPER HOTS RED

0399
ART DIRECTOR(S): SCOTT MCFARLAND
DESIGNER(S): MIKE REHDER
CLIENT: GREATER TORONTO AIRPORTS AUTHORITY
TOOLS: ILLUSTRATOR, PHOTOSHOP, QUARK, MAC
MATERIALS: MEAD WESTRACO 100LB SIGNATURE

0813
ART DIRECTOR(S): SCOTT MCFARLAND
DESIGNER(S): NELSON SILVA
CLIENT: ABER DIAMOND
TOOLS: ILLUSTRATOR, PHOTOSHOP, QUARK, MAC
MATERIALS: SYNERGY FELT TEXT 100LB

THIRTEEN
0221
ART DIRECTOR(S): JOHN UNDERWOOD
DESIGNER(S): JOHN UNDERWOOD
CLIENT: CENTRAL WORKSHOP
TOOLS: ILLUSTRATOR, PHOTOSHOP, QUARK
MATERIALS: WICOTEX CLOTH, MUNKEN LYNX, ARCTIC SILK

0447, 0451
ART DIRECTOR(S): JOHN UNDERWOOD
DESIGNER(S): DANIELLE WAY
CLIENT: BRISTOL REGENERATION
TOOLS: PHOTOSHOP, QUARK
MATERIALS: EUROCHIP ESSENTIAL OFFSET

0452
ART DIRECTOR(S): SUFFIA KHANAN
DESIGNER(S): SUFFIA KHANAN
CLIENT: WHITE DESIGN
TOOLS: QUARK
MATERIALS: G.F. SMITH COLOURPLAN

0454
ART DIRECTOR(S): DANNY JENKINS
DESIGNER(S): DANNY JENKINS
CLIENT: ARNOLFINI
TOOLS: QUARK
MATERIALS: REGENCY GLOSS, MUNCHEN LYNX

0174
ART DIRECTOR(S): DANNY JENKINS
DESIGNER(S): DANNY JENKINS
CLIENT: HITEC-LOTEC
TOOLS: PHOTOSHOP, QUARK
MATERIALS: INDUSTRIAL EPDM FOAM, ANTALIS PRINTSPEED

0571
ART DIRECTOR(S): NICK HAND
DESIGNER(S): NICK HAND, NEIL TINSON
CLIENT: ORANGE
TOOLS: PHOTOSHOP, QUARK
MATERIALS: CONSORT ROYAL SILK

0637, 0981
ART DIRECTOR(S): DANNY JENKINS
DESIGNER(S): DANNY JENKINS
CLIENT: HITEC-LOTEC
TOOLS: PHOTOSHOP, QUARK
MATERIALS: PHOENIXMOTION

0776
ART DIRECTOR(S): DANNY JENKINS, SUFFIA KHANAN
DESIGNER(S): SUFFIA KHANAN
CLIENT: ORANGE
TOOLS: ILLUSTRATOR, PHOTOSHOP, QUARK
MATERIALS: DUTCHMAN

THOMPSON
0061, 0731, 0771
ART DIRECTOR(S): IAN THOMPSON
DESIGNER(S): IAN THOMPSON
CLIENT: THOMPSON
TOOLS: QUARK
MATERIALS: GRAPHIC TEXTURES

0425
ART DIRECTOR(S): IAN THOMPSON
DESIGNER(S): IAN THOMPSON
CLIENT: DESIGN YORKSHIRE
TOOLS: QUARK
MATERIALS: NEPTUNE UNIQUE

0435, 0476, 0872, 0911
ART DIRECTOR(S): IAN THOMPSON
DESIGNER(S): IAN THOMPSON
CLIENT: LEEDS METROPOLITAN UNIVERSITY/ CHARLES QUICK
TOOLS: QUARK
MATERIALS: NEPTUNE UNIQUE

WEBB & WEBB

ART DIRECTOR(S): BRIAN
WEBB
DESIGNER(S): BRIAN WEBB,
CHRIS GLOSTER
CLIENT: LONDON INSTITUTE
TOOLS: PHOTOSHOP, QUARK,
LETTERPRESS TYPOGRAPHY
MATERIALS: G.F. SMITH
BRIGHT WHITE 200GSM
(JACKET), GALLERY SILK
170GSM

ART DIRECTOR(S): BRIAN
WEBB
DESIGNER(S): BRIAN WEBB,
CHRIS GLOSTER
CLIENT: THE ROYAL MAIL,
2003
TOOLS: QUARK, LETTERPRESS
TYPOGRAPHY
MATERIALS: HANDMADE
CARTRIDGE

WILSON HARVEY

ART DIRECTOR(S): PAUL
BURGESS
DESIGNER(S): STEPHANIE
HARRISON
CLIENT: PHILLIPS GROUP

ART DIRECTOR(S): PAUL
BURGESS
DESIGNER(S): BEN WOOD,
PETE USHER, PAUL BURGESS
CLIENT: LIBERTY

ART DIRECTOR(S): PAUL
BURGESS
DESIGNER(S): BEN WOOD,
PAUL BURGESS
CLIENT: LUKE AND LIZA
TOOLS: QUARK, MAC
MATERIALS: 35GSM OFFSET

ART DIRECTOR(S): PAUL
BURGESS
DESIGNER(S): GRAHAM FARR
CLIENT: WENNER-GREN

ART DIRECTOR(S): PAUL
BURGESS
DESIGNER(S): PAUL BURGESS
CLIENT: WILSON HARVEY

ART DIRECTOR(S): PAUL
BURGESS
DESIGNER(S): BEN WOOD
CLIENT: CCD

ART DIRECTOR(S): PAUL
BURGESS
DESIGNER(S): WAI LAU
CLIENT: CCD

ART DIRECTOR(S): PAUL
BURGESS
DESIGNER(S): DANIEL
ELLIOTT
CLIENT: NET BENEFIT

ART DIRECTOR(S): PAUL
BURGESS
DESIGNER(S): PAUL BURGESS
CLIENT: MUTINY

ART DIRECTOR(S): PAUL
BURGESS
DESIGNER(S): EMMA
GARNSEY, PAUL BURGESS
CLIENT: PFIZER
MATERIALS:
POLYPROPYLENE

ART DIRECTOR(S): PAUL
BURGESS
DESIGNER(S): DAN ELLIOTT,
PAUL BURGESS
CLIENT: OLWEN DM
MATERIALS:
POLYPROPYLENE COVER

XAX CREATIVE

ART DIRECTOR(S): ZACK
SHUBKAGEL
CLIENT: WORKING SPACES
TOOLS: ILLUSTRATOR,
INDESIGN, MAC
MATERIALS: COUGAR WHITE
80LB COVER

YAEL MILLER DESIGN

ART DIRECTOR(S): YAEL
MILLER
DESIGNER(S): YAEL MILLER
CLIENT: LE BELGE
CHOCOLATIER
TOOLS: ILLUSTRATOR
MATERIALS: UNCOATED
COLORED TEXTURED PAPER,
HOTSTAMPED RIBBON

ART DIRECTOR(S): YAEL
MILLER
DESIGNER(S): YAEL MILLER
CLIENT: ASTOR CHOCOLATE
TOOLS: ILLUSTRATOR
MATERIALS: VELVET PAPER,
FINE GOLD CORD

ART DIRECTOR(S): YAEL
MILLER
DESIGNER(S): YAEL MILLER
CLIENT: ASTOR CHOCOLATE,
VENETIAN HOTEL, LAS VEGAS
TOOLS: ILLUSTRATOR
MATERIALS: COATED STOCK,
FOIL STAMP

ZIGZAG DESIGN

ART DIRECTOR(S): RACHEL
KARACA
DESIGNER(S): RACHEL
KARACA
CLIENT: ZIGZAG DESIGN
TOOLS: ILLUSTRATOR, MAC
MATERIALS: RUBBER COVERS,
CLOTH RAG

ZIP DESIGN

ART DIRECTOR(S): PETER
CHADWICK
DESIGNER(S): PETER
CHADWICK
CLIENT: SKINT RECORDS
TOOLS: PHOTOSHOP, QUARK
MATERIALS: DIE-CUT CD
WALLET

ART DIRECTOR(S): PETER
CHADWICK, TIM DELUXE
DESIGNER(S): NEIL BOWEN
CLIENT: UNDERWATER
RECORDS
TOOLS: PHOTOSHOP, QUARK
MATERIALS: SPIRO-BOUND
HARDBACK CD BOOKLET

ART DIRECTOR(S): PETER
CHADWICK
DESIGNER(S): NEIL BOWEN
CLIENT: UNDERWATER
RECORDS
TOOLS: PHOTOSHOP, QUARK
MATERIALS: SPIRO-BOUND
HARDBACK CD BOOKLET

ART DIRECTOR(S): PETER
CHADWICK, TIM DELUXE
DESIGNER(S): CAROLINE
MOOREHOUSE, NEIL BOWEN,
DAVID BOWDEN
CLIENT: HED KANDI
TOOLS: ILLUSTRATOR,
FREEHAND
MATERIALS: CARD DIGI
PACK AND CLEAR ACETATE
SLIPCASE

ART DIRECTOR(S): PETER
CHADWICK
DESIGNER(S): CAROLINE
MOOREHOUSE, HANNAH
WOODCOCK
CLIENT: OBSESSIVE/BMG
RECORDS
TOOLS: PHOTOSHOP, QUARK
MATERIALS: DOUBLE WHITE
REVERSE BOARD

ZULVER & CO.

ART DIRECTOR(S): DAVID
KIMPTON
DESIGNER(S): LEON TORKA
CLIENT: REGALIAN
PROPERTIES
MATERIALS: JOB PAVILOX,
MATT WHITE 170GSM

ART DIRECTOR(S): ANDREW
ZULVER
DESIGNER(S): DAVID
KIMPTON, GRAHAM BIRCH
CLIENT: GHM ROCK
TOWNSEND
MATERIALS: SKY DXM XENON,
MUNKEN LYNX

ART DIRECTOR(S): ANDREW
ZULVER
DESIGNER(S): GRAHAM BIRCH
CLIENT: REGALIAN
PROPERTIES
MATERIALS: 300GSM PARLUX
SILK

ABOUT THE AUTHOR

WILSON HARVEY IS A LONDON-BASED
INTEGRATED DESIGN AND MARKET-
ING AGENCY WORKING ACROSS A
WIDE RANGE OF DESIGN DISCIPLINES
SUCH AS BRANDING, IDENTITY, COL-
LATERAL, ADVERTISING, DIRECT
MARKETING, PUBLISHING, AND NEW
MEDIA. COLLECTIVELY THEY HAVE
DESIGNED MORE THAN 500 BOOKS FOR
A VARIETY OF PUBLISHERS AND ARE
THE AUTHOR/DESIGNERS OF *THE BEST
OF BROCHURE DESIGN 7.* THEY HAVE
RECENTLY JOINED FORCES WITH
FIVE OTHER LEADING MEDIA AGEN-
CIES UNDER THE BANNER OF THE
LOEWY GROUP, CONTINUING THE LEG-
ACY OF THE GREAT RAYMOND LOEWY.
PAUL BURGESS IS COFOUNDER AND
CREATIVE DIRECTOR OF WILSON
HARVEY. HE HAS BEEN WORKING
AS A MULTIDISCIPLINED GRAPHIC
DESIGNER FOR MORE THAN 14 YEARS
WITH B2B AND B2C CLIENTS ALIKE.
PAUL HAS BEEN PUBLISHED IN MORE
THAN 20 DIFFERENT INDUSTRY
TITLES.
BEN WOOD IS A SENIOR DESIGNER
AT WILSON HARVEY. BEN'S WORK HAS
BEEN RECOGNIZED BY THE DESIGN
INDUSTRY, ACHIEVING A D+AD
STUDENT GOLD AWARD.